D1521620

Clean Hands?

Clean Hands?

Philosophical Lessons from Scrupulosity

JESSE S. SUMMERS
WALTER SINNOTT-ARMSTRONG

OXFORD
UNIVERSITY PRESS

OXFORD
UNIVERSITY PRESS

Oxford University Press is a department of the University of Oxford. It furthers
the University's objective of excellence in research, scholarship, and education
by publishing worldwide. Oxford is a registered trade mark of Oxford University
Press in the UK and certain other countries.

Published in the United States of America by Oxford University Press
198 Madison Avenue, New York, NY 10016, United States of America.

Library of Congress Cataloging-in-Publication Data
Names: Summers, Jesse S., author. | Sinnott-Armstrong, Walter, author.
Title: Clean hands? philosophical lessons from scrupulosity /
Jesse S. Summers and Walter Sinnott-Armstrong.
Description: New York : Oxford University Press, 2019. |
Includes bibliographical references and index.
Identifiers: LCCN 2018061613 (print) | LCCN 2019980264 (ebook) |
ISBN 9780190058692 (cloth : alk. paper) | ISBN 9780190058722 (ebook)
Subjects: LCSH: Scruples. | Psychiatry—Philosophy.
Classification: LCC BJ1278.S37 S86 2019 (print) |
LCC BJ1278.S37 (ebook) | DDC 155.2/32—dc23
LC record available at https://lccn.loc.gov/2018061613
LC ebook record available at https://lccn.loc.gov/2019980264

1 3 5 7 9 8 6 4 2

Printed by Sheridan Books, Inc., United States of America

to Mara, manager of anxiety

to Liz, my obsession and compulsion

Contents

Preface

When Walter first asked me several years ago, not long after we'd met, whether I'd ever heard of "moral OCD," I imagined moral OCD in exactly the naive way that many people think of OCD more generally, as being *overly concerned* with something: those with hand-washing OCD want very clean hands, cleaner than most, and they clean them far beyond what anyone else would tolerate. They are "obsessed" with hand-washing the way someone might be "obsessed" with *Star Wars* or with making to-do lists: they love it and are very, even overly concerned with it. When people casually refer to themselves as being "a little OCD about" something like having their books arranged in a certain way, what they have in mind is this naive understanding of OCD. Of course, someone who is "a little OCD about" how their books are lined up on the bookshelf won't stay up all night with a ruler going over the same shelf multiple times. For that matter, someone who is "a little OCD about" having clean hands will stop washing before they've rubbed their hands entirely raw. So this naive understanding of OCD is misleading. People with OCD aren't just very concerned with something. They also have problems controlling their thoughts and actions.

Both Walter and I had previously, separately, worked on addiction, another kind of irrational behavior in which people fail to control their actions. What's puzzling about addiction is that addicts often know they should quit, even say that they want to quit. They see the costs of their addictions. Yet they don't quit; or if they do quit, they later relapse. People with OCD similarly often know they shouldn't act as they do, even say they don't want to act this way, yet they continue to do it. What's different from addiction is that, as we'll see, there is a widely accepted explanation of why those with OCD act as they do: anxiety. The role anxiety plays in OCD is complicated and sometimes subtle, but anxiety is what ultimately unifies explanations of OCD. A person with hand-washing OCD doesn't just want her hands to be clean: she is anxious that they're not clean or about what might happen if they're not clean.

The question for us, then, was whether *moral* OCD—or Scrupulosity—could be understood in this way. If so, Scrupulosity seems very different from sainthood. Saints aren't motivated to be moral by anxiety, are they? Those who are worried about going to hell if they're sinners aren't worried about morality: they're worried about hell. They might or might not act the same as someone motivated by morality, but motivation by anxiety seemed fundamentally incompatible with motivation by morality.

As I said, though, motivation by anxiety is complicated and subtle, and our understanding of how anxiety motivates both Scrupulosity and morality developed significantly as we worked on this project. At the University of Arizona's Workshop in Normative Ethics (WiNE), where we presented on Scrupulosity and moral judgments, Liz Harman and Hallie Liberto perceptively asked why genuinely moral judgments *couldn't* be motivated by anxiety, while Charlie Kurth presented on the positive role that (non-pathological) anxiety can play. These exchanges, among many others, ultimately led us to develop a far more nuanced position on the role of anxiety than we had held up to that point—and one more nuanced than the position we published in some of our earlier articles on this topic.

What distinguishes Scrupulosity from ordinary moral judgments isn't, we came to see, the mere presence of anxiety or even the fact that anxiety is motivating. This is because there are ways in which anxiety might plausibly play some motivating role in a moral judgment. Doing something good because of your anxiety about otherwise going to hell might not be moral, but doing something good because of your anxiety about otherwise doing the wrong thing might be.

What we came over time to believe distinguishes Scrupulosity from ordinary morality is not the motivating anxiety alone but the distorted features of moral judgments that anxiety causes. Anxiety—at least in those with OCD—makes people focus on what will legitimate or reduce their anxiety. That focus corrupts what might otherwise be a perfectly normal moral judgment, and makes it into something that, at its most corrupted, is plausibly no longer a moral judgment at all. The implications of that central thought expanded to shape the rest of what is written here.

Of course, our work on this topic over the years has also benefited in many other ways from many other influences. Walter and I owe thanks to enough people who have discussed this topic with us over the years that we cannot hope to remember and thank everyone. Neither of us is scrupulous enough—fortunately or unfortunately—to keep track of every useful interaction we've had on this topic. Here are at least some of the people who helped us think more carefully about this topic: Jon Abramowitz,

Nomy Arpaly, Laura Crosskey, Julia Driver, Iskra Fileva, Gary Gala, Molly Gardner, Harlin Gradin, Christine Lille, Daniel Moseley, Lauren Olin, Roger Perilstein, David Shoemaker, Liz Sinnott-Armstrong, Holly Smith, Chandra Sripada, and audiences at the American Philosophical Association, the Moral Psychology Research Group, the Southern Society of Philosophy and Psychology, Beth El Synagogue, and the Universities of Alabama, Oxford, and Pennsylvania. Thanks to Lizzie Schechter for coming up with the book title. Thanks to the members of MAD lab and the Kenan Institute for Ethics for repeated feedback and support. Special thanks to Michael McKenna for arranging and the University of Arizona philosophy department for hosting an amazing extended discussion of the entire manuscript, to Fr. Thomas Santa for allowing us to visit one of his retreats for people with Scrupulosity, and to its participants for sharing their experiences with us.

Special thanks also to my wife, a much more prolific writer than I'll ever be, who agrees to a 5:30 A.M. alarm and free time together that is often spent reading and writing. I've been very fortunate to be with someone who values the life of the mind and doesn't make me feel like I'm choosing between family and work, even when I am. I'm sure the time I used on this project made me miss some things that I would have loved.

A propos of which, the first draft of the first presentation I wrote on Scrupulosity began shortly before my son was born. I spent the winter before his late-February due date rushing to read and write as much as possible on this new topic, knowing that it would be hard to sustain the work once he was born. That much was correct. But, of these two projects born at around the same time, I'm happy that this one is concluding so that I have more (anxiety-limited) time to spend with the other.

A final thanks and note on authorship: the book is a genuine collaboration and, except for these prefaces, was co-authored in its entirety. I wrote the first drafts, except for the introduction, sent the drafts to Walter, who heavily edited and rewrote, then sent them back to me, and so it continued back and forth for many, many drafts, revising and editing, substantially at times, discussing when necessary, presenting together at conferences and workshops, and publishing earlier versions of several chapters. Walter has been a fantastic collaborator and editor, writing quickly and patiently shepherding long and incoherent initial thoughts into clear and readable ones, and pushing us to explore areas I would have ignored. When we disagreed significantly—which wasn't often—what emerged was much better and clearer than it would have been without the disagreement. It would be impossible to disentangle authorship further at this point, except to say that Walter insists that the word "might" refers to possibility and "may" refers to permission, so almost every instance of "might" throughout the book was written by Walter, and any instances of "may" that survived were written by me. I take full responsibility for this and all other grammatical mistakes. As for any more serious mistakes that *might* remain, I hope we'll worry no more than necessary about those.

Jesse S. Summers
August 2018

I second all of Jesse's thanks and add my own gratitude to my wife, Liz, whose devotion to helping people with mental illnesses is inspiring. Thanks also to Jesse for years of fruitful and fun collaboration. And thanks for financial support from the Kenan Institute for Ethics and the John Templeton Foundation. Of course, the contents of this book are solely the responsibility of the authors and do not necessarily represent the official views of the Kenan Institute for Ethics or the John Templeton Foundation.

Walter Sinnott-Armstrong
August 2018

Clean Hands?

Introduction

Moral Psychiatry

Morality is central to our personal and social lives. Without morality, our lives would be "solitary, poor, nasty, brutish, and short," as Hobbes (1651) said of life without society. Hobbes's solution was an authoritarian monarch enforcing strict laws. However, even Hobbes knew that force alone cannot ensure morality. It is just too easy and tempting to violate moral rules without getting caught. If all we're afraid of is being punished, wouldn't we commit crimes when we know that we are unlikely to be caught and punished by authorities?

The main reason we avoid doing what's wrong even when we know we won't be punished is our sense of morality. Either we appreciate the immorality of an act, and that realization stops us, or we know that, even if we're not punished, our family, friends, co-workers, or even just strangers will know we acted immorally. Even if we are sometimes not moved by moral concerns, we still want those around us to care about morality, since that will make them less likely to hurt us when they know they can get away with it. Morality thus restricts misbehavior even when the law is ineffective or punishment is impractical, and it is in large part because of these internal moral motivations that our lives are less "solitary, poor, nasty, brutish, and short."

Because morality is so important in every part of our lives, it's no surprise that we want to understand it. Morality is hard to understand, though. First, morality is complex. It involves choices, actions, reactions, emotions, motivations, character traits, dispositions, practices, institutions, and people. Its content varies from harm and fairness to sanctity, loyalty, and respect for authority (Haidt, 2012). It varies in its functions and its neural bases (Sinnott-Armstrong, 2016). Moreover, morality might have no single unifying definition, so it can be hard even to know where to start our examination.

In order to understand such a multi-faceted phenomenon fully, we need to look at morality from as many perspectives as possible. This point was put with his usual flair by Nietzsche when he said,

> There is *only* a perspective seeing, *only* a perspective "knowing"; and the *more* affects we allow to speak about one thing, the *more* eyes, different eyes, we can use to observe one thing, the more complete will our "concept" of this thing, our "objectivity" be. (Nietzsche, 1966)

We do not need to agree with Nietzsche that all seeing and knowing is perspectival in order to accept his point that we see and know better—more completely and objectively—when we view a complex phenomenon from many perspectives. Morality is no exception. We cannot understand morality fully or even adequately by means of any single discipline.

Morality is already studied using a wide variety of methods, including philosophy, psychology, neuroscience, biology, sociology, anthropology, theology, and so on. Philosophers and theologians endorse normative moral theories whereas psychologists, neuroscientists, and sociologists try their best to keep their theories morally neutral. Sociologists and anthropologists study trends and patterns in large groups whereas psychologists sometimes look for internal mental processes and factors that are common across societies and cultures. Neuroscientists bring culture and psyche into the world of the brain. Thus, we already know a lot about morality from a wide diversity of disciplines.

Still, other perspectives are yet to be explored. One new perspective that needs to be added to this collection is moral psychiatry. There is already a huge literature on moral psychology (Sinnott-Armstrong, 2008). However, most studies in moral psychology investigate moral judgments and decisions in normal people without psychiatric illnesses. There are also already tons (literally!) of work on the philosophy of psychiatry (Fulford et al., 2015). However, not every mental illness is about morality. Some delusions (such as Capgras and Cotard) and phobias might be morally relevant in affecting moral responsibility, but the contents of those delusions and phobias are not distinctively moral. So moral psychiatry, as we propose it here, is distinct from philosophy of psychiatry more generally.

Moral psychiatry, as we see it, specifically focuses on mental illnesses whose content is closely related to morality, and it uses those psychiatric conditions to illuminate aspects of morality and to test theories of morality that originated in other fields. This is the field that we want to help develop in this book.

Psychiatric conditions are well suited to illuminate morality, partly because so many moral theories are idealized. Moral philosophers are sometimes prone to unrealistic views of how humans form moral judgments and make moral decisions. (We have in mind particularly the rationalist, often Kantian views of moral agency like those found in Korsgaard, 2009, though this is not a problem unique to any one approach.) Such moral theories either do not apply or need to be stretched in order to apply to real humans who are mad, bad, or sad to varying degrees. We are not the first to make such a critique; other philosophers (such as Arpaly, 2000; Doris, 2015) have taken them to task for their extravagances.

We can extend and concretize these critiques of abstract, unrealistic moral theory by learning about mental illnesses, especially those with an essential connection to morality. This is because mental illnesses are often continuous with ordinary mental life, and, to the extent they are discontinuous, mentally ill individuals still retain enough of their ordinary, rational mental capacities for the illness itself to shed light on normal functioning. In this way, moral psychiatry can bring moral theory into closer contact with real life.

The field of moral psychiatry is most illuminating when it focuses on real, concrete examples of mental illnesses, but not all mental illnesses throw the same light on morality. Many psychiatric conditions, like Alzheimer's and frontotemporal dementia, can cause abnormal moral judgments under some circumstances. Nonetheless, abnormal moral judgments are not essential to those mental illnesses. Patients can have those disorders without having any abnormal moral judgments. In other conditions, like depression, abnormal moral judgments are common and—depending on which judgments we count as "moral"—might even be necessary to cause or sustain the condition. In some conditions, though, abnormal moral judgments are clearly essential. Psychopathy and Scrupulosity are paradigm examples.

Psychopathy has been well studied already, and it has shed a great deal of light on ordinary moral judgments. It's sometimes tempting to think of psychopaths as lacking a sense of morality, but the truth of their condition is much subtler and more interesting (Kiehl & Sinnott-Armstrong, 2015). It might also be tempting to think of Scrupulosity as the opposite of Psychopathy, that psychopaths care too little and people with Scrupulosity care too much about morality. Again, though, this contrast is too simple and overlooks what makes Scrupulosity so interesting for morality, as we will see. Each mental illness needs to be understood in detail and on its own terms.

There has been little work by philosophers on Scrupulosity so far (e.g., Schroeder, 2015; Shoemaker, 2015; Pickard, 2016; Bommarito, 2018), so the temptation to understand Scrupulosity only in caricature remains. This gap in the literature is a shame, and it keeps us from drawing the conclusions (or prompts us to draw the wrong conclusions) that caricatures encourage. This book will start to fill that gap.

Our goal is to use the case study of Scrupulosity to illuminate morality and to test philosophical theories of morality. Scrupulosity teaches a number of important lessons.

First, Scrupulosity illustrates problems in assuming that mental illnesses can be diagnosed without assuming and applying substantive moral judgments. Psychiatrists usually think of themselves as morally neutral. However, if Scrupulosity is a mental illness, as we will argue, then it presents the clearest case of a diagnosis that appears to rely essentially on the psychiatrist's own evaluation of whether a person is too moral. We will ask whether that is what psychiatrists in fact do, but regardless of the answer, this raises larger questions about whether psychiatry is or should be morally neutral.

Second, we distinguish people with Scrupulosity from people with admirable character traits who might perform the same actions. The difference, as we will see, lies in anxious motivation and the ways in which that anxious motivation affects the actions. The lesson from this contrast is that admirable character traits cannot be defined merely by behavior—and in some cases, not even by a simple account of the person's motivation. "He washed his hands because he thought they were still dirty" describes the motivation of both ordinary hand-washing and obsessive-compulsive disorder (OCD) hand-washing. To see a difference requires looking more carefully at *why* individuals have that motivation and what other motivations they have or lack. These differences in motivation, which can be quite subtle to describe correctly, affect whether a character trait is admirable or disordered.

Third, moral judgments need to be targeted at (or responsive and reactive to) morally relevant features of acts. That much is fairly uncontroversial. If an employee gives to charity only to impress friends, then his judgment about whether and how much he should donate is at least very different from paradigm and proper moral judgments, and perhaps not a genuinely moral judgment at all. Similarly, moral judgments should not be targeted at relieving one's own anxiety. When they are mistargeted in this way, the judgments will be distorted in characteristic ways that rationalize or relieve the person's own anxiety rather than remaining focused on the morally relevant features of the situation. This motivation at least distorts the moral judgments and, at the extreme, might make them no longer genuine moral judgments at all.

Fourth, we consider whether patients with Scrupulosity are responsible for their acts that harm other people. Scrupulosity raises challenges for popular theories of moral responsibility that suggest that people with Scrupulosity who are reflective and ego-syntonic are just as responsible for their actions as people without any mental illness. If we believe that those with Scrupulosity are less responsible than those without any mental illness, theories of moral responsibility that emphasize reason-responsiveness will more easily explain this conclusion. Scrupulosity thus provides a test case for deciding between popular and plausible theories of moral responsibility.

Fifth, Scrupulosity also raises questions about the ethics of practicing psychiatrists and therapists. Patients with ego-syntonic Scrupulosity might not want to enter treatment and might resist the kinds of therapy that the therapist recommends. Is this a case of a therapist imposing her own moral views about what's right and wrong on a patient? Nonetheless, this book will defend some treatments even against certain kinds of moral objection. This conclusion raises doubts about any principle that says it is morally wrong to do something morally wrong intentionally as a means to achieve a good end.

We hope that this book overall will impart to readers a greater understanding both of Scrupulosity and of morality in general. We also hope that readers will see the value in moral psychiatry as a general field. There are many more philosophical lessons to draw from examining other mental illnesses closely and thinking carefully about what humans—in all our real, sometimes unpredictable variety—are like, instead of understanding moral agents as idealized versions of ourselves. Theorizing about a morally ideal person who always asks "What ought I to do now?" runs into difficulties when we see what such a person looks like in practice. Whether those with Scrupulosity exemplify any moral ideals will have to wait until we better understand this fascinating disorder.

1

Cases

Consider the following vignettes. The first ones are cases of Scrupulosity. When you read them, feel free to speculate on what they have in common. We will begin our own answers to those questions soon enough. But don't skip ahead, for two reasons. First, we will refer back to these cases throughout the book, so study them carefully now to evaluate what we say in what follows. Second and more important, reflecting on cases is crucial to understanding this or any other psychiatric condition. We'll explain why after the cases.[1]

Adam

[Adam is a] patient whose Scrupulosity focuses on the theme of honesty[; he] has obsessive thoughts that a "grocery store cashier may have made an error in favor of the patient." The patient then engages in a compulsion: "Receipts are taken home and laboriously checked item by item, even if totals involve hundreds of dollars. Some receipts are kept for months, with the patient hoping that the urge to check will eventually decline and he can throw them away." (Ciarrocchi, 1995: 42)

Benjamin

[Benjamin is] a 33-year-old married man with three children. Following his marriage when 20, he became preoccupied with the thought that he had not had sufficient concentration during the

---

[1] All names of people with Scrupulosity discussed in this book—except the autobiographical account of Jennifer Traig (2004)—are pseudonyms: some of our own creation, and some taken from existing literature.

wedding ceremony, rendering the marriage invalid. He went to see the rabbis about it, until a second ceremony was arranged.

After this, he became preoccupied with his wife's menstrual cleanliness. The thoughts filled his mind all day, although he tried to dismiss them. Although he was aware that this preoccupation was excessive, he would question his wife many times a day as to whether she had become menstrually unclean. If she dismissed his question, he would decide that she was not taking the matter seriously and he would remain tense. He consulted rabbis very frequently as to whether—given his doubts—he was permitted to be with his wife, and they always permitted it. Nevertheless, he avoided touching his wife whenever possible, and intercourse was very infrequent. He only agreed to intercourse because of the commandment "Be fruitful and multiply," but on occasion his wife "forced" intercourse on him.

In addition, he took a long time to complete the portions of daily prayer that are considered to be especially important and requiring particular devotion, every such line adding an extra 10 minutes to his prayer. (Greenberg, Witztum, & Pisante, 1987: 32)

Big John

John worked in a huge government agency that employed thousands. He believed that loving one's neighbor meant that he was obligated to greet with a "Good morning" or nod of his head each and every worker he passed. He could pass, conceivably, hundreds of persons any time he stepped out of his office. If he missed greeting someone, he felt an impulse (and sometimes acted on it) to circle the corridor to catch up and greet the person.

Using the Biblical story of the good Samaritan in which Jesus answered the question of who is one's neighbor, he eventually realized that, when walking the corridors, he only had to extend himself to those in true need. This solution, however, generated a whole new set of problems in dealing with the dozens of homeless and panhandlers who accosted him on his daily ride on the subway. Were not these modern-day equivalents of the victim in the good Samaritan story? Did he have to contribute money to each?

Later, he was helped⁄m to resolve this issue, when one afternoon he spotted one of the regular "cripples" at his subway stop walking rapidly down the street with his crutches slung over his shoulders. (Ciarrocchi 1995: 15–16)

Bob

Bob was changing his daughter's diaper when the thought, idea, or image (he wasn't quite sure which) flashed through his mind—"touch her private parts." The first time it happened, he shuddered, tried to dismiss the idea, and hurriedly completed diapering her. All day he tried not to think about it. The next time he changed her diaper, however, the idea came back, but this time in the form of a graphic picture of Bob engaging in the dreaded behavior. This time he felt nausea, became dizzy, and called his wife to finish, saying that he thought he was ill and would pass out. The idea began to torment Bob. He found himself not wanting to be alone with his daughter, lest he "give in" to this impulse. He refused to bathe her or change her diaper. . . . He talked to his rabbi who tried to reassure him that he was not a child molester and should dismiss the thoughts. When Bob could not do this, the rabbi referred him to a psychiatrist. Therapy explored several possibilities. One was that Bob was ambivalent about child-care, that his symptoms represented an unconscious attempt to escape being a "modern" father. This "secondary gain" allowed him to avoid distasteful aspects of child-care. He and his therapist also explored how "incestuous" feelings are commonplace. Still Bob was not comforted. He sought out a therapist in a community mental health clinic. When Bob revealed the depth and extent of his imagery, the counselor wondered whether he would have to make a formal report to the state's Department of Child Welfare. Bob never returned. (Ciarrocchi, 1995: 7–8)

Bridget

At a restaurant where Bridget worked as a waitress she had a recurring fear of accidentally poisoning her customers. Accordingly, she checked the containers of cleaning solvents stored in the kitchen cabinets to ensure she did not inadvertently powder the food she served with a lethal garnishing of chemicals. Despite the fact that her position never involved contact with the solvents, making her involvement in such a fatal faux pas a virtual impossibility, she was tormented by the idea and correspondingly checked the containers at almost every order. . . .

Another behavior occurred upon the passing of ambulances. When hearing the sound of ambulance sirens she dropped whatever she was doing, crossed herself several times—sometimes a specific number of times—or looked to the sky. If driving, this often required pulling over to the side of the road either to cross or to pray with clasped hands for the ambulance passenger. If she was unable to perform these behaviors, she felt anxious and guilty, fearing that the condition of the afflicted passenger would worsen, or that the person would even die, and that she would then be morally responsible.

In the same vein, she often had intrusive thoughts about her younger brother dying from illness or getting into a fatal car accident. Consequently, she would cross herself and pray ritualistically when the thoughts randomly arrived and in response to antecedents such as her brother catching a cold, or when he left the house with his friends on weekends. These fears sank roots deeply into her sense of self, with her fearing that if she failed to avert harm this meant she was a selfish, uncaring, and even evil person. (Garcia, 2008: 7–8)

Ezekiel

The bar mitzvah at 13 years of age represents the passing into manhood, when the Jewish male becomes responsible for his own religious practice. At this time, [Ezekiel] started spending excessive time in prayer and its preparations. His prayers took up to three hours daily, about three times longer than his peers. Despite the time spent, the content was abbreviated, less important parts being omitted, so that the significant sections could be said at the correct time. When he said the most important sentence, he doubted if he had complete faith at that moment, or he was assailed by a desirous thought of a female neighbour. He would go back over this line in his mind for up to 10 minutes. Similar difficulties over another section would cause this prayer to take up to 20 minutes, at least four times the average. . . .

He considered his rituals to be excessive, but experienced no resistance to carrying them out, and said that he would have put up with them were it not for his wife, who was contemplating divorce. (Greenberg, Witztum, & Pisante, 1987: 33)

Jacob

[Jacob] began [as an adolescent] to keep a diary of his sins which he maintained for five years. For the last 10 years, his main fear has been of not being clean in the rectal area, resulting in meticulous cleaning for half an hour whenever he uses the toilet . . . and is continually thinking "Am I clean?" . . . This anxiety increases before and during any prayer, Bible study, benediction or eating for which cleanliness is necessary. In addition, he will not say benedictions at home unless he has checked there are no rags or garbage to be seen, and the baby has had its diaper changed. (Greenberg, Witztum, & Pisante, 1987: 34)

Jennifer

Jennifer reports of her own Scrupulosity that it:

made even regular museums agony. I had decided not to look at any paintings of people; they were graven images, and if I was going to do that I might as well go ahead and build a golden calf. Worse still were the religious paintings, idols all. My parents had seen this coming and had warned me not to try anything funny. "If we pay eight dollars to get you into a museum you're damn well going to look at everything they have there," they insisted. I placated them by pretending to look at the artwork; I was actually just looking at the frames. (Traig, 2004: 200)

Linda

Linda reports,

I am troubled with bad thoughts and desires. I am afraid to bathe or brush against my breast for fear I will feel sexual pleasure. I have harmful and envious thoughts about others. I am afraid to watch TV because of the bedroom scenes. I'm even afraid I'm abusing my health by getting so upset about these things and maybe that is a sin also. My common sense tells me that these are either no sin at all or, at most, venial sins, but I'm never sure, so I stay away from Holy Communion. When I see so many people receiving Communion, I want so badly to go, but I can't because I feel so unworthy. (Santa, 2007: 137)

Mary

[Mary is a] 31-year old wife and mother of three, . . . an Orthodox Jew and the daughter of an Orthodox rabbi. She worked in the home, raising her children. Mary's main OCD symptoms included recurrent, persistent doubts that she had not completed religious prayers and other rituals properly. Thus, she engaged in such behaviors repeatedly until satisfied that they had been performed correctly. For example, before eating, she felt compelled to recite (to herself) the ritual blessing 18 times (18 is a significant number in Judaism). If she experienced any stray thoughts, or if there were any distractions during the ritual, she would stop and start over from the beginning. When she was unable to finish rituals, she kept a mental note and completed them after the rest of her family had gone to bed. Frequently, Mary spent several hours each night repeating prayers and other religious rituals that she was unable to complete during the day. Mary was experiencing difficulties staying awake during the day, reported significant depressive symptoms, and expressed hopelessness and suicidal ideation. (Abramowitz 2008: 159)

Peter

Peter was a 33-year-old Mormon who was employed as a sales representative with a pharmaceutical company. He described being
tormented by one particular obsessional doubt that began following
an incident four years earlier during which he had obtained an erec-
tion while embracing his girlfriend, Sue. Although both Peter and
Sue were fully clothed during the embrace (and there was no ejac-
ulation), Peter became obsessed with the possibility that he had
impregnated Sue, who may have subsequently (a) aborted the un-
born child or (b) raised this child to be agnostic. Peter engaged in
compulsive reassurance seeking with fertility specialists to ascer-
tain whether a pregnancy could have taken place. He also repeatedly telephoned Sue (whom he no longer dated) to ask questions
about her lifestyle and checked with Sue's work supervisor to make
sure she had not missed any days for maternity leave. He had even
checked local hospital admission records. Peter believed that if he
ignored any opportunity to find out whether there was a pregnancy,
he was acting sinfully. (Abramowitz 2008: 158)

These cases raise questions almost immediately. Why are these people
like this? Do they really believe what they say? Are they mentally ill or mistaken? If they're mentally ill, what is wrong with them? If they're mistaken,
what are they mistaken about?

Experts have diagnosed all except the case of Jennifer as Scrupulosity—
Jennifer's was a self-diagnosis. The cases display a great variety in what the
people are concerned about, how they react to those concerns, whether they
sought treatment on their own because they recognize a problem or only
because they were compelled to go. This variety makes it worth spending
time figuring out what the cases have in common.

At least one feature that they have in common is pretty obvious: these
people are all focused on issues that we can describe generally as moral
or religious—or at least on what they take to be moral or religious issues.
In addition, there is something extreme about the way that they approach
those issues, though it might be hard to characterize what makes it extreme.

Beyond that broad generalization, though, it's hard to know what they
have in common. Some of the people seem to be mistaken about something,

like how babies are made or what makes a person likely to molest an infant. Some of them seem mistaken about what they morally or religiously ought to do in some circumstances, like how many times it's necessary to repeat a prayer or whether looking at a painting counts as worshipping an idol. Some of them are making subtler mistakes, like how many times you need to check a receipt to be sure there's nothing wrong on it: double checking is safer, and triple checking is safer still. But it's not clear in some of the cases whether they're making a mistake or whether we are: what does it mean to love one's neighbor as oneself? Does that not require at least saying hello to everyone we work with?

In the next chapter, we'll point out some similarities within the cases that are not as immediately apparent. We'll also begin considering what kinds of mistakes occur consistently in these cases—as well as whether these people might be right to have such high moral or religious standards.

Before we do, though, consider some contrasting cases, cases that would not be diagnosed as Scrupulosity but that share extreme concern with morality or religion:

João

[A]fter suffering a health crisis in 1990, at age 49, [João] wanted to live differently. "I saw death from close up," he would often say. "Now I want to be in high spirits." And nothing made him happier than giving. . . . [H]is new outlook resulted not from a spiritual awakening but from brain damage caused by a stroke. Among other symptoms, he became a chronic insomniac and lost his sex drive; he started forgetting things and had trouble focusing; his movements slowed. And, his neurologist says, he became "pathologically generous"— compulsively driven to give. . . .

João's neurologist . . . talked extensively with João's family about what João had been like before the stroke, and he concluded that the desire to give had always existed inside him . . . : he had the same basic traits before and after, but his latent generosity came to the fore and began to dominate. . . .

João quit his job and began selling french fries from a street cart. . . . João often served them up for free. All you had to do was ask, and he'd scoop some into a box, no charge. What money he did take in, he frequently gave away to children begging in the street or used to buy them sweets. Day after day, he came home to his wife and son without a single [Brazilian] *real* in his pocket. . . .

His carefree attitude toward money led to confrontations with his family, especially his brother-in-law, who co-owned the french-fry cart. But even when his family berated him, and the cart went out of business, and he was reduced to living on his mother's pension, João refused to stop. (Kean, 2015; passages rearranged)

Zell Kravinsky

About 1400 people have donated their "spare" kidney to someone whom they didn't know before the donation, with no incentive greater than their desire to help someone who needed a kidney. One of those people is the former millionaire—he gave away most of his $45 million fortune to charity—Zell Kravinsky (Parker, 2004). There are some differences between these living anonymous donors and others. For example, living anonymous donors are more likely to have a spiritual belief system and are more perceptually sensitive to others' fearful facial expressions—but these differences are well within the range of the normal, and no one has found that Kravinsky or the other living anonymous donors suffer from anything like a mental illness (Henderson et al., 2003; Marsh et al., 2014). Indeed, if they were mentally ill, that would raise a serious ethical barrier against accepting their donations.

Jains

Practitioners of this religion make central to their lives nonviolence or non-injury (*ahimsa*) of all living beings. This includes avoiding causing injury, physical and otherwise, to other humans, but also to animals, including insects, and even to plants to the extent possible. Jains are vegetarian if not vegan, but they are best known for the sometimes extreme measures they will take to avoid killing insects, or even to avoid the risk of killing an insect. Some will sweep the paths they are about to walk or where they are about to sit to avoid crushing insects and will cover their mouths with cloths that keep them from inadvertently inhaling and therefore killing any microorganisms. Although Jainism today has relatively few adherents, it has existed for millennia and has flourished at times.

If we think that what all the people above have in common is that they have extreme moral or religious beliefs or actions, there are many, many such "scrupulous" cases. Someone finds a lost wallet and searches extensively for its owner, long after his friends tell him it's not worth all this effort. Someone prays or meditates for an hour every morning, or goes to church for hours every week, giving up sleep, time with family, or even just time pursuing hobbies. Someone becomes a doctor to help others and then leaves behind a comfortable middle-class life as a doctor to serve those who are neediest, perhaps people they've never met and have no connection to. People live on far less than they earn so that they can donate to people with less. (MacFarquhar, 2015, explores several such extreme cases in detail.) Many people have strong concerns about remaining sexually pure, whatever they take that to mean, and they delay or avoid sexual pleasure to do so; perhaps they avoid even thinking about it. Agnostics and atheists, when faced with serious illness and the threat of death, find themselves engaged in religious rituals that they might not themselves fully understand. (The atheist writer James Morrow opined on this subject: "'There are no atheists in foxholes' isn't an argument against atheism; it's an argument against foxholes.") And countless religious values and rituals appear extreme, compulsive, and bizarre to nonadherents: candle lighting, prayers, quiet sitting, dancing, special clothes, greetings, required and forbidden foods, relationships. In short, there is no problem finding cases that are similar, at least in some ways, to the extreme ones listed here.

Whatever this condition is, then, something like it is fairly widespread. Many people have and act on extreme, compulsive, even bizarre (at least to non-adherents) religious or ethical beliefs. In such concerns, we see something of the motivation of those diagnosed with Scrupulosity: we know why Adam wants to check his receipts, why Big John wants to love his neighbor, and why people worry so much about things they've done wrong. But there is something different about the diagnosed cases of Scrupulosity, even if we can't neatly distinguish their acts from more ordinary ones. Or, at least, that's what we'll argue in this book. The question is: What distinguishes the similar cases from the cases of Scrupulosity, and why we should care about that distinction?

From here on out, we will draw this distinction in part by using the capital "S" to distinguish the disorder "Scrupulosity" from traits that are scrupulous in a more ordinary sense, i.e., careful, fastidious, concerned with one's rectitude, etc., but not necessarily disordered or part of a mental disorder. A person with Scrupulosity will have scrupulous traits, but most people with scrupulous traits will not also have Scrupulosity. Also, to avoid confusion and to avoid characterizing people as only their disorder, we won't refer to people with the disorder Scrupulosity as "Scrupulous people."

Although we're going to draw a distinction between Scrupulosity, the disorder, and those scrupulous traits that are more widely shared, we have to acknowledge right from the beginning that we will not provide diagnostic tools, and it will be very hard to draw the distinction in some cases. We could present any number of ordinary cases that are hard to distinguish, but consider the following case, which is presented in the literature as a case of Scrupulosity. Nevertheless, based on the minimal description given here, the case is at best a borderline case of Scrupulosity, for reasons that will become clearer throughout the book.

Little John

John is a serious fifteen-year-old boy who is active at Church in Sunday school and attends as many adult education meetings as he can. He has become particularly sensitive about social justice issues: hunger in the world, the disparity between rich and poor nations, unemployment in his country, etc. John is driving his otherwise placid family to distraction. He eats a minimum amount of food each day (using his allowance for food relief in Africa). What disturbs his parents the most, however, are his constant harangues to his seven year old sister and five year old brother whenever he notices they waste food. They refuse to eat when he does, and more than one meal has ended with some of the little ones running from the table crying. When the parents raised this problem with their pastor, she replied that she wished all the teenagers in the congregation had John's social conscience. (Ciarrocchi 1995: 15–16; cf. Salwen & Salwen, 2010)

Little John was diagnosed with Scrupulosity based on more than this short vignette, but it's worth considering why this description alone isn't enough to determine that he has Scrupulosity. We need more details to know whether the case is closer to Scrupulosity or closer to those with (merely) scrupulous traits. It will soon be clearer what kinds of details might do that.

Many other cases are similarly difficult to categorize, and even the cases of Scrupulosity that we consider here could, with only slight adjustments, be made to sound much less like clear cases of Scrupulosity. The exercise of trying to decide whether any of the above cases are cases of Scrupulosity or not is therefore instructive, but reading the cases should prompt more general questions: what would need to change or be clearer in each of the Scrupulous cases in order for them not to seem disordered, or in the non-Scrupulous cases for them to seem Scrupulous? Did we divide the cases correctly? The answers to these questions will depend on what more we have to say about what makes this condition unified, unique, and distinct from the conditions of those who only have scrupulous traits.

These cases together function much like data to be unified under a theory that shows what they have in common. Of course, we must be cautious in starting with so few cases since a handful of cases cannot claim to be representative without some strong background assumptions about how the cases were chosen. We do make those assumptions here because the reports, which we present just as they were reported by clinicians and religious authorities, were chosen by those researchers because they are both evocative and illustrative of this general disorder. We chose the particular cases we did from the available cases in the literature because these were described at enough length to allow us more insight into the details of the mental processes, and also because they reflect the variety of cases in the literature. We also believe they are representative of the general discussions in the literature, and we will supplement these cases throughout with shorter vignettes and anecdotes, as well as with other data, but these initial cases will give enough of a background for now.

Of course, one should immediately ask: If we already know that these are real cases of Scrupulosity, then aren't we begging the question? We must have a generalization in mind if we can present examples of it. Right? Well, yes, to some extent we do. The examples aren't chosen entirely at random, and we can cull these cases from the literature on Scrupulosity precisely because there *is* a literature on Scrupulosity. Thus, researchers have at least a general working definition—what we should perhaps call a "characterization," rather than a definition—of Scrupulosity. We will consider that characterization in the next two chapters.

The reasons to avoid stating a characterization before giving the cases, though, are two. First, you, the reader, likely do not know that characterization, so we are inviting you to do what we and the authors of these vignettes can no longer do, namely, read the cases without preconceptions about what kind of a disorder is shared by those described. This gives you a chance to assess what we have to say more critically than if we began with an abstract characterization that shaped your reading of the cases.

The second reason is that we hope to go beyond the characterization to consider some philosophical issues that arise from Scrupulosity. So we don't mind drawing on a general characterization, since it is helpful in assembling cases that have some similarities. But we don't want to say more about what those similarities are until we've given the reader a chance to mull them over. We encourage you to do that before moving on to the next chapter.

We'll move on from these cases to a more abstract discussion of the disorder, in order to consider some philosophical issues that the cases raise: Are these people demonstrating a mental illness or a strong moral character? Are they making genuine moral judgments, or only judgments that they wrongly believe are moral? Are they responsible for their actions and any harms they cause? Should they be treated, or should we respect that their moral beliefs are simply very different from or much stronger than our own? Our goal here is to understand those issues in a way that uses the empirical research on these cases to shed light on these more general moral topics. First, though, we'll consider what the psychological research tells us about the condition uniting these cases.

2

Obsessive-Compulsive Disorder

A Little History

Scrupulosity might be found as far back as ancient Rome. Plutarch speaks of "the superstitious man" who "turns pale under his crown of flowers, is terrified while he sacrifices, prays with a faltering voice, scatters incense with trembling hands, and all in all proves how mistaken was the saying of Pythagoras that we are at our best when approaching the gods. For that is the time when the superstitious are most miserable and most woebegone" (Plutarch, 1951: 373, 375–376; cf. www.ocdhistory.net/biblio.html).

Judaism also refers to apparent cases of Scrupulosity in the Talmud (redacted by 500 CE) and to pretty clear cases of Scrupulosity by the 11th century (Greenberg et al., 1987; Greenberg & Huppert, 2010; cf. Mora, 1969). The 13th-century rabbi Nachmanides says about a particular matter of ritual purity, "It is not good for a person to be too strict, looking into doubts to invalidate [the ritual purification] for a light matter, for there is no end to the matter. . . . One should not insert his head into [these] serious, interminable doubts" (Laws of Niddah, 9:25). Nachmanides here echoes a similar sentiment from over 700 years before that a person shouldn't worry about whether some unobserved rodent might have dragged leaven into a house during Passover, when all leavened products are prohibited from the house: "there would be no end of the matter!" (Mishnah Pesachim 1:2)— whether there were people with such worries from 700 years before wasn't recorded, but by the time of Nachmanides there apparently were.

Scrupulosity is clearer in the Catholic tradition by the time of Ignatius of Loyola, the 16th-century Catholic founder of the Jesuit order, who had problems much like those of the cases in the first chapter. For example, after carefully confessing all of his sins, his dictated memoirs record:

Even though the general confessions he had made . . . had been quite carefully done and all in writing, . . . still at times it seemed to him that he had not confessed certain things. This caused him much distress, because although he had confessed them all, he was not satisfied. Thus he began to look for some spiritual men who could cure him of these scruples, but nothing helped him. . . .

[H]is confessor ordered him not to confess anything of the past, unless it was something quite clear. But since he found all those things to be very clear, this order was of no use to him, and so he continued with the difficulty. . . . He persevered in his seven hours of prayer on his knees, getting up regularly at midnight, and in all the other exercises mentioned earlier. But in none of them did he find any cure for his scruples, and it was many months that they were tormenting him. (Loyola, 1991 [1553–1555]: 77–78)

This is one of the earliest recorded cases of apparent Scrupulosity in Catholicism,[2] and our understanding of the disorder owes much to the Catholic tradition. The term "Scrupulosity" in fact comes from the Latin "scrupulosus," from which we get the word "scruple"; but this word comes originally from a word referring to a pebble, which was then used figuratively to refer to a cause of uneasiness—in the way that a small pebble caught in one's shoe would make one consistently uneasy without causing serious pain.

Protestantism also records cases of Scrupulosity perhaps as early as its founding, with many of Martin Luther's concerns and discomforts about whether his confessions were complete anticipating Ignatius's worries by only a few decades (Erikson, 1958). A century later, the English cleric Jeremy Taylor wrote in 1660 of those persons who "dare not eat for fear of gluttony; when they are married they are afraid to do their duty, for fear it be secretly an indulgence to the flesh . . . and yet they dare not omit it for fear they should be unjust." A generation later Bishop John Moore referred to what we now call "Scrupulosity" as "religious melancholy." He describes those with Scrupulosity as having a

fear, that what they do, is so defective and unfit to be presented unto God, that He will not accept it. . . . [They experience] naughty, and sometimes

---

[2] Not everyone agrees that this case is one of Scrupulosity: the symptoms in this short excerpt suggest Scrupulosity, but we won't consider the case in more detail. Fr. Thomas Santa, a Catholic priest and expert on Scrupulosity distinguished (in conversation) cases like that of Ignatius as cases of a "tender conscience," not of Scrupulosity. Nothing we say here depends on whether Ignatius the person would be diagnosed with Scrupulosity, only whether certain descriptions given of him are characteristic of Scrupulosity, though we will continue to probe the distinctions between Scrupulosity and non-disordered forms of religious or moral life.

Blasphemous Thoughts . . . [which] start in their Minds, while they are exercised in the Worship of God . . . [despite] all their endeavors to stifle and suppress them. . . . The more they struggle with them, the more they increase.

Interestingly, Moore noted of them as well: "They are mostly good People . . . for bad men . . . rarely know anything of these kind of Thoughts" (Moore, 1692: 252–253).

This historical context raises a crucial question: If these people are "mostly good" (as Moore said) and sometimes even literal saints (like Ignatius), then why do modern psychiatrists treat Scrupulosity as a mental illness? Do we really want to say that a saint was mentally ill, or that Protestantism or the entire Jesuit order arose out of a mental disease?

Maybe we will want to say that—you'll have to keep reading—though it is worth asking how those facts would matter if they are true. Does it tell us anything about a religious or any other social group or movement if one of the founders had a mental illness? What if the mental illness prompted a founder to make certain rules or set up certain structures: Would that forever blemish the group? Or can we set aside the mental states of the founders and consider the movements on their own merits?

These are difficult questions that, for now, we'll gently sidestep in order to flesh out Scrupulosity more completely. Our understanding of Scrupulosity and of mental disorders in general has developed significantly since Scrupulosity was first recognized. So let's look more closely at how we understand it now.

Obsessions

Scrupulosity is currently understood as a form of obsessive-compulsive disorder (OCD),[3] so we begin by explaining OCD in general. OCD is

---

[3] Although Scrupulosity does not have its own diagnostic category in the official psychiatric handbook (*The Diagnostic and Statistical Manual of Mental Disorders*), the three most recent versions (*DSM*-IV, *DSM*-IV-TR, and *DSM*-5) do mention being "scrupulous" among the criteria for obsessive-compulsive personality disorder (OCPD), e.g., if the patient "is overconscientious, scrupulous, and inflexible about matters of morality, ethics, or values (not accounted for by cultural or religious identification)" (*DSM*-5: 678). Being scrupulous is not enough to qualify one as having Scrupulosity. For someone to be diagnosed with OCD or Scrupulosity, that individual must display "true obsessions and compulsions" (*DSM*-5: 681; cf. p. 242).

characterized, as its name suggests, by obsessions and compulsions. Persons who have OCD have recurrent and persistent, intrusive and unwanted, unjustified, and anxiety-evoking thoughts or "obsessions." They resist or reduce those obsessions by repeatedly performing some behavior or "compulsion," which can be mental or physical. For example, an OCD sufferer might be unable to stop imagining a break-in at his house, which causes great anxiety; to quell the thought, the person repeatedly and compulsively checks the locks to doors of the house or repeats a particular thought. Another OCD sufferer might be constantly anxious about contamination by germs, so she washes her hands many times each hour and avoids touching others.

The central role of anxiety in this syndrome explains why *DSM*-IV-TR classified OCD as an anxiety order. *DSM*-5 later introduced a separate chapter titled "Obsessive-Compulsive and Related Disorders" immediately after its chapter on anxiety disorders. Nonetheless, because of the central role of anxiety regardless of the classification, we will continue to refer to OCD as an "anxiety disorder" (Abramowitz & Jacoby, 2014).

OCD needs to be distinguished from a different condition with a similar name: obsessive-compulsive personality disorder (OCPD). Whereas OCD is an anxiety disorder, OCPD is a personality disorder, i.e., a disorder in those stable traits that make up one's personality. Because anxiety is aversive, people with OCD are generally opposed to their condition. People tend not to be similarly opposed to their own personalities, even when the personality causes distress, so those with OCPD are often not similarly opposed to their own condition. In psychological terms, OCD tends to be "ego-dystonic" and OCPD tends to be "ego-syntonic," although it is not clear whether these distinctions are categorical (e.g., Coles et al., 2008; Eisen et al., 2013).[4] In any case, the official distinction between OCD and OCPD lies in "the presence of true obsessions and compulsions in OCD" (*DSM*-5: 681; cf. 242).

The official definition of OCD thus requires the "presence of obsessions, compulsions, or both" (*DSM*-5: 237), which are both related to the presence

---

[4] Scrupulosity blurs the OCD-OCPD distinction, because it is plausibly an anxiety disorder like OCD, but people with Scrupulosity often see their anxiety as morally justified, so their condition is ego-syntonic like OCPD. Therefore, we will let the OCD-OCPD distinction slip into the background while continuing to highlight the basic issues that distinguish OCD from OCPD: obsessions, compulsions, ego syntonicity, and perhaps a different role for anxiety.

of anxiety in the sufferer. We'll return to the role of anxiety, but let's first consider what obsessions and compulsions are. *DSM-5* (p. 237) diagnoses obsessions as the following:

1. Recurrent and persistent thoughts, urges, or images that are experienced, at some time during the disturbance, as intrusive and unwanted, and that in most individuals cause marked anxiety or distress.
2. The individual attempts to ignore or suppress such thoughts, urges, or images, or to neutralize them with some other thought or action (i.e., by performing a compulsion).

The requirements, then, are that obsessions are (1) recurrent and persistent, (2) unjustified (3) thoughts, urges, or images that are (4) intrusive and unwanted, (5) anxiety or distress evoking, and that (6) prompt compulsions. Let's look at these features in turn.

Recurrent and Persistent

Some individuals might imagine their houses being broken into. Maybe they've just been reading about another break-in, or maybe the thought springs to mind for no obvious reason. Maybe they imagine it vividly. Maybe they imagine something sentimental being stolen or a loved one being assaulted. However they imagine it, they immediately feel great anxiety that pushes their other thoughts off to the side. It's a fleeting thought, though: the thought and the anxiety soon go away without any effort on their part, and they go back to their ordinary life and thoughts.

If the incident is isolated and short-lived, as we've described it, then, however disturbing it might have been in the moment, it's not an obsession. It's just a disturbing thought. If the thought arises again, however, with the same accompanying anxiety, or if similar thoughts arise, or if the thoughts persist for longer, then the thoughts begin to look like obsessions. The thoughts don't need to be always about the same thing, but obsessions will often be on the same topics. For example, the thoughts may center on security and violation, or on death, on contamination of various sorts, on sex and purity, or, in the cases we'll focus on here, on moral or religious violations or contaminations, on sin and spiritual or moral value. What's important to note here is that no one thought on its own is an obsession;

obsessions are part of a pattern of thoughts. And, while any one obsession may be easy enough to dismiss or ignore, the pattern as a whole is not easily dismissed or ignored. It is this repeated pattern that creates a problem for the person.

Unjustified

The requirement that obsessions are unjustified is unstated in the diagnostic criteria, but it's worth making this background assumption explicit for our purposes. Fear, anxiety, and intrusive thoughts about danger and potential loss are sometimes very reasonable. Someone who lives in a community with lots of crime might be very afraid of crime, or she might have particularly valuable and irreplaceable possessions, such as family heirlooms, that she isn't able to secure or that no amount of insurance could replace. An organ transplant patient with a compromised immune system should be very worried about avoiding germs. A soldier in an active war zone is reasonably unable to sleep out of worry about her safety. These higher-than-average levels of fear are entirely reasonable, understandable, and justifiable. Even if the thoughts are slightly exaggerated relative to the actual threat, the thoughts and worries are still justified.

In order for anxiety-inducing thoughts to support a diagnosis of OCD, however, the anxiety must not be a proportionate response to a reasonable and accurate assessment of a danger, threat, or genuine potential for losses. It's normal and justifiable to feel anxious at the thought of a break-in, even one that's very unlikely to happen. Not everyone gets anxious, but it's unsurprising when someone does. And the amount of anxiety a person experiences is justifiable when it's more or less proportionate to the likelihood of a break-in and to the loss—however that loss is measured—that one would suffer. There's obviously no clear formula for determining how much anxiety is proportionate, and reasonable people will differ about what it is reasonable to feel in various situations. Nevertheless, certain levels of anxiety are too much for a given situation.

We don't need to be prescriptive about how much anxiety is merited in any particular situation. People vary in reasonable and idiosyncratic ways. But we should point out two distinctive ways in which anxiety might be unjustified in OCD.

One's anxiety might be unjustified because it wasn't justifiable to form the anxious thoughts or judgments in the first place. This is a common way in which OCD reasoning precedes: there is some small possibility that something bad will happen, and the person fixates on that possibility and responds as if the possibility were serious and severe. For example, I worry that I might have hit someone with my car while driving, despite there being absolutely no real evidence that I did so, or that anyone was hit where I was driving, and no evidence that anyone sober and attentive (as I am) has *ever* hit someone without realizing it. It's of course possible that I hit someone—possible, though so unlikely as not to be worth the thought. The thought and related anxiety about having hit someone are reasonable *if I have some justification that I might have hit someone*, but, given that I have no such justification, the thought and related anxiety are also unjustifiable. What is unjustified is having the thought to begin with, so its subsequent anxiety is unjustified as well.

This raises the second way in which anxiety is unjustified in OCD cases. An anxious thought is not justified when there is only the merest *possibility* that a bad thing could happen. Someone with OCD might put forward elaborate justifications for why it's *possible* that something worth worrying about has occurred or might occur. It is *possible* that one ran into a pedestrian when driving despite finding no evidence that anyone was hit. Why stop with these possibilities? It is *possible* a tornado will take out my house tomorrow—or even a few minutes from now!—despite the calm forecast. It is *possible* that a black hole could form on Long Island from the experiments being done there that would then destroy Earth.[5] These are all possible!

The reason such anxieties aren't justified is because there are infinitely many harmful possibilities that a person could worry about. If a worry were justifiable merely in virtue of its being a possibility, there would be literally no end to the amount of anxiety that could be justified. But we don't have an infinite capacity for anxiety. If we are extremely anxious about something with a minuscule probability of a moderate harm, it's impossible for us to feel proportionately more anxiety for something that is equally harmful but somewhat likely, and we cannot then easily distinguish the serious cases

---

[5] https://www.bnl.gov/rhic/docs/rhicreport.pdf.

from the frivolous ones. Ideally, one's worries should be proportionate to the magnitude of the possible harms and their probability. At a minimum, one's worries should be in proportion to each other.

Feeling disproportionate anxiety isn't limited to those with OCD, since many of us worry more about, say, an unlikely plane crash than about the far likelier car accident we could have on the way to the airport; or we worry more about a harm of an incredibly unlikely terrorist attack than the far likelier harm of slipping in the bathroom. Our disproportionate worry is unjustifiable in all of these ordinary cases, though such disproportionate anxiety is especially characteristic of OCD anxiety, and it's unjustified in part because it's disproportionate.

There are lots of explanations of why someone could have such unjustified thoughts. The most interesting cases for us, though, are those in which individuals have some level of anxiety that prompts them to make a judgment that in turn rationalizes and even reinforces the anxiety. Here's an example of what that means. I have some justification—not much, but some—for my anxious thought that my house could be broken into, but I started thinking about my house being susceptible to a break-in because I was anxious, rather than having anxiety in response to realizing that I was susceptible to a break-in. I might now have very accurate judgments about the break-in rate in my apparently safe neighborhood, and it turns out that the crime rate here is higher than people in the neighborhood would have guessed. But I realized what the crime rate was because I was nervous, and I then looked for evidence to justify my nervousness. I looked at police reports, read the papers, talked to neighbors, drove around the neighborhood late at night, and so on. I then came to believe that we should all be worried about break-ins. And I might even be right that having some anxiety is better justified than my neighbors' complete naive indifference, but the anxiety *arose* without a justification, and I then found a justification for the anxiety. The anxiety did not arise in response to the data, but instead the search for the data was guided by the anxiety: both my search for any evidence at all despite safe appearances and the way that I conducted the search. I deliberately sought out data to show that burglaries do happen in my neighborhood. (If I hadn't found that data, would I have felt reassured, or would I have looked for data from another source?) I thus legitimate my prior anxiety with data that I otherwise would have no reason to examine, since nothing about the neighborhood would suggest to the typical person in my situation that it is dangerous.

The anxiety, then, could be unjustified in several ways. For one, the level of anxiety might be disproportionate to the related thought that one has. More interestingly, though, the thought that apparently causes the anxiety might not itself be justified. Perhaps the judgment is not justified because one failed to look at enough data to justify concluding that anxiety is warranted. (Are break-ins most likely to occur in houses like mine, e.g., with alarm systems and near a street light?) If one's judgment is justified only in the sense that there is *some* evidence in support of it, but it ignores any possible counterevidence, then one's anxiety is unjustified.

Even if the judgment is indeed supported by all of the evidence—one's house really is more likely to be broken into than her neighbors realize—and even if one's anxiety is proportionate to the evidence she has discovered, that anxiety is still compatible with the diagnosis of OCD if the thought arose from a desire to legitimate that prior anxiety (Taylor & Brown, 1988, 1994). After all, if I'm anxious and spend enough time looking for reasons to be anxious, I can surely find *some* reason to be anxious. This kind of subtle connection among beliefs, evidence, and anxiety will arise throughout our discussion.

Thoughts, Urges, or Images (or Beliefs?)

The *DSM* characterizes obsessions as "thoughts, urges, or images." A person with lock-checking OCD might, for example, constantly think that his door is not locked, feel an urge to lock it, or perhaps have an image of a burglar entering his house. A person with hand-washing OCD might constantly think of germs, feel an urge to wash, or imagine germs or tiny bugs crawling on her hands.

It is not clear whether to classify such obsessive "thoughts, urges, or images" as beliefs. These mental states might be emotions, imaginings, pretendings, or some other non-belief state (Levy, 2016). Perhaps at least some obsessions are non-belief states that nevertheless lead to action much as a belief would (cf. Grayson, 2014), but other obsessions might be genuine beliefs.

There is no simple and widely agreed upon definition of "belief" that will settle this issue. Generally speaking, a belief is an attitude we have toward something that we take to be true or that we rely on in deciding to act. But that leaves unanswered all the difficult questions about beliefs: Does a thought count as a belief if I'm only slightly committed to it? What if I don't realize I hold it? What if I would even explicitly deny that I believe it? Can I have a belief that I only barely hold, don't realize I hold, and would explicitly deny that I believe?

Fortunately, we do not need to answer these questions or determine how to define belief. Our interest is instead in what most people are likely asking when they ask whether persons with OCD "genuinely believe" their obsessions: Do they take these obsessive thoughts to be *true* or do they just *act* as if those thoughts are true? For example, do people with OCD who rewash their hands many times actually *believe* that there are still microbes on their hands that need to be washed off, or do they wash their hands *as if* they might still be dirty, perhaps imagining dirt on them, or fearing dirt on them, but not actually believing that they're dirty? The question, then, is whether the person takes the thoughts as true or only as on them.

This narrower question is still difficult to answer. For one thing, some thoughts can't even be true or false. In the example of Bob, a "thought, idea, or image (he wasn't sure which) flashed through his mind—'touch her private parts.'" If an *image* flashed into his mind, then he couldn't believe that the image is either true or false. Statements, sentences, and propositions can (generally) be true or false although one relevant exception is that imperatives like "touch her private parts" are neither true nor false. Images, on the other hand, can be more or less accurate, more or less vivid, more or less appealing, etc., but not more or less true. Thus, if it's an image of touching his infant inappropriately that flashed through Bob's mind, Bob cannot consider the image to be "true." He might believe that the image truly represented the future or truly expressed his desires, but these are not the same as believing that the image itself is "true." Similar remarks apply if his "thought" is an urge or a feeling, like fear or anxiety. Feelings can be fitting or appropriate, aversive or pleasant, strong or weak, but they cannot be true. So a person's images, urges, and feelings cannot themselves be beliefs.

What about thoughts that are about—or caused by—a vivid image or urge? Suppose Bob thinks "I want to (or will) touch my infant inappropriately" or "I am thinking about (or obsessed with) molesting my daughter." Now the question is whether Bob believes that. How can we answer this question?

We cannot simply ask Bob what he believes and take his answer to tell us definitively what he believes. Our access to our own mental states is limited and biased under the best of circumstances, and what we know about

Bob makes us less justified than usual in relying on his self-reports or self-understanding.

If we ask Bob what he believes, we can still use his answer to help us figure out what he believes if we think of his answer as behavior—the behavior of speaking some words—that we have to explain, just as we have to explain the rest of his actions. Under ordinary circumstances, beliefs explain actions, so, if you want to know whether I believe that the light switch in my office works, ask me whether it works and also see whether I flip the switch when I walk in and it's dark. It's not a perfect way to determine what I believe, since there is always more than one explanation of my behavior: maybe I believe the switch doesn't work but I mistakenly said "yes" and then flipped the switch out of habit. Still, at least in principle, we can refine our explanations over time by observing more behavior.

Unfortunately, this strategy is unhelpful in cases of OCD, since the question we are considering is precisely whether the person with OCD actually *has* a belief or *acts as if* he has a belief. This test of checking how a person behaves can't distinguish those two: if we assume that an action reveals a person's belief, then we aren't distinguishing believing from acting as if it's true. So actions aren't definitive tests of whether obsessions are beliefs.

Another potential test looks at the person's evidence. Beliefs that something could be true or false generally respond to evidence. If you see a friend wandering around the parking lot with car keys in hand saying to himself, "Maybe it was stolen," what does your friend believe about his car? Does he believe that it was stolen or is he merely entertaining a distant possibility? The answer might depend on what evidence he has available to him. Did he see broken glass where he remembers parking his car? Does he think of this parking garage as secure? Does he regularly forget where he parked his car? You might say that he doesn't *really* believe his car was stolen because he knows he always forgets where he parks and he doesn't see evidence that it was stolen.

Analogously, someone with hand-washing OCD might have no evidence of actual dirt or germs on her hands, and she might recognize her lack of evidence for this. Whether this person believes in the presence of dirt or germs then depends on the criteria we use for beliefs and also on what evidence is available to the person. Even this notion of when evidence is available is complicated in cases of OCD: on some views, people with OCD have such difficulty breaking their focus away from their obsessional thoughts that they do not—perhaps *cannot*—notice counterevidence.

To add to these complexities, the person's "belief" in OCD cases is often only that something is *possible*. Individuals with hand-washing OCD think it's possible that their hands are still dirty, not because they see dirt on them or even saw them under a microscope, but because they are worried that they *might* be dirty despite a *lack* of evidence. Now, being worried about something can be evidence when one's worries are reliable: worry that I left the stove on is evidence that I *might* have left the stove on, but only if this worry generally arises only when I've actually left the stove on and goes away after I check the stove.

In short, we cannot say in general that the mental states of those with OCD are or are not beliefs. The answer depends on the specific thought we're examining as well as the criteria we use for beliefs and the evidence that is available to the person.

What is perhaps more interesting than asking whether those with OCD have genuine beliefs is noticing that those with OCD who do not really believe their obsessions at first might come to form genuine beliefs over time. This conversion can happen in at least two ways.

First, obsessions can change what evidence one seeks out or what data one considers as evidence, so one ends up with evidence, even though the search for that evidence was unjustified. The person who is worried about the safety of his neighborhood discovers that the neighborhood isn't as safe as he'd hoped. The person who has an obsessive thought about her dirty hands could begin to do research on how hard it is to get all of the microbes off of her hands and discover that, as she feared without justification, it's almost impossible to get every single microbe off of her hands even with very hot water, lots of soap, and intense scrubbing.

Second, a person's belief needn't be that her hands *are* dirty or that she *will* make others sick: she doesn't have evidence for that. Nonetheless, she still might believe that *it's possible*, or that her hands *might be* dirty and that those microbes *could* make others sick. A belief about even a very low probability requires more than merely entertaining the thought that something is possible, which requires no evidence beyond its not being entirely impossible. But weak beliefs about low probabilities can be held on the basis of correspondingly weak evidence. Of course, we can still ask whether someone has even weak evidence, especially if the supposed evidence is only a negative feeling that her hands are dirty and there is evidence that such a negative feeling is unreliable.

These complications suggest that at least some obsessions may be or become beliefs, even if others are not and do not. The variety of cases together with changes over time leave a cloud of uncertainty around whether any particular obsessional thought should be classified as a belief.

Luckily, this classification does not matter much for our purposes. This is in part because complicated cases like obsessions demand nuanced categories, like "in-between" beliefs (Zimmerman, 2007; Schwitzgebel, 2010). It's also because our concern isn't classification as much as understanding. When we want to understand whether someone with an obsession "believes" that obsession, we can ask several questions: Does she think there is evidence for the obsession? Does the obsession change in response to evidence? What is the role of anxiety in sustaining the obsession? We'll return to these questions later, especially when we consider when and how anxiety can count as evidence.

Intrusive and Unwanted

Obsessive thoughts are also intrusive. By various measures, intrusive thoughts are reported to be present in as much as 90% of the population at one time or another (Rachman & de Silva, 1978; Salkovskis & Harrison, 1984; cf. Rassin & Muris, 2007). Almost all of us have worried at some point about whether we locked a door, for example, or left on a stove or a light, and such thoughts can be hard to shake even when we have no evidence for the thing we're worried about. Intrusive thoughts are likewise unbidden and unwelcome.

The intrusive thoughts of OCD vary by case, but one common type of thought—which is also common in cases of Scrupulosity—is the thought of contamination (Fergus, 2014). Contamination can be by dirt or microbes or something else physical; but, more interestingly, the "contaminated" item might be physically completely clean. Its perceived contamination comes from something else, like its history, an association, or its symbolism: maybe it is a shirt once worn by a Nazi or a painting that hung in a convicted pedophile's house. The person with OCD might have no reason to believe that the shirt or painting was physically tainted in any such way, but she still cannot dismiss the thought that the item might somehow be unclean. The thought is unwelcome and incompatible with her other beliefs, yet she cannot shake it. If she does shake it for a while, it returns.

Concerns about non-physical contamination are present in non-pathological cases as well: many of us would be hesitant to wear a shirt worn by a Nazi or a pedophile, no matter how many times it was washed. Thus, aversion to non-physical contamination is not by itself pathological—or, at any rate, it is widespread. What makes a thought intrusive is that it's both unwelcome and inconsistent with one's other beliefs and desires, and it persists despite being both unwelcome and inconsistent.

What does it mean that intrusive thoughts are generally inconsistent with most of one's other beliefs and desires? If I have an unexpected thought that I'm probably going to flunk the test I'm about to take, but I also know I didn't study enough, the painful thought that I'm about to fail isn't intrusive, even if I would prefer not to have it and even if I would perform better on the test if I had higher confidence. What would be an intrusive thought is the thought that the exam was yesterday and I've missed it, despite my having confirmed that the exam is tomorrow and having no other evidence that I've missed it this time.

Intrusive thoughts are also unwelcome. My sudden, unbidden thought as I talk to my boss that I should seduce him might be unprompted and inconsistent with my thoughts about what will make my life and career go best, but it might not be intrusive: I might find it funny that I have such inappropriately lewd thoughts, or I might wonder why my mind reacts to authority in this way, rather than finding the thought unwelcome.

In contrast, an intrusive thought is unwelcome or troubling and it doesn't easily go away when I realize it's intrusive. Consider this same unwelcome sexual thought when I'm talking to a parent or to a sibling. It's harder to shake that thought, which is equally unbidden in the way it arises, and even less consistent with my other desires and beliefs, especially my moral beliefs about incest. It's also less welcome because it's far more troubling. The longer it sticks around, the more troubling it is. I would like to get rid of the thought; even once I get rid of it, I want never to have had the thought, and I might want to find some way to nullify it. This raises a further, crucial element of intrusive thoughts.

Anxiety or Distress Evoking

Although most of us have intrusive thoughts at one time or another, we usually react to them in one of the following four ways (Wells & Davies,

1994). (1) We check the evidence. We look at the knobs on the stove to be sure they're switched to "off." (2) We shift our attention to something else. If we have a thought while at work that we left the door at home unlocked, we might decide just to think about something else instead. (3) We try to analyze why the thought occurred. My unbidden thoughts about seducing my parent makes me think about the ways in which biological urges direct my thoughts and desires in ways that I don't endorse. (4) We discuss the thought with other people. Even if we're unable to dismiss or make sense of the thought, we can at least find others with similar thoughts who reassure us that we're as normal as they are.

In contrast, those with OCD are more likely to react in two other ways (Moore & Abramowitz, 2007; Wells & Davies, 1994). (1) They respond to the thought with anxiety. They worry about what it means that they even had the thought. They worry about whether it makes them a bad person. They worry about whether the thought will itself cause some bad effects in the world. They even worry that the thought itself has contaminated their mind in some way. These worries repeat and build up until they interfere with the person's life.

Or, they do more than merely worrying: (2) They punish themselves in some way for having the thought. The punishment may be physical or mental. It might have the goal of preventing negative effects of the thought or it might serve as retribution for even having had the thought. One way or another, they give themselves the punishment that they think they deserve.

Why do some react in these stronger, more punitive ways to an intrusive thought? We'll focus here on the anxiety that attends the thought. The thoughts feel serious, worrisome, and therefore harder to ignore or dismiss. If that's true, then why would they seem so serious and worrisome? To answer this question, we need to consider what anxiety is.

A range of emotions could count as anxiety. Given how common the word is, we suspect that clinicians—like the rest of us—use the term in various, related ways. Importantly for our purposes, one of the ways in which we use the word "anxiety" refers to a benign sense of excitement and anticipation that one feels when facing something unknown: anxiety about a blind date, performing onstage, or running the race that one trained for. All of these events prompt anxiety, but not because one believes that they will go poorly. One might believe the event will go very well but won't know until it's over. It is this unknown element that prompts anxiety.

On the other hand, anxiety is sometimes prompted by something that could be terrible, like a long-delayed dental appointment, or something that *at best* will turn out to be only mildly bad. Anxiety about a bad outcome is similar to fear about a bad outcome, but the difference is that anxiety is about nothing in particular, whereas fear is of some particular thing. I can be anxious about what is in the tall grass, but I fear the snake that I see. What distinguishes anxiety from fear is that anxiety typically involves uncertainty about a possible threat, and fear is of something determinate.

In anxiety disorders,[6] the person takes the anxiety to be strongly aversive. Its being aversive—like pain or disgust—means only that the person who feels it strongly wants not to feel it.[7] What a person *does* as a result isn't determined simply by its being aversive: pain is aversive, but one may react to a headache by taking an aspirin, taking a nap, trying to ignore it, complaining about it, or going to the doctor. Similarly, most ways of reacting to anxiety are ordinary and unremarkable. If I'm anxious about whether I left the stove on, then I can go back to check, I can think about how likely it is I've actually left it on, I can wonder why I just had that thought, or I can tell my friend about it. But anxiety can also lead to spiraling compulsions and increasing harm. Anxiety about my stove can cripple my life by forcing me to check again and again.

Why do people with OCD respond to intrusive thoughts with such high anxiety? There are, broadly, three reasons for these pathological reactions.

First, in some cases, the person's beliefs may be exaggerated. A person might think her house is *likely* to be broken into, when it is merely *possible* that it will be broken into. For probabilistic beliefs in particular, the person's thought that it's possible to transmit a disease with an unwashed hand, while true, might seem much more likely to the person with OCD than it actually is. Or someone might believe that the risk of burglary is much higher than it really is or that the harms it would cause would be catastrophic, rather than merely inconvenient. In short, they might overestimate the probability or the degree of harm. If their thoughts were accurate, and the harm really

---

[6] Again, we're using the term "anxiety disorders" broadly to include what the *DSM*-5 includes as OCD and as anxiety disorders—all disorders that centrally involve anxiety.

[7] We ignore here cases in which people seek out pain or other aversive states, either because they enjoy the pain itself or enjoy something about keeping oneself in the aversive state, e.g., the feeling of mastery over the pain, or the way that the pain distracts from other aversive states. Such exceptions to our general claims about aversive states will matter in discussions of other psychological disorders but are generally a concern neither with OCD nor with Scrupulosity, so we ignore them in our generalization here.

were more likely, then they would be worrying the appropriate amount. But their thoughts are not accurate.

Second, instead of the thoughts themselves, the problem might lie in the accompanying emotions. The emotions of people with OCD might be stronger or more persistent than others', even for the same thought. I know it's possible that my house will be broken into when I'm gone, but, while the thought is uncomfortable for me just as it is for someone with OCD, it doesn't prompt strong or persistent anxiety. If I instead had strong or persistent anxiety about this possibility, it might be impossible for me to trust that the locks are in fact secure, perhaps unbearable even to leave the house. This doesn't change the thoughts or beliefs, but only the accompanying emotion. So a second possibility is that those with OCD feel extreme anxiety in the face of normal risks and normal beliefs about risks.

Within this area, we should ask whether anxiety always arises from one's thoughts or whether anxiety sometimes causes people to fixate on thoughts that justify why they feel so much anxiety. We will return later to this question, but one common theory of OCD is a cognitive theory, according to which obsessive thoughts cause compulsions (O'Connor & Robillard, 1995; Salkovskis, 1999), and, while the person may be predisposed to feel anxiety, the obsessive thoughts prompt further anxiety. But the alternative causal story is also possible to tell. Anxiety could be a major cause of an obsession if anxiety causes someone to search for a way to rationalize that anxiety. In actual cases, there is also feedback and mutual support between anxiety, obsessions, and compulsions, such that there is no simple causal story to tell about whether anxiety causes the anxious thoughts or anxious thoughts cause the anxiety. It is even complicated to say that either the thoughts or the anxiety is itself "the" cause of a person's subsequent compulsions.

Finally, a third reason for a pathological reaction to intrusive thoughts is that people with OCD might have less ability to shift their attention consistently away from an obsession (Levy, 2018). In our example, they might have normal beliefs and normal initial anxiety reactions but lack a normal ability to ignore, influence, or behaviorally control those anxieties or their responses to the anxiety. They might not even try, either because they assume they would fail or because they don't know any techniques to try. In that case, they might actually have the ability to shift their attention away from the intrusive thoughts, but they don't know that they have this ability, or they don't exercise it. Either way, they don't succeed in shifting their attention or otherwise controlling their anxiety.

Of course, all three of these proposed explanations can interact. If one is unable to control or change one's attention, this might lead one to attend only to certain pieces of evidence (e.g., the fact that there was a break-in down the street), which might lead to false beliefs (e.g., that a break-in here is likely). Or, the difficulties of attention might keep one's focus on one's anxieties, which might reinforce and increase them. Intense anxiety might keep one's attention focused on the object of that anxiety, so feeling anxious about whether the door is locked might be a regular reminder to check it. Mistaken beliefs might both cause anxiety and be caused by anxiety and by attention focused on highly selective evidence. The explanations aren't mutually exclusive and can reinforce each other, so there is often little point in trying to distinguish the best explanation in a particular case.

Compulsions

The final requirement for OCD is that obsessions cause compulsions. *DSM*-5 (p. 237) defines a compulsion as

1. Repetitive behaviors (e.g., handwashing, ordering, and checking) or mental acts (e.g., praying, counting, repeating words silently) that the individual feels driven to perform in response to an obsession or according to rules that must be applied rigidly.
2. The behaviors or mental acts are aimed at preventing or reducing anxiety or distress, or preventing some dreaded event or situation; however, these behaviors or mental acts are not connected in a realistic way with what they are designed to neutralize or prevent, or are clearly excessive.

As presented, it sounds as if anxiety or an anxious thought causes the compulsion, but how they do so is complicated. The ways that people respond to anxiety vary, even in non-pathological cases. People vary in what sorts of things they think will soothe their anxiety. Some anxious people will repetitively wash and others will repeat phrases to themselves. Both of those compulsions could come from anxiety about cleanliness and contamination. So already we see that the story is not a simple one that can predict how or whether anxiety will result in compulsion.

What we can say as a generalization, though, is that compulsions, like obsessions, are unjustified. Obsessions can reduce anxiety in the short term, so they are justified in that way. But they lack a realistic, proportionate connection to reducing one's anxiety overall; and worse, they serve to reinforce the anxiety. So they end up being counterproductive.

This makes it especially strange that people continue to have compulsions. Checking the lock on my door makes sense if it's a sticky lock that sometimes doesn't shut correctly, but how does one develop a lock-checking compulsion when the lock has never failed? If compulsions worked overall, it would make sense that anxious people have them. So how do they arise and why do they stick around?

The key to understanding this is that a compulsion did, at one point, reduce anxiety for the person. It has the opposite effect, of increasing anxiety, only over time. Let's see how that might develop in a case of lock-checking OCD.

An obsessive thought of a break-in evokes (or legitimates, or makes sense of) anxiety, and the person discovers that checking the lock temporarily reassures him and soothes the anxiety. The connection between the worry and the soothing checking behavior is straightforward and reasonable. This reassurance is brief, however: his underlying anxiety about the house's security—or perhaps a more general anxiety—returns, or even persists through, the checking. The obsessive thought will return. When it returns, with the attendant anxiety, this leads to more compulsive behavior in an attempt again to soothe the anxiety. But it turns out that this will develop into an especially vicious circle in the person with OCD. To complicate our lock-checking example, the more often this routine occurs, the more, well, *routine* it feels to check the lock in response to feeling anxiety. And this also makes the routine feel less reassuring. If the initial routine fails to soothe the anxiety, then these individuals may develop compulsive rituals that are less reasonably responsive to the initial anxiety: they develop a particular way of checking the lock that feels more reassuring. They check it a certain number of times or while holding a certain neutralizing thought in mind. Or they develop the belief that the house will remain secure if they always lead with the right foot when stepping into the house or never touch the doorknob with the left hand. These more complex compulsions turn the checking, which initially responded (albeit excessively) to a specific anxiety about the vulnerability of the house, into a ritual that is more than just a temporary reassurance that the lock remains locked.

Indeed, the individuals might perform some compulsive lock-checking ritual as a way of staving off anxiety before any anxiety is felt (Salkovskis, 1999). When they walk near the front door, they check its lock just in case, though not in response to any felt anxiety about a break-in. Or they engage in other compulsions, such as strenuously avoiding vulnerable parts of the house, or seeking excessive reassurance from locksmiths or security companies that the house is secure from break-in. At this point, the ritual takes on a life of its own and becomes increasingly divorced from the initial anxiety that might have led to it. The result is a clear case of OCD.

What Else Is Required?

In addition to the mere presence of obsessions or compulsions, the official definition of OCD also requires that the obsessions or compulsions are time-consuming, cause clinically significant distress, or impair some important area of functioning. These requirements, the last two of which typify all mental disorder diagnoses, keep the definition of OCD from applying to habits and patterns that are like OCD but without being harmful or disruptive to one's life. For example, a proofreader should worry about overlooking a misspelling. That's a normal and productive part of a proofreader's life, so it shouldn't be diagnosed as OCD. But if it causes impairment or distress by keeping the person from being able to write down anything at all for fear that it would be a grammatical mistake, then it looks more like OCD.

These requirements also ensure that the disorder is significant enough to merit treatment. If I love one of my pens so much that I feel "compelled" to search through my bag for it instead of using the first one I find, this could be mildly stressful, mildly impairing, and mildly time consuming; but all of these are so inconsequential that my "pen-preference disorder" shouldn't be diagnosed in this more serious psychiatric category of OCD.

The definition further adds that the symptoms must not be attributable to any substance use, medical condition, or other mental disorder. These requirements ensure that OCD is a distinct mental disorder by reminding us that not all OCD-like symptoms are an expression of the same underlying disorder.

What is not required in these criteria is that the person lack insight into her own condition. A person with OCD might in fact have a good recognition that her obsessive beliefs are probably not true and that the compulsions will probably not remedy anything but her own anxiety for a short time. Alternatively, the person might have poor insight into her own condition, think the obsessive beliefs are probably true, and that the compulsions are effective. If the person genuinely has no insight at all, believes that her obsessions are true, her compulsions are effective, and her emotions are appropriate, then it's also possible that she has more than just OCD. She might, for example, be delusional. But OCD does not necessarily involve any delusions or even mistaken beliefs.

3

Scrupulosity as a Form of OCD

Some descriptions of Scrupulosity make it seem very different from OCD. Informally, Scrupulosity is sometimes characterized as "seeing sin [or immorality] where there is none" or "focus[ing] on minor details of the person's religion, to the exclusion of more important areas" (Nelson et al., 2006: 1072). There is something to these characterizations. People with Scrupulosity do, indeed, see some form of wrongdoing where there is none or much less than they believe. They often do fixate on minor details of their religion to the exclusion of more important values and practices.

Nonetheless, Scrupulosity is also more complicated and more closely connected to OCD than these characterizations suggest. What these informal descriptions leave out are the obsessions and compulsions that structure the disorder. People with Scrupulosity report obsessions like these:

> At times when trying to fall asleep, either when I first go to bed or after I awaken, thoughts of cursing and swearing flash through my mind. I do not use this type of language and would be happy if these thoughts never came. But I'm not sure whether I should confess them or not. (Santa, 2007: 144)
>
> When I look at the crucifix or think about Jesus I often get impure thoughts in my mind about Christ. I seem more likely to be this way when I am upset or afraid. These thoughts come at the most unlikely times, and I don't want them. Sometimes it seems that the more these thoughts upset me and the more I try to push them out of my mind, the more of them I have. (Santa, 2007: 136)

People with Scrupulosity also have compulsions. These are the more visible aspects of the disorder. Recall Adam's checking his receipts again and again, Bridget's checking container after container before serving her customers their meals, Big John's greeting all his fellow workers, Jacob's cleaning his rectal area, or Ezekiel and Mary's repeatedly praying. Such compulsions are part of what justify counting Scrupulosity as a form of OCD.

As with OCD more generally, it has long been recognized that the underlying explanation of Scrupulosity's obsessions and compulsions is the person's anxiety, not a misunderstanding about the way the world is. As researchers said half a century ago about the disorder (without distinguishing fear from anxiety, as we did above): "The basic factor in a scrupulous conscience is not so much error as fear" (Jone & Adelman, 1959: 38).

Despite sharing these general features of OCD, Scrupulosity has its own peculiarities. In particular, scrupulous obsessions and anxieties have a distinctive content. Scrupulous people are focused on moral or religious concerns, harming themselves or others physically or spiritually, or breaking moral or religious rules. They worry about going to hell or about displeasing God. Sometimes they and people with other forms of OCD worry about the same things: sexual purity, contamination, or death, to take three prominent examples (Olatunji et al., 2005). Even when they share these obsessions, people with Scrupulosity react to those anxieties with moral or religious compulsions that are not shared with other forms of OCD. So, while Scrupulosity shares significant overlap with other forms of OCD (cf. *DSM-5*: 238–239), Scrupulosity still differs from other forms of OCD enough to constitute a distinct form of OCD.

All that said, not every case of OCD can be clearly classified either as Scrupulous or as some other form. Someone might repeatedly and excessively wash her hands and also repeatedly and excessively confess her sins to a priest, and both of these might come from a general feeling that she is unclean, both physically and spiritually. Classifying psychopathology in general is no easy task and raises important issues that we have avoided here (Kincaid & Sullivan, 2014). Scrupulosity is no exception. But enough cases are clear and distinct to make Scrupulosity worth an inquiry on its own.

The PIOS-R Scale

The distinctive content of obsessions in Scrupulosity is represented in the topics raised by the questions in the Penn Inventory of Scrupulosity-Revised—or, in a wonderfully appropriate acronym, the PIOS-R (Abramowitz et al., 2002). The PIOS-R scale—in addition to asking for demographic information, including religious affiliation, belief, and practice—asks for responses on the following short series of statements.

Instructions: The following statements refer to experiences that people sometimes have.

Please indicate how often you have these experiences using the following key:

0 = never; 1 = almost never; 2 = sometimes; 3 = often; 4 = constantly.

1. I worry that I might have dishonest thoughts.
2. I fear that I might be an evil person.
3. I fear I will act immorally.
4. I feel urges to confess sins over and over again.
5. I worry about heaven and hell.
6. I worry I must act morally at all times or I will be punished.
7. Feeling guilty interferes with my ability to enjoy things I would like to enjoy.
8. Immoral thoughts come into my head and I can't get rid of them.
9. I am afraid my behavior is unacceptable to God.
10. I fear I have acted inappropriately without realizing it.
11. I must try hard to avoid having certain immoral thoughts.
12. I am very worried that things I did may have been dishonest.
13. I am afraid I will disobey God's rules/laws.
14. I am afraid of having sexual thoughts.
15. I worry I will never have a good relationship with God.
16. I feel guilty about immoral thoughts I have had.
17. I worry that God is upset with me.
18. I am afraid of having immoral thoughts.
19. I am afraid my thoughts are unacceptable to God.

Scoring is simple: the higher one scores on the test, the more scrupulous traits one has. This test is not diagnostic of Scrupulosity. There is no cutoff above which a person would be diagnosed. But those with higher scores are more likely to have Scrupulosity. The scores are also useful in finding other correlations with scrupulous traits, e.g., between scrupulous traits and religiosity or religion.

There is a lot to say about each of these items (Olatunji et al., 2007), but we will confine ourselves here to a few simple observations. Many of these items refer to negative feelings. Items 2, 3, 9, 10, 13, 14, 18, and 19 mention fear. Items 1, 5, 6, 12, 15, and 17 mention worrying. Items 7 and 16 refer to guilt feelings. Items 7, 8, and 11 suggest disabilities. All of these items pick out scrupulous traits that involve some kind of harm. Items 1, 8, 11, 14, 16, 18, and 19 refer directly to obsessive thoughts, though many refer to the contents of obsessive thoughts. Items 4 and 6 mention compulsive actions. These items thus look for obsessive-compulsive traits.

Scrupulosity is often described primarily as religious, so it shouldn't be surprising that many items on the PIOS-R scale mention "God," "hell," or other religious beliefs and practices. This includes at least items 5, 9, 13, 15, 17, and 19. However, as a result of wording the questions this way, the questionnaire might miss people with scrupulous traits who are not religious and would not report their anxieties in this way. Someone with scrupulous traits who has no religious beliefs; whose religious beliefs do not involve beliefs in a god, hell, divine laws, or sin; or whose religious beliefs and activities are otherwise significantly different from the ones suggested here will not score high on these religious items. Since the religious items comprise a large proportion of the total list of questions, these secular people will not score high overall, despite having lots of scrupulous traits. The PIOS-R scale is thus most useful in communities that share the religious beliefs identified here, which are most obviously Christian. Without a second scale to validate the data, however, it is harder to know how accurate it is with non-Christian populations.

In order to capture secular and non-Christian people with Scrupulosity, we composed a secular variation on the PIOS-R. We went back to the much longer, original list of questions that were validated for the PIOS-R, rephrased or translated each one into a secular statement that captured as closely as possible the same thought, then, after testing, emerged with a narrow list of the following questions:

1. I am afraid my thoughts are morally unacceptable.
2. Immoral thoughts come into my head and I cannot get rid of them.
3. I fear I have acted inappropriately without realizing it.
4. I fear I will act immorally.
5. I am very worried that things I did may have been dishonest.
6. I worry that I have harmed others.
7. Trying to follow moral rules is a source of anxiety for me.
8. I feel anxious when people talk about moral issues with me.
9. Making moral decisions frightens me.
10. I worry that I will never be a morally good person.
11. I spend excessive time making sure that I adhere to moral rules.

In preliminary testing, we find that this revised scale captures substantially the same population as the PIOS-R, while also finding a secular population that was not captured by the original PIOS. Future research on Scrupulosity should incorporate a secular questionnaire like ours to quantify scrupulous traits in an individual if that research hopes to capture non-religious Scrupulosity.

Religious Versus Secular Forms of Scrupulosity

Scrupulosity often—but not always—has religious obsessions and compulsions. The examples in the opening chapter included excessive praying, disproportionate attention to religious minutiae, and repeated reassurance-seeking from religious authorities. Mary and Ezekiel, for example, had recurrent, unjustified, unwanted, intrusive, anxiety-inducing thoughts about whether they had completed religious rituals correctly, and Benjamin had similar worries about whether he was adhering correctly to religious laws. Such religious presentations are the most commonly observed kind of Scrupulosity (Abramowitz, 2008; Nelson et al., 2006).

Scrupulosity can also have secular content, such as in the example of Bridget. Bridget's anxieties concerned harming others, which is not distinctively religious. Bridget was herself religious, and she did develop a number of religious rituals, such as making the sign of the cross to stave off harm to strangers and loved ones. However, her central concern—avoiding harm to others—is equally shared by the religious and the secular. Likewise, Bob is concerned about harming his infant, and Peter is concerned about being a neglectful father, which are both secular concerns even if both Bob and Peter were in fact themselves religious. Finally, some cases, like Adam, may not be religious at all.

What makes a case of Scrupulosity religious is not only that the person has religious beliefs or practices or that the person understands her anxieties in religious terms. Otherwise we would count as Scrupulosity any OCD expressed in a religious context, such as a compulsion to check the lock on the door of a church or to line up the prayer books (cf. Tek & Ulug, 2001). For religious Scrupulosity, instead, religious beliefs direct and structure the obsessions and compulsions, meaning that religion significantly shapes the anxiety, obsessions, and/or compulsions of a person with religious Scrupulosity (Yorulmaz et al., 2009; Inozu et al., 2012). The thoughts or actions must therefore have, or have been significantly shaped by, some distinctly religious content, such as blasphemous or sacrilegious thoughts, doubts about dogma or about one's sinfulness, fears of damnation, or religious acts like prayer or religious ritual.

Religion can even give one entirely new things to worry about, as when a religion specifies something as obligatory or forbidden that one otherwise would not have noticed as significant at all. Dietary laws forbid certain foods, and what would have been ordinary actions—from waking up and washing hands to having sex and going to sleep—take on religious meanings. If the person were to have been exposed to another religion, or to no religion at all, then her anxieties may have developed in entirely different ways—and perhaps not developed at all. Once the action (food, thought, etc.) is made salient by the religion, though, the person may no longer be able to ignore it, and this may create or shape one's anxiety. Nobody would become religiously scrupulous in these ways without the religious context (cf. Hacking, 1996).

If Scrupulosity can develop in religious or non-religious ways, why is its religious presentation more common than its secular presentation? Certainly, the research on subtypes of religious Scrupulosity is common, while there is so far no research distinctively on secular Scrupulosity—though secular cases are spread throughout the religious Scrupulosity literature. But nothing in the existing literature indicates the religiously scrupulous have been exposed to religion in systematically different ways from others, apart from being exposed to their own religion. Even if there were some such research, we would be wary of drawing broad conclusions given that our research comes almost exclusively from those with Scrupulosity who also seek treatment: the members of the group who seek treatment might not be a representative sample (Berkson, 1946). They might differ in systematic ways that make it hard to draw conclusions about differences. Those in religious communities might pursue religious counsel instead of more formal therapy, or the nature of religious counsel might dispose them to seek out other counsel. We could only speculate about such differences at this point. Moreover, even if they are open to therapy, as we will discuss below, a very moral person and someone with Scrupulosity can be quite similar superficially, which would keep friends, family, and psychiatrists from noticing that a scrupulous person might be more than just very concerned with morality and might instead have a genuine disorder. Without further research, we can't know how those who end up in treatment differ from a more representative sample, and that adds to our hesitancy to consider why some forms of Scrupulosity have a religious presentation and others do not.

Moreover, it is possible that a secular presentation of Scrupulosity is less likely to be recognized as a form of Scrupulosity, even by therapists. If we expect Scrupulosity to be religious, as many have, we will overlook secular cases. Or, if we do notice them, we might interpret non-religious moral concerns as religious. Religious people often explain their concerns in religious language even when those concerns are themselves not based in anything peculiar to religion. For example, one might interpret Bridget's worries about causing harm as an expression of her religious beliefs, even if such moral beliefs show no particular connection to her religious background. She herself might understand her moral worries that way, if she finds it easier to think of moral issues in religious terms. Big John defends his desire to greet everyone as a fulfillment of the golden rule to love one's neighbor as oneself, but his interpretation is a stretch, to say the least, and we might wonder whether Big John is using religious language to capture a non-religious desire. If he is using religious language to capture a secular desire, should we classify his as a secular or a religious case? The answer isn't obvious. We therefore not only have a very poor estimate of how many secular cases of Scrupulosity there are, but we also face serious obstacles in making an estimate.

If, however, it turns out that Scrupulosity is more likely to develop a religious presentation than a secular presentation, and that explains why there are so many more religious cases than secular ones, we should hypothesize why there is such a discrepancy. Perhaps the religious are more prone to develop OCD. They might be more prone either because those with a predisposition toward OCD tend to be attracted to religion or because common and manageable intrusive thoughts and worries get magnified when people adopt certain religious beliefs and practices. Those hypotheses would have to be developed and defended, of course. Alternatively, many more people are religious than entirely secular, at least in some countries, and the religious use their religion to rationalize their anxieties and compulsions. Or perhaps people don't generally distinguish morality from religion, so anything that feels like a moral concern is understood as religious. At this point, of course, we can only speculate. Secular scrupulosity remains largely a topic for future research.

What's Special about Scrupulosity?

Scrupulosity shares with other forms of OCD the features in the previous section, as well as other features that we won't consider at length here. For example, OCD obsessions often concern sex, death, or contamination of various kinds, and these concerns are present for Scrupulosity as well. What distinguishes Scrupulosity from other forms of OCD are that its obsessions or compulsions are primarily religious or moral. Psychiatric subcategories like these are somewhat porous, so we should not be surprised that someone who clearly receives an OCD diagnosis has diverse obsessions and compulsions, some scrupulous and some not; but, in practice, a person's obsessions do tend to cluster around common issues, and the same compulsive behavior may respond to diverse obsessions. There are enough markers to distinguish someone with Scrupulosity from someone with other forms of OCD, even if some cases are unclear.

Given that what distinguishes Scrupulosity as a form of OCD is that a person has religious or moral obsessions or compulsions, it might be surprising to learn that Scrupulosity has other features that also characterize it and distinguish it from other subtypes of OCD. In particular, Scrupulosity has the following characteristic features: (1) perfectionism, (2) chronic doubt, and (3) moral thought-action fusion (Nelson et al., 2006; cf. Frost & Steketee, 2002; Olatunji, Abramowitz, Williams, Connolly, & Lohr, 2007). We will discuss all three of these distinctive features, particularly the way in which they concern morality.

To be clear, these three features are neither necessary nor sufficient for Scrupulosity—current diagnostic categories rarely allow for simple necessary or sufficient conditions—and we won't claim that these features would diagnose Scrupulosity. In fact, there is also evidence that Scrupulosity could also have other distinctive features, such as a relatively heightened disgust sensitivity, especially toward sex and death (Olatunji et al., 2004; Olatunji et al., 2005), and a greater sense of mental contamination (Fergus, 2014; Melli, 2015). Not enough research has been done to develop these connections in the case of Scrupulosity, and we can't speculate on whether these features are distinctive of Scrupulosity or only of a particular sample of those with Scrupulosity.

Nevertheless, what is interesting about the three features with the most support is this: Scrupulosity is best understood as a form of OCD with moral or religious obsessions or compulsions, so a diagnosis assesses the person's OCD traits. But, having made that diagnosis, it is remarkable that it characteristically has these other, distinctive features. It is therefore worth trying to understand why OCD with moral or religious obsessions or compulsions characteristically has these other features and what that reveals about the condition itself.

Understanding these deeper features of Scrupulosity is also important given that Scrupulosity's obsessions and compulsions do not themselves clearly distinguish Scrupulosity from non-pathological conditions. As we'll see in the following three chapters, some religious and moral views will value each of these conditions, and these features need not always be pathological. Nevertheless, even if neither diagnostic nor necessary, these traits are typical or characteristic of Scrupulosity.

Perfectionism

Perfectionism involves extremely high moral or religious standards for oneself (and maybe also for others) and, correspondingly, a heightened sensitivity to anything that falls short of such standards.[8] This feature is characterized as being

> excessively conscientious, scrupulous, and inflexible about matters of morality, ethics, or values. . . . [Individuals with these characteristics] may force themselves and others to follow rigid moral principles and very strict standards of performance. They may also be mercilessly self-critical about their own mistakes. Individuals with this disorder are rigidly deferential to authority and rules and insist on quite literal compliance, with no rule bending for extenuating circumstances. For example, the individual will not lend a quarter to a friend who needs one to make a telephone call because "neither a borrower not a lender be" or because it would be "bad" for the person's character. These qualities should not be accounted for by the individual's cultural or religious identification. (*DSM*-5: 679–680)

---

[8] Perfectionism in this sense should not be confused with perfectionism as a theory of value or politics; cf. Hurka, 1993.

Psychological perfectionism—though understudied in this context—seems to promote and maintain various psychopathologies, such as anxiety disorders as well as narcissistic and borderline personality disorders (Shafran & Mansell, 2001; Egan, Wade, & Shafran, 2011). This is not surprising: having high standards and being sensitive to whether they are achieved can make one ever-vigilant and anxious about possible failures. In many religious cases, like the cases of Mary and Ezekiel, the person is so sensitive to any (perhaps imagined) defect in nearly perfectly said prayers that she repeats them over and over. Similarly, Jennifer adhered to demanding standards about avoiding idolatry that kept her even from letting herself look at an artwork, so that she would not even come close to worshipping a graven image. And Bridget's perfectionist standards regarding risk of harm to others went well beyond the reasonable concern to avoid poisoning customers when she "checked the containers at almost every order."

As will emerge in later chapters, the distinction between perfectionism as a pathology and having high moral standards or ideals can be difficult to draw. Surely the standards for servers are that they should *never* poison customers, not that they should poison them only occasionally, so what could it mean to say Bridget goes too far? Is it when she checks much more than other servers? Maybe the others are just lax. Is it when she checks so much that she neglects other duties, such as serving her customers quickly? But isn't safety more important than speed? Is it when she creates a personal risk of getting fired? Shouldn't her boss also care about poisoning customers? We cannot and should not assume that all high standards are pathological or an expression of a psychopathology. Nevertheless, some extreme degree of perfectionism is a characteristic feature of many psychopathologies, including Scrupulosity.

Chronic Doubt

The second characteristic feature of Scrupulosity is chronic doubt and intolerance of uncertainty, particularly about the moral or religious status of one's acts and oneself. Many healthy people have some doubts about themselves and whether they are virtuous enough, but these doubts can go too far or can arise in inappropriate contexts. If one is antecedently anxious about sin or immorality, then slight or even imaginary failures can be magnified so that even intense anxiety feels justified. If the doubts and anxieties arise repeatedly, even after reassurances, they are chronic. Mary could not stop doubting that her prayers were acceptable, particularly given the high standards she held for her own prayers, so she needed many, many anxious repetitions before she could feel confident enough that they had been performed adequately. Peter's doubts about whether he had impregnated his girlfriend—particularly given that they had not had intercourse—continued despite overwhelming evidence to the contrary, and he engaged in unnecessary reassuring checking to resolve the small, imagined doubts.

As with perfectionism, chronic doubt itself might not always be a problem. Famous doubters like René Descartes and David Hume extended their doubts far beyond what most people would consider reasonable. Descartes begins his famous *Meditations* by doubting whether everything he senses and believes is real or whether it could all in fact be a dream or the illusory creation of an evil demon. He uses this doubt methodologically to establish what can be known for certain. That is, by first showing that it is possible to doubt even our most basic sensory experiences and beliefs, he can then establish that some beliefs will survive this extreme doubt. We can use these surviving beliefs as foundational in determining what we can know for sure and how we know it.

Hume also introduced extreme and serious doubts in his *Treatise of Human Nature* and later works. As he looked carefully at what his experience and the science of the day revealed, he came to doubt that we ever directly observed one thing causing another and doubted that each of us is (or has) a unified self. He had many other doubts about what we could know and whether our senses could be trusted, just as Descartes proposed. Hume's doubts, like Descartes', are quite extreme, but are they pathological?

Generations of philosophers haven't found them pathological; on the contrary, they have insisted that Descartes was in fact *too quick* to reassure his own doubts by the end of his *Meditations*. Instead of using his doubts methodologically to establish what we know, some philosophers take the doubts seriously and believe that they show us that, in fact, we *should* have such extreme doubts. Hume similarly has no shortage of sympathetic followers who maintain his same doubts even now and have added additional arguments to buttress his doubts against reassurances. Indeed, Hume himself did not even pretend to be able to resolve his own doubts.

He instead responded to them by simply exiting his study and leaving his doubts there, ignoring them rather than answering them.

Therein lies a clue to a difference between the kind of persistent and extreme doubts that are often found in philosophy, particularly in the history of skepticism, and the chronic and extreme doubts found in Scrupulosity. Hume could walk away from his doubts and go about his day with his doubts locked away in his philosophical writing. Descartes assumed his doubts only for the sake of establishing that we in fact do have certain knowledge. If we assume—as we do here—that Descartes' and Hume's skeptical doubts, and those skeptical doubts of many other philosophers, are not themselves simply expressions of a psychopathology, then we should conclude that extreme doubt is not itself necessarily a problem. The problem is where those doubts are found and how they affect the rest of one's life. If Hume were unable to leave his study, crushed by the weight of his skeptical doubts, then that impairment and subsequent distress would signal a psychopathology—perhaps a psychopathology that would make him a talented skeptical philosopher, but a psychopathology nonetheless. Hume, however, not only left his study but had a long, active career (one largely outside of academic philosophy), so extreme doubt by itself was not a problem for him.

It is not just chronic doubt but doubt coupled with intolerance of uncertainty that causes problems. Countless skeptical philosophers and thinkers have doubted. For that matter, successful people in many fields are driven by doubts about whether what they have done is good enough, which keeps them working to improve—being confident leads to its own problems. The exacerbating issue with doubts, though, is how well someone can tolerate those doubts and uncertainty. What do they need to do to resolve the doubts? Do they respond to evidence that something is *unlikely*, or even to evidence that it's *impossible*? Does anything reassure them? And if not, can they live without having their doubts entirely resolved? Can they walk out of the study, so to speak, and leave their doubts behind when they're doing other things, or will the need to resolve the doubts about something lead more broadly to distress, further anxiety, and behaviors designed to resolve the doubts, whatever the cost and however they intrude on the person's life? As with perfectionism, then, extreme chronic doubt and intolerance of uncertainty are not sufficient for Scrupulosity, but their role in inducing and maintaining distress and anxiety is part of what characterizes Scrupulosity.

Thought-Action Fusion

Perhaps the most striking and surprising characteristic of Scrupulosity is thought-action fusion. Thought-action fusion is a broad and not yet well-understood problem with some general connections to OCD (Amir et al., 2001; Berle & Starcevic, 2005; Shafran et al., 1996). There are, in fact, two forms of thought-action fusion: likelihood thought-action fusion and moral thought-action fusion. In both cases, one has difficulty understanding the limitations of one's thoughts and therefore the boundaries between one's thoughts and one's actions.

In *likelihood* thought-action fusion, sufferers believe that their thoughts, merely by occurring, make some bad outcome (such as the act or event that they are imagining) more likely to occur. For example, one patient wrote,

> I have trouble with wishing evil on people. When I was a girl, I wished my neighbor would get sick, and he did. I prayed hard for him, and he got better. One day I got upset with someone and wished her to have cancer. Now she has cancer, and I feel it is my fault. I pray for her a lot. Sometimes I wish that bad accidents would happen and that people would get hurt. I really don't want these terrible things to happen, but these thoughts keep coming anyway. Am I committing sin in having all these evil thoughts? (Santa, 2007: 150)

Remember also Bridget's need to engage in rituals to prevent harm when she "had intrusive thoughts about her younger brother dying from illness or getting into a fatal car accident." Her therapist at the time asserts that "underlying these rituals was the irrational belief that she could ritualistically prevent his death" (Garcia, 2008: 18). She believed that having the thoughts without performing the rituals would lead to harm to her brother.[9] This case seems to exemplify likelihood thought-action fusion. Likelihood thought-action fusion is not distinctively characteristic of Scrupulosity, though it is characteristic of OCD more generally (Berman et al., 2013; Berman et al.,

---

[9] Recall from above that "belief" is ambiguous; we can attribute a belief to someone based on what she does or what she says, and those bases can conflict in OCD. If I sincerely say that I believe that my house is safe regardless of how often I check the stove, yet I continue to check the stove repeatedly "just in case," then it's unclear how to determine what exactly I believe—or even what that means.

2010; Nelson et al., 2006; Rassin & Koster, 2003; cf. Tolin, Abramowitz, Kozak, & Foa, 2001).

In *moral* thought-action fusion, by contrast, people with Scrupulosity fail to distinguish doing something immoral from thinking about doing something immoral and, hence, treat thoughts as equivalent (or close) in moral status to physical actions. They see having unacceptable thoughts, even if they are uncontrollable and intrusive thoughts, as (almost) as bad as having an immoral intention, making an immoral attempt, or even actually performing an immoral action (Abramowitz et al., 2002). The perceived wrongness of having the thought is therefore simply in entertaining its content, however unwillingly.

Linda exemplified moral thought-action fusion when she had "harmful and envious thoughts about others." Linda doesn't necessarily fear that her thoughts will cause harm to those other people. She believes that it is wrong simply to have those thoughts, regardless of any effect. Similarly, Ezekiel saw it as wrong for him to have "a desirous thought of a female neighbor" during his prayers. Again, he never suggests any fear that he will act on those thoughts or that the neighbor will suffer harm. He judged the thoughts themselves as wrong, apart from any consequences.

A more complex example is that of Bob. Although the thought (or idea or image) of his touching his infant's private parts was disturbing to him, Bob was reliably and repeatedly informed that there was nothing wrong about the thought's merely having occurred, particularly because he had no way to stop such thoughts, and the fact that he found them repulsive indicated that the thought was intrusive, not a deep or endorsed desire. Now, if Bob found the thought attractive, or if he had formed an intention rather than entertaining a mere image, or if he chose to entertain the thoughts, then we should reassess the case. But none of that holds in the reported case.

Further, although Bob worried about "giving in" to the idea—which could express some likelihood thought-action fusion—it also seems that he had no desire to do so or history of doing so, and he would presumably be bothered by having such thoughts even if he were far away and had no chance of actually enacting the content of his thoughts. All he had were thoughts (or even just images) of his doing so, but that was bad enough. Bob somehow imbued those thoughts with moral significance, worrying that he was doing wrong merely in having them (cf. Rassin & Koster, 2003).

Thus, Bob seems to be a case of moral thought-action fusion rather than likelihood thought-action fusion—even if the two kinds of thought-action fusion are sometimes difficult to distinguish in practice.

What both likelihood and moral thought-action fusion make more understandable is why people with Scrupulosity, and with OCD more generally, hold themselves to be especially responsible for events that are largely out of their control. For example, someone with hand-washing OCD might say she must wash her hands repeatedly because she might otherwise make someone sick by transmitting diseases. She might; that much is true. But that's very unlikely if she washes her hands regularly and doesn't shake hands with anyone when she's sick or has been interacting with sick people. If she kept those reasonable precautions, we wouldn't hold her responsible for making someone sick if we suspected she did (which, of course, we would never know for sure). She holds herself responsible, though, even for this small chance that she could make someone sick.

Now, imagine what likelihood and moral thought-action fusion do to one's sense of personal responsibility. If I can make someone sick just by thinking about it, I will worry a lot about what I'm responsible for. I might be making people sick with each passing thought! Worse, if it's just as bad for me to *wish* for someone to be sick—or maybe even to *imagine* that they're sick—as it is for me to make them sick, then there is almost no limit to what I will feel responsible for.

Like perfectionism and chronic doubt, moral thought-action fusion has a respectable history in moral and religious teachings. Many religions emphasize keeping one's thoughts pure. Similarly, many moral philosophers—Kant being a prominent example, though certainly not the only one—also consider one's mental states to be paramount in determining an action's moral worth. In Kant's view, the good will (as opposed to any physical action) is the only thing that is unconditionally good and is what determines whether actions are good. What determines whether an action is right, then, is whether the underlying maxim (subjective principle) of the action accords with the categorical imperative, so we morally assess motives and not physical movements or actions themselves (Kant 1997 [1785]). Whether these doctrines, or similar religious doctrines, are a form of moral thought-action fusion are good, provocative questions that depend on difficult Kantian and theological interpretations. Luckily, we do not need to settle those here in order to conclude that moral thought-action fusion characterizes Scrupulosity, though, again, it's not sufficient for a diagnosis of Scrupulosity.

Mutual Reinforcement

Scrupulosity, which is diagnosed as a form of OCD with moral or religious obsessions or compulsions, has these other characteristic features. What we should notice is that this is no coincidence. These characteristic features co-occur because they reinforce each other in a way that will create or at least reinforce this condition. People with Scrupulosity set high moral standards for their actions as well as their thoughts, and then they experience uncertainty and doubt that they meet those standards adequately or often enough (Abramowitz et al., 2002; Ciarrocchi, 1995).

Consider how the reinforcement can happen. Moral thought-action fusion fuels chronic doubt in ways that this Scrupulosity patient makes clear: "How can a person be absolutely certain that he has resisted sufficiently all impure, obscene, or blasphemous thoughts or desires that have come to him? This seems almost impossible to me. But without this certainty, how can peace of mind be achieved?" (Santa, 2007: 153) Moral thought-action fusion also raises the standards for perfection, since our thoughts are much more difficult to control than our actions.

Perfectionism, in turn, reinforces chronic doubt, because perfectionist standards are more difficult than normal standards to know, to meet, or to know that one has met. Perfectionism can even reinforce moral thought-action fusion by raising the standards for moral action so high that one is not only worried about one's actions, and about one's intentions, but even about one's thoughts that are not intentions, so one treats both thoughts and actions equally.

For similar reasons, chronic doubt can also lead to moral thought-action fusion. One might worry about whether one's thoughts were "mere" thoughts or were something more: maybe intentions, or manifestations of deep and immoral desires? In conjunction with perfectionism, there is always room to doubt: Have I recognized everything that I needed to do and then done everything I needed to do in exactly the way I needed to have done it? And chronic doubt can even lead to perfectionism, because uncertainty about whether one has the correct moral standards down to the very last detail can lead one to adopt extreme standards in order to make sure that one did not overlook any immorality.

These interconnections show how the characteristic features of Scrupulosity produce a coherent syndrome and are not just coincidentally related. This will provide the insight we need into why Scrupulosity is genuinely a mental illness, not strong moral character.

4

Mental Illness

Even if Scrupulosity is a form of OCD, as we argued, we still need to ask whether it is a mental illness. We will argue here that it is indeed a mental illness.

This question might seem to be settled already by the fact that OCD is in *DSM*-5, the "bible" of mental disorders. The issue is not so simple. One reason is that Scrupulosity is not itself listed as a mental disorder in *DSM*-5. Second, even though OCD in general is listed there, and Scrupulosity is a form of OCD, Scrupulosity might be an exception that should not be counted as a mental illness (Cefalu, 2010). Moreover, even if Scrupulosity were listed there, the *DSM* (like other bibles) resulted from editorial decisions and compromises, not everyone has faith in it, and the fact that something is listed in or missing from one edition doesn't tell us anything about whether it should be there. Furthermore, unlike other bibles, the *DSM* is revised every few years, and disorders are often added, dropped, or redefined. Therefore, the inclusion or exclusion of a disorder from *DSM*-5 does not tell us for sure whether that disorder genuinely is a mental illness.[10] At a minimum, we need to know *why* it's there (or not there), not simply *that* it's there (or not there). We need to look more carefully at what makes something—including Scrupulosity—a mental illness.[11]

---

[10] A pessimistic induction from previous versions of the *DSM* leads us to expect that at least some items in the manual aren't really mental illnesses. But a reasonable response is that the *DSM* is instead getting more accurate over time, so we should expect fewer and less egregious changes now and in the future. Perhaps, but the pessimistic induction might instead *understate* how likely the *DSM* is to discard current diagnoses in future editions. Major upheavals prompt systemic changes in our understanding of mental illness. This happened in the *DSM*-III's move away from psychoanalytic categories, and it could occur again if our neuroscientific reconceptualization of mental illness develops enough to supplant current classifications.

[11] We might also ask whether all mental illnesses should even be in the *DSM*, or whether there could be some mental illnesses that are not right for inclusion. This line of questioning is about the nature of the *DSM*, its purpose, and how *DSM* editorial decisions are made. The *DSM* certainly plays a role in coordinating treatment and research—whether it is successful in that is less clear (Olbert et al., 2014)—but those practical purposes aren't the same as defining mental illness. We'll focus on what makes for a mental illness and leave aside the question of what should be included in the *DSM*.

What Is a Mental Illness?

One central puzzle about whether Scrupulosity is a mental illness arises because Scrupulosity is characterized by traits that count as virtues in more moderate cases. Adam seems to display honesty, and Big John seems very friendly. So how can they be mentally ill?

To put this puzzle in context, compare another mental illness and how it would contrast with a vice or a bad character trait:

A: Some people are *arrogant*. They often talk about themselves in glowing terms and view others as inferior.

A*: Other people have *narcissistic personality disorder*. Such a person has five or more of these features: "a grandiose sense of self-importance; . . . is preoccupied with fantasies of unlimited success, power, brilliance, beauty or ideal love; believes that he or she is 'special'; . . . requires excessive admiration; has a sense of entitlement; . . . is interpersonally exploitative; . . . lacks empathy; . . . is often envious of others and believes that others are envious of him or her; shows arrogant, haughty behaviors or attitudes." (*DSM*-5: 669–670)

A**: Still other people have *delusions of grandeur*.

Of course, arrogance is a vice, not a virtue, but the point is that like virtues, arrogance comes in degrees and can take on various forms. Arrogance that is a vice but not a mental illness (as in A) can become part of one's personality more generally and would be diagnosed as a personality disorder (as in A*). We don't need to take a stand on whether to count personality disorders as mental illnesses, but some forms of arrogance include features that might eventually become a clear mental illness (as in A**).

Similarly, moody people are not mentally ill, though extreme and prolonged mood swings meet the criteria for bipolar (manic-depressive) disorder (*DSM*-5: 123–154). Recognition of one's own limitations and attention to others' opinions are often admirable, but if these go too far, the person develops avoidant personality disorder (*DSM*-5: 672–673). These cases demonstrate a pattern found in many mental illnesses: a common and even admirable trait is part of a mental illness only when it's in an extreme form, which then often produces other symptoms as well.

This pattern is common even outside of clear diagnoses. Reasonable fears can make a person very careful, but being very careful is not a mental illness. Even unreasonable fears might be widespread but not clinically significant and not indicative of a mental illness. For example, fear of a terrorist attack is unreasonable for almost every private citizen: most people will never be affected by one, and rarely are people as afraid of those many dangerous events, like car accidents, that are much more likely to affect them. Yet an unreasonable fear of terrorism is hardly worthy of therapy just because it is unreasonable. If the fear becomes debilitating or is part of a constellation of debilitating, unreasonable fears, then it could be worthy of therapy; but, again, this is not just in virtue of being unreasonable. Yet unreasonable fears, especially when they are extreme or have lost contract with reality, also form phobias and paranoia.

Let's look at this pattern in Scrupulosity:

> B: Some people are deeply morally committed with high standards. They might even be very virtuous and good people who contribute a great deal of time and money to help the needy and fight long and hard against corruption, injustice, and human rights abuses (e.g., MacFarquhar, 2015).
>
> B*: Other people are so morally demanding and perfectionist that they are diagnosable as having a scrupulous version of obsessive-compulsive personality disorder (*DSM*-5: 678–679).
>
> B**: Still other people have scrupulous obsessions or compulsions that meet the criteria for obsessive-compulsive disorder (*DSM*-5: 237).

These conditions might receive increasingly high scores on the PIOS-R scale, described above.

These alternatives illustrate that the features that characterize Scrupulosity can vary in ways that affect whether Scrupulosity should be classified as a mental illness. As a result, it is easy to answer this question: Does every person who is morally or religiously scrupulous about any part of her life have a mental illness? No. Some features that characterize Scrupulosity are entirely normal, and many of those features that are rare or uncommon fail to qualify as a mental illness. The more difficult and interesting question is whether *any* cases of Scrupulosity are extreme enough to count as mental illnesses. It is even more difficult to say *when* cases of Scrupulosity become extreme enough to count as mental illnesses. And what is it about those cases that make them mental illnesses instead of admirable extreme character traits?

In order to answer these questions, we need to know in general what a mental illness is. This issue deserves a whole book itself (e.g., Graham, 2010), but we can at least look at a few candidate general accounts of mental illness.

Skepticisms

Let's start with some skepticism about mental illness. The skeptical position is that nothing should count as an illness of any kind unless it is similar enough in crucial respects to paradigm cases of physical illnesses. Mental illnesses, on this view, aren't close enough to the paradigm cases. Two aspects of those paradigm cases, which are not shared by mental illnesses, are often emphasized.

First, physical illnesses have physical markers. As Thomas Szasz puts it, they require "a derangement in the structure or function of *cells, tissues, and organs*" (Szasz, 1999: 38). Those "derangements" are then manifested in symptoms. The physical markers of influenza are fever and chills, indicating the presence of the virus. The physical marker of diabetes is high blood sugar, which manifests a disregulation of insulin production. The physical marker of glaucoma is intraocular pressure, which may result from one of several different physical causes. A paradigm physical disease is identifiable by some physical mark that manifests an underlying physical derangement.

Second, to identify a physical illness, doctors don't need to depend on any of their own values or moral judgments. An ophthalmologist diagnoses a patient as having glaucoma without making any assumptions about whether intraocular pressure or damage to the ocular nerve is good or bad, and she certainly doesn't need to know whether the patient is responsible or morally good or bad in order to make the diagnosis. Ophthalmologists assume that glaucoma is bad, but they do not use that value judgment in making their diagnoses. They could make the same diagnosis if they thought glaucoma were good. They simply perform tests designed to measure intraocular pressure.

Admittedly, diagnosis is more complicated than that. Ophthalmologists have to determine whether there is *too much* pressure in the eye. The term "too much" introduces a value judgment of some kind. The threshold chosen is the one above which pressure is *dangerous*, which means that it involves an *unacceptably high danger* or likelihood of *damage* to the ocular nerve, and such *damage* is a problem for the patient. All of this assumes value judgments about what is acceptable, what counts as danger or damage, and what patients want, e.g., to keep their vision. Moreover, good ophthalmologists use more than a simple threshold of intraocular pressure. They will look for confirmation, alternative causes, and question whether their tests were accurate. They decide whether they have good enough evidence to make a diagnosis and what might happen if their judgment is wrong. Which evidence is good enough also depends on evaluating—that is, making value judgments about—the quality of the evidence. Nonetheless, other than evaluating the evidence, an ophthalmologist can diagnose glaucoma without any further value judgments about the patient or the patient's actions, certainly without any reflection on the patient's moral character or responsibility.

Now, if these two features—physical markers and value-free diagnoses—are essential to physical illnesses, and if mental conditions should not be classified as mental illnesses unless they resemble paradigm physical illnesses in these respects, then we have two necessary conditions of mental illness. Mental illnesses need physical markers and need to be diagnosable without relying on any moral or value judgment about the person or the person's actions.

Scrupulosity cannot meet these requirements. We are nowhere near knowing the physical markers of Scrupulosity or knowing whether there is any physical underlying derangement. As we'll discuss, not every mental problem one has reflects an underlying disorder: if I'm distraught that I don't have enough money to pay rent, the underlying problem is probably financial, and neither psychological nor neurological. If I'm angry that you stole from me, the underlying problem isn't my emotional response but your stealing. Likewise, although Scrupulosity's symptoms are distressing, we can't simply assume that they therefore reflect an underlying physical derangement (cf. Sinnott-Armstrong & Summers, 2019).

It also seems impossible to diagnose Scrupulosity without assuming some value judgments about the person or the person's actions. If scrupulous rituals (compulsions) and constantly thinking about morality (obsessions) are indeed morally required, and if perfectionism, moral thought-action fusion, and chronic doubt about moral judgments are normal and justified, even when extreme, then people with Scrupulosity are moral ideals, not mentally ill. Hence, we cannot determine whether someone has Scrupulosity without assuming moral judgments about which actions, thoughts, and characters are appropriate or ideal.

This difficulty is part of why we cannot diagnose Little John, who insists on giving away much of what he has, and also insists that others do the same. We cannot say how much is too much to give away. João and Zell Kravinsky both give away much more than Little John, but João and Zell Kravinsky are not diagnosable with Scrupulosity, whereas Little John was diagnosed. Our reluctance to agree with that diagnosis based on the description here is not because we don't know precisely how much Little John gives away: no amount would be large enough, on its own, for us to conclude that he has Scrupulosity. Or, in the case of Big John, the relevant question in diagnosing Big John is not how many people a person should greet. There is no number over which a person should be diagnosed with a mental illness. We have to decide in another way whether the number of people that Big John greets is excessive. Thus, if all mental illnesses must have morally neutral diagnostic criteria, then Scrupulosity is not a mental illness.

The problem is not just in diagnosing Scrupulosity. Almost no mental illness can meet these requirements. We know of no specific physical markers for many paradigm mental illnesses, from delusions and depression to eating disorders, phobias, or schizophrenia. Even of those mental illnesses that might have physical markers, the diagnosis is done via psychological and behavioral criteria and rarely, if ever, appeals to those physical markers.

Could we someday characterize mental illnesses entirely as physical disorders? Perhaps, but probably not the same mental illnesses that we currently recognize (Sinnott-Armstrong & Summers, 2019). In order to study neurological disorders—brain disorders with physical, neurological markers—instead of psychological disorders, we have to change the subject, sometimes subtly, but sometimes dramatically, from the psychological disorders we currently use and study. For example, instead of studying addiction, which we characterize behaviorally and by psychological criteria like craving, we would study overactive dopaminergic areas and damaged executive areas. (And we would have to specify "overactive" and "damaged" in purely physical terms, not as the simple equivalent of psychological criteria.) It's hard to predict what the end result of this change of subject would be, but many psychological disorders are almost certain not to survive as unified neurological disorders. There is therefore no reason to suspect this is a threat to our claim that mental illnesses *as we currently understand them* are not entirely physical.

We also cannot diagnose many paradigm mental disorders without relying on values or morals. Everyone goes through rough patches from time to time, so everyone has some reason to be down—to be "depressed" in the non-clinical use of the term. Psychiatrists cannot therefore diagnose clinical depression without determining whether patients are *too sad* or sad for *too long*, given what has happened to them. Weeks of debilitating sadness after a death, a job loss, or a bad breakup might or might not be appropriate, but we can't determine that without first determining what the person lost and how serious the loss was. The phrases "too sad" and "too long" again introduce value judgments, since appropriate sadness or grief is, by definition, grief that's not *too* much grief, and hence cannot be diagnosed as depression. This value judgment of how much sadness is appropriate might be implicit or explicit, but to diagnose this paradigm mental illness (and many others) is impossible without relying somehow, somewhere on a value judgment about the person or the person's values or actions.

Well, then, mental illnesses don't—or at least don't all—have these two features of physical illness. What does this show? Eliminativists draw the strong conclusion that, if mental illnesses lack these defining features of illnesses, then all mental illness is a myth (Szasz, 1961; Pickard, 2009; Pearce and Pickard, 2009). Mental conditions are not real illnesses. Instead, eliminativists see mental illness diagnoses as veiled social, political, or moral judgments of deviant reactions to "problems of living" (Szasz, 1961: 114). If they are right, then Scrupulosity is not really a mental illness, because nothing is. The whole category of mental illness should be avoided as "the proper heir to the belief in demonology and witchcraft" (Szasz, 1961: 117–118).

Why might someone be tempted to such an extreme position? Recall what serious mental illnesses look like. A delusional schizophrenic's condition is as disruptive to good mental functioning as a physical illness is to good physical functioning, regardless of any social standards. When people close themselves in their houses and collect weapons because they feel that their neighbors are plotting to kill them, and when they hallucinate people walking through the walls of their houses to attack them, and when they quickly dismiss or refuse to listen to any reasons that might undermine these delusions, their condition is certainly a problem in living, but it is not *only* a problem in living. It's hard to draw a precise line between delusions and eccentric beliefs, some societies might better deal with and encourage mental diversity, and some cases are harder than others to determine. Nonetheless, as Samuel Johnson is reported to have quipped, "The fact of twilight does not show that there is no difference between day and night." Clear instances of mental illness aren't disproven by less clear "twilight" cases. And if delusional schizophrenia is a genuine illness, in the same way that physical illnesses are, then knowledge of the physical cause is irrelevant to whether something is an illness.

Our inability to identify any physical abnormality underlying schizophrenia, OCD, Scrupulosity, or any other disorder might simply reflect our temporary ignorance. After all, we are also ignorant of the precise physical basis of some physical ailments, like fibromyalgia, Tolosa–Hunt syndrome, irritable bowel syndrome, and Behçet's disease. These are all diagnoses without clear etiologies, but we have no doubt that *something* causes those clusters of symptoms. Even for diseases that do, in general, have clear etiologies, sometimes the normal cause isn't present—the diseases are idiopathic—though that also needn't change the diagnosis.

At other times, we simply haven't yet dedicated the resources, however minimal, to determining a disease's cause. Imagine, for example, that a patient has co-occurring rash, weakness, and fever. We haven't yet run any tests, so we are temporarily ignorant of what disease has caused these symptoms. Is that person not ill until we discover the cause of the symptoms? If so, then we had better not run any tests, since the test results could make him sick! But ignorance of the physical cause of some particular symptoms does not entail that there is no disease present. If this can be true for physical illness, it can be true for mental illness. As we devote more resources to discovering the causes of various mental illnesses, we may discover their physical causes. In the meantime, they are still illnesses.

The eliminativist can concede that there can be causes of illnesses that we're ignorant of. They still have their more fundamental position that if, in fact, there is no physical abnormality that causes a so-called mental illness, it cannot be an illness. Although our argument here doesn't require us to make the following claim, we will object to the assumption that a physical abnormality is necessary for a mental illness (cf. Graham, 2010). To see why we find this claim dubious, distinguish the following two claims: (1) mental illnesses have physical causes and (2) those causes are themselves physical abnormalities. We can (and do) accept that all mental illnesses have physical causes without also believing that those physical causes are themselves physical abnormalities.

For example, addiction results in significant part because the reward system of the brain is functioning just as it evolved to function, but the addicted brain has been exposed to substances that are much more rewarding than anything that shaped the brain's evolutionary development. Similarly, post-traumatic stress disorder (PTSD) is caused by our having a memory that functions best when it remembers most clearly the most emotional and stressful events. When that memory is exposed to an overwhelmingly stressful event, it will create debilitating, strong memories. Addiction and PTSD are more complicated than this, but this illustrates how the physical causes of a mental problem are not clearly problems themselves. They become problematic in certain circumstances. Therefore, to assert not only that mental illnesses need to have physical causes but also that those physical causes themselves need to be abnormalities entails that all mental illnesses are necessarily also physical illnesses. That would beg the question, absent some further argument.[12]

What about the other requirement of eliminativists: value-free diagnosis? As we indicated above, mental illnesses are not significantly different from physical illnesses in this respect. We need to rely on some value judgments in order to diagnose many paradigm physical illnesses. How high is too high for blood sugar in diabetes? Blood sugar levels are too high when they cause an unacceptably high likelihood of harm, but we cannot identify which probabilities are unacceptable or which effects are harms without resorting to value judgments. Thus, this rationale for claiming that mental illness is a myth also seems to extend to many paradigm physical illnesses.

A difference remains, however. The value judgments needed to diagnose physical illnesses are not moral judgments about the person or the person's actions. To say that it is bad for a diabetic to suffer from neuropathy is not to say that the diabetic did something wrong, much less that the diabetic is a bad person or that anything is immoral. People sometimes blame

---

[12] A variant on this claim is that a psychological condition is not a genuine illness unless it can be treated physically. However, we don't know whether all physical illnesses will respond to physical treatments. Sometimes lifestyle changes are more effective or have fewer side effects than drug treatments: if one is allergic to peanuts, avoiding peanuts is a better path to health than injecting oneself with epinephrine after each peanut butter and jelly lunch. So the requirement that genuine illnesses are treatable in a particular way is no more defensible than a requirement that all illnesses have a known physical cause.

a diabetic for failing to taking medications properly or even for bringing about the condition by making certain dietary and lifestyle choices, but those judgments are irrelevant to the diagnosis of diabetes.

In contrast, psychiatrists cannot diagnose a patient with Scrupulosity on the basis of the person's perfectionism and doubt without assumptions about which actions are morally required of people in general and which actions go too far. If the person's apparently compulsive acts are in fact morally required, then those acts would not go too far and would not count as evidence of Scrupulosity or of any illness. This diagnosis thus depends not simply on a value judgment but also on a moral judgment about the person or the person's actions.

The eliminativist claims that this dependence on moral judgment is a problem for classifying Scrupulosity as a mental illness. If it is, then it is equally a problem for several other mental illnesses. We already saw that a diagnosis of narcissistic personality disorder depends on judgments of which acts are "exploitative" and "arrogant." Those also require moral judgments. In addition, psychiatrists diagnose patients with antisocial personality disorder (ASPD) on the basis of "deceitfulness . . . reckless disregard for the safety of self or others . . . consistent irresponsibility . . . lack of remorse" (*DSM*-5: 659). None of these symptoms can be identified without moral judgments. Since we all sometimes deceive, disregard some others, and fail in some responsibilities, psychiatrists cannot diagnose antisocial personality disorder without relying on assumptions about how much deception is too much so that it becomes "deceitfulness," about how much disregard for safety of others is too much so that it becomes "reckless," about what counts as "irresponsibility," and about how much remorse is required or appropriate. These are moral judgments, and similar moral judgments are found throughout the *DSM* criteria, so Scrupulosity would not be the only mental illness that needs moral assumptions for diagnosis (see Pickard, 2009; Pearce and Pickard, 2009).

Psychiatrists don't think of themselves as making moral judgments about their patients when they diagnose them, and they want to remain morality-free in order to be scientific. In order to avoid relying on their own moral judgments, they might therefore want to give criteria for these symptoms in terms of social norms. Instead of diagnosing antisocial personality disorder by asking whether the patient displays *too much* deceitfulness or irresponsibility, they might ask instead what that patient's society would *consider to be* too much deceitfulness or irresponsibility. If so, then maybe Scrupulosity is similarly diagnosable by reference to, say, what a patient's society would judge to be too much perfectionism, without the therapist claiming that the person is actually too perfectionist.

This reply suggests an extreme version of social constructionism, which claims that what counts as a mental illness depends on whether people in the society (where they live?) would classify it as extremely deviant (Sedgwick, 1973). For example, Jains, whose behaviors and norms are extreme by our society's standards, would be mentally ill when they live in our society but perfectly sane when they live in a community with only other Jains. But then they can become mentally ill by moving to our society and cure themselves by moving back home. (One wonders what their therapist should say when they call from abroad.) These implications are absurd, so this crude form of social constructivism is indefensible. More sophisticated versions of social constructivism might be able to address this obvious problem, but then they will find it harder to avoid making any moral judgment. As we'll discuss in the final chapter, these problems show why psychiatrists need to rely on real moral judgments instead of mere descriptions of social norms.

Other psychiatrists might try to avoid this conclusion without appealing to a moral evaluation by appealing to the patient's own standards. They can claim that deceitfulness, irresponsibility, or perfectionism go too far not when they violate some independent standard, but instead when they start to undermine the patient's self-interest, health, or some other non-moral value. This move seems to work in some cases. Of course, we first have to establish that these values are in fact non-moral and that we're not just making a moral evaluation of something else: Are these people interfering with their own goals *too much* or *excessively* hurting their own health? Still, in some cases, this strategy might avoid moral evaluations or at least depend on only widely shared moral evaluations—health, autonomy—that are relatively uncontroversial.

It's unlikely, though, that such a strategy will work for Scrupulosity. A crucial part of what makes Scrupulosity a mental illness is associated anxiety and distress. Anxiety and distress feel bad, but anxiety or distress on their own, without excessive perfectionism and other features that likely require moral evaluation, will not count as Scrupulosity. Otherwise, many healthy people with anxiety or distress would be diagnosable with Scrupulosity. It is only unjustified anxiety that supports a diagnosis of Scrupulosity. Hence, psychiatrists would still need to make moral judgments in order to diagnose patients with Scrupulosity, even if this is not true for all mental illnesses.

Eliminativists will, of course, use this reliance on moral judgment to argue that Scrupulosity is not a mental illness. However, similar moral judgments are also needed in order to diagnose other mental illnesses. Moreover, it is not clear why moral judgments are more problematic in this role than other kinds of value judgments—like whether a person is "healthy" or "functioning," or even whether she has "desires" or "beliefs"—which are needed to diagnose physical illnesses.

We can now draw the following conditional conclusion. Even if eliminativism or social constructionism were correct, Scrupulosity would still have a claim to be a mental illness in the same way that schizophrenia, bipolar psychosis, depression, phobias, and other forms of OCD do. If Scrupulosity belongs in the same class as those paradigm cases of mental illness, then forget whether we should call them "mental illnesses" or the ways in which they are like physical illnesses: the real question is whether Scrupulosity might reduce responsibility and warrant psychiatric treatment just as much as those other conditions do. That is what matters to us when we ask whether it is a mental illness. Eliminativists often doubt that mental illnesses should be taken to reduce responsibility and warrant treatment either, but those are topics we'll return to in the last two chapters, when we ask more directly if we should hold people with Scrupulosity morally or legally responsible, and if we should suggest or even require psychiatric treatment. We don't have to take a position on mental illness more generally to ask those questions.

Unity

One final objection by eliminativists questions the unity or coherence of mental illnesses. Schizophrenia might result from any of several, unrelated brain disorders. The symptoms are the same, but the underlying physical causes are very different. For the eliminativist, this shows that it is not a single disorder.

Our response is twofold. First, if true, this only shows that our current understanding of schizophrenia is imperfect. But who would have thought otherwise? As we learn more about underlying neurological causes, we might distinguish different types of schizophrenia. We might even decide that what we currently think of as one disorder was actually several different disorders with similar symptoms. Our understanding of disorders is revisable, but it doesn't follow that our current, general understanding isn't of something "real" or that we should put our psychological research on hold until neurobiology tells us which disorders are the "real" ones.

Second, what it means for a disorder to be "unified" isn't as clear as these opponents assume. What if it turns out that, even though the symptoms of schizophrenia are caused in one of several different neurological ways, every single type of schizophrenia is successfully treated in exactly the same way? Or what if this cluster of symptoms, however it is caused, reduces responsibility in exactly the same way? This finding would not mean that it is a unified disorder when considered neurologically, but it would be a unified disorder when considered in terms of treatment or responsibility.

This response could be taken a step further. If functionalism about the mental is true—meaning, roughly, that neurological states are the states they are in virtue of what mental states they cause—then saying that several different neurological states cause the same mental symptoms could amount to saying that there are several neurological instantiations of the same mental disorder. Therefore, disorders are unified mentally because they correspond to the same mental state, and any neurological disunity is no more significant than the disunity we find with any other mental state: pains, beliefs, desires, emotions, etc. The ways in which each of our brains encode the sentence "The sun is a star" differ, but those neurological differences alone don't show that we have different beliefs about what the sun is.

The same point about the unity of a disorder goes for Scrupulosity. As we learn more, we might revise our understanding of the condition and how to diagnose it. Future research might teach us that Scrupulosity is really a bunch of separate mental illnesses, each with its own distinctive neural basis. Scrupulosity would be like anemia, which can result from many distinct causes. The treatments for Scrupulosity might be more effective by addressing each type's neurological causes. Nonetheless, we might not revise our views of the psychological condition of Scrupulosity. We might continue to see it as unified, just as we still coherently talk of "anemia" despite knowing the various ways it could be caused and treated. We will still wonder whether those with the disorder are responsible and how they differ psychologically from the non-scrupulous.

Or, perhaps, we might someday completely throw out our current understanding of Scrupulosity. We can't predict how our understanding of psychology and neuroscience will change. Further research will show whether this genuinely is a neurologically unified disorder or whether there are many forms of Scrupulosity that are only superficially related. Regardless, we don't have to know all of the underlying causes in order to consider the acts that are distinctive of Scrupulosity, whether they result from a mental illness—or from many related mental illnesses—and what implications these distinctive acts have for moral issues like character, judgment, and responsibility. Those questions are the central ones here.

Definitions of Mental Illness

Although eliminativism and social constructivism cannot show that Scrupulosity is *not* a real mental illness, our responses also do not yet show that Scrupulosity really *is* a mental illness. For that, we need to define mental illness and show that Scrupulosity fits that definition.

Let's start by being clearer about the term "illness." Some theorists talk about "illness" while others refer to "disease," "disorder," or "malady." People with mental illnesses are also sometimes—less formally, and more pejoratively—called "insane," "crazy," "mad," and "sick." These terms are not all synonymous, but what matters for our purposes is not the term but whether Scrupulosity is relevantly similar to schizophrenia, clinical depression, OCD, and other paradigms of mental illness. Hence, we will talk primarily about whether Scrupulosity is a mental illness, and to the extent we use any other term it shouldn't be taken to introduce a distinction unless we make that explicit.

Philosophers and psychiatrists have developed a wide variety of definitions that purport to tell us which features are common to and distinctive of mental illnesses. We will discuss an example or two from each of the main approaches to defining mental illness. (Our discussion here owes much to Nadelhoffer & Sinnott-Armstrong, 2013.)

Dysfunction

One popular approach to defining illness focuses on dysfunction (e.g., Boorse, 1975; Scadding, 1990). When an organism is functioning properly according to its biological "design," it is healthy. When an organism is not functioning properly according to its biological "design," it has an illness (or at least it meets one condition of illness). Thus, this view claims that every illness—physical or mental—can and should be understood in terms of some biological dysfunction. This general biological model of illness includes mental illness due to dysfunctions in either mental capacities themselves or their underlying neural processes. Just as medical doctors identify and then treat physical dysfunction, psychiatrists should also strive to identify and treat mental dysfunction.

According to this account, then, Scrupulosity is a mental illness only if it involves some mental or neural dysfunction. Let's consider OCD first. Although it is not clear precisely which kind of function is relevant, OCD likely involves some dysfunction:

> Biological models of obsessive-compulsive disorder posit abnormalities of some neurotransmitter systems, such as the serotonin system, and dysfunctional circuits in the orbito-striatal area. These models still fail to account for symptom heterogeneity. The cognitive-behavioural model of obsessive-compulsive disorder emphasises the importance of dysfunctional beliefs and appraisals. This model has some empirical support but is insufficient to fully explain the disorder. Thus, despite some promising models, what causes obsessive-compulsive disorder remains unknown. (Abramowitz, Taylor, & McKay, 2009: 497)

In short, researchers have tried to establish, with limited success, that OCD involves biological dysfunction in specific neural circuits or, with more success, psychological dysfunction in beliefs (or belief-like states). If such research is correct, OCD would meet the dysfunction condition in the definition of mental illness.

We cannot be sure, because the research on the biological basis of OCD is itself very limited. Nevertheless, it is plausible to assume there is some dysfunction, as long as we keep in mind the following distinction: a dysfunction *in* the brain needn't be a dysfunction *of* the brain (cf. Graham, 2010). That is, when we say that there is something wrong with someone's brain, we need to be clear about whether we're saying that there is something biologically wrong—a tumor, or a neuroreceptor malfunction—that can be identified without knowing anything about how the brain (or the person) is supposed to function; or whether we're instead saying that what is wrong is that the brain (or the person) isn't functioning the way that is best for the person. Remember the example above of the addictive brain: the reward system responds in biologically appropriate ways to the presence of an over-whelmingly rewarding substance, but that's bad for the person who then pursues the drug to the exclusion of family and friends. Similarly, what goes wrong in OCD may not be due to a biological malfunction of the brain that we could identify independently of the symptoms. It could instead be due to a brain that responds in a biologically appropriate manner in a dysfunc-tional environment.

Presumably, the research on other forms of OCD will apply to Scrupulosity, although there is so far almost no research on the biological basis of Scrupulosity. The relevant brain systems and beliefs facilitate both personal and social functioning, and those functions are undermined in Scrupulosity and in OCD. As we will explain in more detail below, anx-iety steers us away from real dangers, and perhaps even evolved because it helped our ancestors avoid potential risks. Doubt keeps us from jumping to false or unjustified conclusions too quickly. However, anxiety and doubt in Scrupulosity go too far, because most of the feared dangers and risks are not real or not significant enough to warrant the responses. As a result, they block instead of facilitate personal and social functioning. That is what makes such beliefs and the corresponding brain systems dysfunctional in OCD and in Scrupulosity.

Harm

One problem for the functional definition of mental illness is that some dysfunctions are not harmful; and, if not harmful, then they do not seem like illnesses. Consider the physical condition of being albino. Albinism is associated with underlying biological dysfunction in melanin production, but it does not seem to be an illness in most circumstances, since it causes no harm. (Albinism is typically associated with some harms, like vision problems, but let's focus strictly on the lack of pigment in the skin and hair, which is itself not harmful.) Should such harmless cases count as illnesses? If not, then perhaps biological dysfunction is not sufficient for illness: harm is also required. If dysfunction and harm are both required, then the defini-tion might look something like this:

A condition is a disorder if and only if (a) the condition causes some harm or deprivation of benefit to the person as judged by the standards of the person's culture (the value criterion), and (b) the condition results from the inability of some internal mechanism to perform its natural function, wherein natural function is an effect that is part of the evolutionary explanation of the existence and structure of the mechanism (the explanatory criterion). (Wakefield 1992: 384)

Notice that Wakefield explicates natural function in terms of an evolutionary explanation, but functions needn't be understood in terms of evolutionary history—we take no position here on how to understand a mechanism's function. Wakefield also takes harm to be relative to "the person's culture." We've suggested some problems with culture-dependent definitions for mental illness, and this definition would have similar problems. We could alternatively define illness in terms of objective harm (Gert & Culver, 2004).

Regardless of whether harm is objective or socially determined, Scrupulosity will meet the condition of harm. First, Scrupulosity brings anxiety and distress, which, although sometimes useful, are excessive in those with Scrupulosity. Second, and as a result of this anxiety and distress, Scrupulosity causes other disabilities. Bridget is unable to serve her customers, and Big John is not able to enjoy a relaxed walk down the street. Jennifer is not able to enjoy an art museum with her family, Bob cannot change his daughter's diaper, and Linda cannot watch TV or go to Holy Communion, even though she "want[s] so badly to go." These are the harms, whether objective or socially relative, that Scrupulosity brings to oneself and others, thus meeting this second necessary condition of mental illness.

The DSM-5 Definition of Mental Illness

Many other definitions and necessary conditions of mental illness have been proposed. We cannot discuss them all here (but see Nadelhoffer & Sinnott-Armstrong, 2013). Instead, we will close our discussion by looking at the definition of mental disorder in *DSM-5*. The *DSM-5* definition incorporates dysfunction, harm, and some other plausible features that we have not directly addressed here:

A mental disorder is a syndrome characterized by clinically significant disturbance in an individual's cognition, emotion regulation, or behavior that reflects a dysfunction in the psychological, biological, or developmental processes underlying mental functioning. Mental disorders are usually associated with significant distress or disability in social, occupational, or other important activities. An expectable or culturally approved response to a common stressor or loss, such as the death of a loved one, is not a mental disorder. Socially deviant behavior (e.g., political, religious, or sexual) and conflicts that are primarily between the individual and society are not mental disorders unless the deviance or conflict results from a dysfunction in the individual, as described above. (*DSM-5*: 20)

To determine whether Scrupulosity ever fits this definition, we need to ask a series of questions about the crucial terms in this definition.

First, does Scrupulosity involve a "disturbance"? A disturbance is some kind of change for the worse—or potentially for the worse. Without speculating more generally on what "disturbance" means in the *DSM*, though, Scrupulosity is likely to include a disturbance: Scrupulosity brings harms, including anxiety, distress, and disability, which all disturb the person's life and make the life worse. That is enough to include Scrupulosity as a disturbance within any ordinary meaning of the term.

Second, what is this disturbance a disturbance in? The *DSM-5* definition refers to a disturbance in "an individual's cognition, emotion regulation, or behavior." Our previous discussion suggests that people with Scrupulosity have all three kinds of disturbances. Their disturbances in cognition include abnormal moral judgments and sometimes delusions about the causal power of their thoughts, such as when Bridget believes that her "intrusive thoughts about her younger brother dying from illness or getting into a fatal car accident" make him more likely to die. Their disturbances in emotion include anxiety and distress. Their disturbances in behavior include repeated rituals and compulsions. Thus, Scrupulosity involves disturbances in all three areas, any one of which is enough to fulfill this condition in the *DSM-5* definition.

Third, are these disturbances "clinically significant"? Yes, at least in cases where people with Scrupulosity seek help. These individuals suffer "significant distress or disability in social, occupational, or other important activities," which is why they seek or are referred for therapy. For example, when Bob tried to change his daughter's diaper, "he felt nausea, became dizzy, and called his wife to finish, saying that he thought he was ill and would pass out." His Scrupulosity made him unable to have a normal relationship with his daughter and wife. We will return to this topic in the final chapter, but there does seem to be good evidence that Scrupulosity also meets this condition in the *DSM-5* definition.

Fourth, do these disturbances reflect "a dysfunction in the psychological, biological, or developmental processes underlying mental functioning"? As we discussed above, Scrupulosity also meets this requirement.

Fifth, are these disturbances "an expectable or culturally approved response to a common stressor or loss, such as the death of a loved one"? It's unclear whether the disorder arises in response to a common stressor or loss, but, even if so, the responses are not expectable or culturally approved. This is a delicate point, since we expect and to some extent approve many strange and extreme reactions when someone suffers a tragedy. Following a tragedy, a person could become deeply religious or focus on trying to exert some control over other things in her life. We lack evidence that Scrupulosity generally begins in such trauma or tragedy; and, even if it turns out that it does begin this way, we doubt that it is expectable or culturally approved to react in the stronger ways that are typical for Scrupulosity. What we see in Scrupulosity goes well beyond, for example, a person's becoming more religious after the loss of a loved one. Therefore, this condition on mental illness will not rule out Scrupulosity.

Sixth, does Scrupulosity consist only in "conflicts that are primarily between the individual and society"? Sometimes. Ezekiel indicates that his primary concern is not whether he's doing something wrong, but with his wife's response to his actions. However, many cases involve purely internal conflict. If anything, society tries unsuccessfully to reassure people that their internal anxieties are unfounded. Bob's rabbi and psychiatrist are both unable to reassure him that he could change his daughter's diapers without touching her inappropriately. Bob agrees with society that inappropriate touching is extremely serious and deserves some anxiety, but he condemns himself for having those thoughts. Similarly, Adam is not trying to start a revolution to make society more concerned about honesty, nor is society trying to inhibit his honesty. Thus, at least some cases of Scrupulosity are not primarily social conflicts.

Moreover, to the extent that there is social conflict, this is compatible with Scrupulosity's being a mental illness if "the deviance or conflict results from a dysfunction in the individual, as described above." This points to the central question of Scrupulosity: Are the problems encountered by those with Scrupulosity problems of their being genuinely moral in an immoral world? Someone who suffers because of a commitment to social justice, for example, shouldn't count as mentally ill. We assume that being concerned with morality is not itself a dysfunction. (Some, like Nietzsche, would disagree. There's no making Nietzsche happy. We'll leave our assumption undefended.) We do not think the problems of Scrupulosity come primarily from being moral in an immoral world, but we will have to make good on this claim in the rest of the book. We will instead continue to argue that the deviance in Scrupulosity does arise from "a dysfunction in the individual," so, even if some of the person's problems do come from being moral in an immoral world, Scrupulosity will still count as a mental illness.

Overall, then, Scrupulosity fits the conditions in the *DSM*-5 definition of mental disorder, which further confirms our more abstract consideration of why it should be considered a mental illness. Of course, other definitions of "mental illness" have been proposed, and our goal is not to show that Scrupulosity fits any possible definition. What we've shown is that the cases of Scrupulosity we discuss here will fit any definition of mental illness plausible enough to include paradigm mental illnesses. We conclude on that basis that Scrupulosity is a mental illness.

5

Character and Virtue

Scrupulosity raises special concerns about the nature of mental illness. Unlike most disorders, Scrupulosity might appear to be an admirable character trait. After all, Adam, who checked and rechecked his grocery receipts, is trying to be honest and to pay his debts, more so than most of us, who don't worry if a small mistake was made in our favor at a store. Honesty is admirable! Similarly, it's friendly and polite to greet everyone, as Big John does in his workplace, even if he goes further than most of us would. Friendliness is praiseworthy! Peter wants to be completely sure that he performs his duties as a father, if he is one. Fulfilling one's parental duties is laudable! He seems confused about how easily conception occurs, but inadequate sex education isn't what makes his action problematic. In these cases (and many more), the actions that characterize Scrupulosity are actions that usually indicate some virtue, such as honesty, friendliness, and parental devotion. Why would the condition that produces virtuous actions in those with Scrupulosity be a mental illness? That is the puzzle of this chapter.

The simple answer is that people with Scrupulosity go further than people with virtuous character traits. They are not just scrupulous (in the ordinary sense) about, say, praying or giving to charity, but are Scrupulous (in the clinical sense) about those same things. This difference allows that Scrupulosity still lies on the same continuum as moral virtue even if it becomes a clinically significant problem as it approaches the extreme end of the spectrum.

That simple answer cannot be the whole story, however, because many people with extreme admirable character traits do not have the mental illness of Scrupulosity. Moral saints take admirable character traits to an extreme, but they would not be diagnosed with Scrupulosity. We saw a few examples in the first chapter, and Larissa MacFarquhar (2015) has profiled more such moral saints, finding that they are motivated by a keen and sometimes overwhelming sense of duty to sacrifice and devote large parts of their lives to others. They give away almost all of their income, move to the poorest areas, help those in the worst conditions, devote their entire lives to helping others, usually with no hope of recognition. We certainly don't want to assume that people are mentally ill just because they perform extreme moral actions. To the contrary, let's start with the assumption, at least for the sake of argument, that Scrupulosity and moral sainthood are distinct. Then we can ask how to distinguish the two.

It will also be unhelpful to say that the difference is that those with Scrupulosity have a mental illness. People with Scrupulosity might possess both an extreme admirable character trait and a mental illness. We already argued that Scrupulosity is a mental illness. Hence, our question here is only whether their Scrupulosity is also an admirable character trait. Our answer will be that Scrupulosity is not a moral virtue, partly because people with Scrupulosity are actually concerned with moral behavior neither for its own sake nor for the sake of other people but only as a means to reduce their own underlying doubts and anxiety. That goal distinguishes people with Scrupulosity from moral saints and people with moral virtues.

Scrupulosity Versus Religious Devotion

To avoid diagnosing good people as mentally ill, we need first to distinguish Scrupulosity from religious devotion. We have already explained that Scrupulosity needn't be religious, but even when it is primarily religious, it differs from extreme devotion to a religion (Taylor, 2002).

One might be tempted to draw this distinction by citing harm. Scrupulosity, as we argued above, is harmful at least to a person who has it, whereas extreme religious devotion needn't be. That response is too simple. The Jains allow themselves to be harmed in order to respect *ahimsa* (non-injury). Being a Baha'i in Iran is (arguably) more harmful and debilitating than is being a scrupulous Christian in the United States, because of the persecution of Baha'is in Iran. And someone with Scrupulosity might be in a community that supports his condition and keeps it from being too harmful. How harmful Scrupulosity and religiosity are depends so much on external conditions that it cannot be the sole difference between Scrupulosity and extreme religious devotion.

Alternatively, could we distinguish extreme religious devotion from Scrupulosity because genuine devotion is based on positive emotions like admiration (e.g., for religious leaders or texts), love (e.g., of the divine, of members of a religious community, of ritual), and joy (e.g., during religious ceremonies), whereas Scrupulosity derives from negative emotions like anxiety, distress, and doubt? Probably not, because this oversimplifies the nature of extreme religious devotion. Genuinely religious people might rely on their religious practice out of despair or doubt or even worry, and religion certainly helps people with those negative emotions. We can't therefore claim that the difference between Scrupulosity and religious devotion is the valence of the emotion.

A subtler version of this view, however, is correct. We'll develop this position in the next chapter, but the difference can be summarized as follows. Some negative states, like anxiety, explain Scrupulosity because they are what the Scrupulous acts attempt to relieve. This attempt to relieve anxiety distorts the religious practice. For example, a devout Muslim prays five times each day, reads the Koran, fasts during Ramadan, refrains from alcohol, and so on. Why do devout Muslims do all of this? In short, because they think these practices are religiously required and make them better people. Their religion might also relieve despair, doubt, and loneliness. It might make them happy. But that is not why they follow it. Instead, they follow their religion because they think it is right to do so. In contrast, Muslims with Scrupulosity might fast excessively on Ramadan even when it threatens their health. Or they might fast after Ramadan "just in case" they didn't fast successfully on one of the days of Ramadan. They might do this even after being reassured by religious authorities that this post-Ramadan fasting is unnecessary. They also believe it is right to do, but this belief is not the best description of their motivation. This motivation is better understood as an attempt to relieve anxiety about their sinfulness, and some of their religious practices serve as compulsions that are means to that end (Abramowitz, 2002; Greenberg, 1984; Traig, 2004). This is not what motivates true religious devotion, which is not undertaken and sustained primarily as a means to eliminate anxiety.

This underlying difference affects moral and religious judgment and practice in several ways (to be explored in the next chapter). Here is one. Religious Scrupulosity sufferers often fixate on one or a few religious values or rituals even when their fixation makes them neglect other people and projects, including other moral or religious practices that may be even more important. One source explains religious compulsions in Scrupulosity like this:

Compulsive behavior has a narrow focus. Persons may direct their attention to one aspect of religious experience, but exclude others—for example, spending all their energy avoiding sexual misconduct. . . . In a similar vein, compulsive behavior often focuses on what is trivial to religious practice. . . . As a result of scruples' narrow focus, important areas of religious life are ignored. The person may be rigid about external rituals, but pays little attention to commandments relating to love of neighbor. (Jone & Adelman, 1959: 51)

For example, Mary "spent several hours each night repeating prayers and other religious rituals that she was unable to complete during the day. Mary was experiencing difficulties staying awake during the day, reported significant depressive symptoms, and expressed hopelessness and suicidal ideation." In order to pray properly, Mary seems to forget about the rest of her life and obligations. Fixation of this kind is not an admirable character trait. Nor is it an expression of normal religious devotion.

The distinction between Scrupulosity and extreme religious devotion is, admittedly, less clear in many cases. One could be both extremely devoted to a religion and also have Scrupulosity, just as one could be both extremely concerned with home security and also have a lock-checking form of OCD. Ignoring such complications here, though, it is clear that Scrupulosity is very different from extreme religious devotion and religious extremists are not ipso facto mentally ill.

Scrupulosity Versus Moral Character

The anxiety underlying Scrupulosity also shows the difference between people with moral obsessions and compulsions and those with extreme moral character. When we talk about "character," this is not what we mean when we say that someone is "a real character." Instead, it is what we mean when we say that someone "has character" or "has a good character": the person has (or is) a stable, predictably virtuous or admirable character.

It is notoriously difficult to define moral character, but it includes at least two things. First, the person shows attention to, concern for, and responsiveness to morally relevant features of situations, acts, and people. That concern is very much shared by people with Scrupulosity. One trait that reliably comes up in conversations with therapists and counselors who work with those who have Scrupulosity is that they are, as a group, extremely kind and considerate.

Second, moral character requires a stable set of underlying traits and beliefs that non-coincidentally lead to the appropriate motivations and endorsements. If I regularly and despite inconvenience give wholeheartedly to charity in order to help the needy, this act of giving suggests that I have a generous character. In contrast, suppose that I give just as much to a charity, but I do so on a whim, or grudgingly, or because my boss tells me that I will not get promoted unless I donate to her favorite charity. Or suppose I give to charity because it relieves my guilty feelings about being rich—feelings that I view as irrational but inescapable if I don't give. Those are not the descriptions of generous, virtuous character. Similarly, when a friend snaps at me because he has a headache, I excuse him because his momentary slip is only "his headache talking." It does not reflect what he is really like as a person, or his typical responsiveness to morally relevant features of a situation. Thus, moral character is not primarily about one's actions—though actions certainly matter—but instead about the person's motivation and the stability of that underlying motivation (cf. Bommarito, 2018).

Do people with Scrupulosity have the right motivation, and are the motivation and their attendant values stable enough to qualify them as having an extreme but admirable moral character? We'll answer this complex question by first dividing people with Scrupulosity into two groups: ego-dystonic and ego-syntonic. Scrupulosity is *ego-dystonic* when people with this condition are distressed and reject and resist their symptoms. It is *ego-syntonic* when they do not reject or resist their symptoms.[13]

Ego Dystonia and Character

Consider ego-dystonic Scrupulosity first. These people are distressed by their condition. Of course, they might be distressed by thinking that they are not moral *enough*. That will certainly be true of many with Scrupulosity, but it will also be true of many ordinary people, those who reflect on their

---

[13] OCD is paradigmatically ego-dystonic whereas OCPD is paradigmatically ego-syntonic. We are here using the ego-dystonic/ego-syntonic distinction *within* cases of Scrupulosity but we're not thereby assuming that ego-dystonic cases of Scrupulosity are OCD and ego-syntonic ones are a personality disorder. Our interest here is not in whether or how this distinction within Scrupulosity maps onto the OCD/OCPD distinction.

own lives during a church sermon, read books on how to be better people, or consider how they could be better friends or better stand up to injustice. Wanting to be a better person and believing that one can be a better person don't distinguish those with Scrupulosity from ordinary cases of self-improvement.

What comes closer to distinguishing those with Scrupulosity from those without is that those with Scrupulosity think of themselves not only as needing moral improvement but also as morally bad people. Many of us want to improve, but we don't also think that, lacking such improvement, we're generally bad. We're fine, if flawed; we can be better, but we could also be much worse. So, most of us are not distressed about how much we could improve, since we know we're not especially bad. If we never improve, we're still fine or adequate. No one will canonize us, but no one will burn us in effigy either.

Those with Scrupulosity are more likely to think of themselves as sinners or deeply flawed, but there's not enough evidence about how most of the population thinks of itself to know whether this is a significant distinction between those with Scrupulosity and those without. Most of us don't agonize about how bad we are, but maybe only because we're lazy or unreflective and not because we think we're fine. After all, many religious teachings suggest that people are unworthy, fundamentally sinful or flawed, or otherwise exceptionally bad, and it is only through some religious act or grace or belief that anyone becomes genuinely good or good enough.

We suspect from how widespread such religious belief is that many people, especially if prompted in a religious context, would describe themselves similarly to how those with Scrupulosity would describe themselves. They're sinners and need to improve themselves. If ego dystonia means that people believe they're sinful and need radical improvement, that view might be broadly shared, even if persons with Scrupulosity exaggerate this thought and the accompanying feelings.

There is another way in which Scrupulosity could be ego-dystonic, and this way will distinguish Scrupulosity from most ordinary views of morality. A person with Scrupulosity might want to be less concerned about morality. People with OCD (and especially those in treatment) generally want to be less concerned with their obsessions. So, perhaps Scrupulosity is ego-dystonic because one wants to be less concerned about, or at least less bothered by, moral issues. This would distinguish Scrupulosity from ordinary views of morality, but is it relevant to determining whether one has a moral character?

We need to ask whether one's stable traits are part of one's character even when one doesn't want to have those traits. Whether the trait is moral or not, isn't ego dystonia evidence that what one rejects isn't part of one's (deep, real, or true) character? The addict who actively resists a desire to drink shows, by that rejection, that the desire is not part of the addict's character. Right?

That's not obvious. The mere fact that a trait is ego-dystonic does not by itself prove that the condition is not a character trait: one might want to change one's character. One might want to change bad features of one's character, like weakness of will or excess compassion (cf. Strohminger et al., 2017). The alcoholic may view her alcoholism as something that's not part of her character, or she might view it as a part of her character that she actively fights to change. The fact of wanting to change it, of disliking it, or of being unhappy about it doesn't show that it is distinct from one's character.

This is even true of good features of one's character from which one might feel estranged or actively resist. One might wish to be less sensitive to the suffering of others, even while realizing that empathy with others' suffering is a good character trait. Doctors in overwhelmingly impoverished areas, for example, might need to compartmentalize their empathy or compassion, if not actively ignore the plight of many of their patients, so that they are not overwhelmed. Lottery winners might want to be less sensitive to the needs of their friends and family than they were before winning so they don't squander all their winnings too quickly on requests of friends and family. Courageous people who become parents, or mutual fund managers, or bus drivers may want to temper their boldness and be more risk averse, and they may view their courageous character as an impediment to their new responsibilities.[14]

Moreover, we cannot even be sure that we know which of our own traits we're resisting. Those who are very conscientious workers might, just in virtue of that trait, be sensitive to the ways in which they fail to be

---

[14] The defender of the virtues here will note that the virtue of, say, courage requires that one be as bold as the situation requires, but no more and no less. Courageous soldiers who become courageous bus drivers will thus take fewer chances than they would have as soldiers but will remain exactly as courageous. Nevertheless, given how character traits are internalized, courageous soldiers will have to make some effort to change those courageous "instincts" formed in the military, which means that they will, for a while anyway, be opposed to aspects of their character that they think are good but not well suited to this new environment.

conscientious workers. Therefore, they might mischaracterize themselves as lazy and try to resist their lazy characters. Or generous people might give to charity because they are in fact sensitive to how much more they have than they need and how much less others have; but, cynically, they erroneously believe that they are giving to alleviate their guilty feelings (cf. Arpaly, 2003).

Scrupulosity's being ego-dystonic, when it is, does not therefore demonstrate that scrupulous traits are not part of a person's character. Nevertheless, some traits that are genuinely not part of our character are also traits that we will find troubling. If I'm generally conscientious and occasionally lazy, I might be bothered by the occasional laziness. And being bothered by it would indicate that I'm not generally lazy. But being bothered by it is also compatible with my being lazy more generally. So there isn't much of a generalization to make about ego dystonia and character. If people's Scrupulosity is ego-dystonic, either because they believe their scrupulous traits are bad or because they believe the traits are good but ill-suited to the present environment, the ego dystonia establishes neither that those traits are part of their character nor that they are *not* part of their character. The truth, which will emerge later, is that the anxiety that largely explains why Scrupulosity is ego-dystonic itself might suggest that such traits are not part of one's character. But that conclusion will have to wait until we can address Scrupulous anxiety more directly.

Ego Syntonia and Moral Saints

What about ego-syntonic Scrupulosity, in which people see their extreme moral standards and anxiety as justified and perhaps even endorse them? The fact that I like something about myself is some evidence that it's part of my character, but this evidence is not infallible. What I like about myself might be an exceptional feature, one that doesn't fit with who I reliably am most of the time, but only the person I wish I could be. I might like my industriousness on that rare occasion on which I'm industrious, but my character is decidedly louche. It would be convenient for theorizing about ourselves if we liked and endorsed all of our character traits and if all of those traits we liked and endorsed were representative of our character. But who we are is not the same as what we find distressing or endorsable about who we are. If we're lucky, they're at least correlated.

Nevertheless, if people with ego-syntonic Scrupulosity both endorse their high moral standards and recognize that their standards exceed what most other people see as required by morality, that is evidence that they have a high moral character, and not just a mental illness. This, in fact, is probably the best description of many moral saints, who are perfectly aware that their own standards are unusually high, aware that there are alternatives to acting according to such high standards, even that it would be both socially acceptable and more convenient to change, but, who, nevertheless, endorse this part of their character. If we assume that moral saints are acting out of strong moral character—a reasonable enough assumption—then the question is whether ego-syntonic Scrupulosity is a form of moral sainthood in this way.

To answer this question, we need to delve more deeply into cases of ego-syntonic Scrupulosity. Remember Ezekiel: "He considered his rituals to be excessive, but experienced no resistance to carrying them out." Let's assume that he considers his rituals to be excessive only in the sense that they exceed what is normally seen as required but not in the normative sense of going beyond what is good. If so, Ezekiel is to this extent ego-syntonic with his Scrupulosity. He does feel distress and has practical problems as a result, but this could be because his excessive standards go far beyond what is normally thought to be required.

That's also true of people with strong moral character. Compare the tireless devotion of a saint—whether a literal saint or just an extremely moral person—who gives far more of herself than most of us could ever do and does so out of a sense of duty. Or, for that matter, consider someone who spends many hours tracking down the owner of a lost wallet, much more time than most of us would spend.

Like these people with high moral character, when people who have Scrupulosity are excessive, their standards quite often appeal to the same features that we all (or those who share their religious view) see as morally (or religiously) relevant. Those who share Ezekiel's religious beliefs don't disagree with his desire to carry out rituals properly, only how long it takes him to carry them out and why he doubts that they have been carried out correctly. We all agree with Bridget's concern about poisoning strangers and Adam's concern to be honest. The fact that they act on their standards while recognizing that they far exceed normal standards might seem to point toward their high moral character.

Differences

Despite these similarities between Scrupulosity and ordinary morality and religious practice, there are several reasons to suspect that people with Scrupulosity have something other than an extremely strong moral character—at least in the matters concerning their Scrupulosity. (They still might have a strong moral character on some other matters.) Roughly, this is because the concern that shows up in their Scrupulosity is only superficially or derivatively about the morally relevant features that genuine moral character is concerned with. We'll close this chapter by surveying five reasons for this claim.

Fixation

First, people with Scrupulosity fixate on or assign disproportionate weight to certain issues to the exclusion of other important issues. Little John illustrates this point (whether or not he has Scrupulosity). His concern with the hungry and his aversion to wasting food are admirable, but he seems to forget his duties to his own family when he "harangues" his younger sister and brother for wasting food: "More than one meal has ended with the little ones running from the table crying." He is fixated on only one aspect of morality—an important part, to be sure, but not the only part. Since the food that his siblings wasted at that meal would not have helped the hungry, any limited benefits of his actions are not enough to justify treating his siblings this way.

Saints are also often focused on just one or a couple of issues to the exclusion of others, though we might wonder if they are better able to respond to other issues when necessary. Owen Flanagan says of Gandhi, Martin Luther King Jr., and Desmond Tutu that they were

> guided by a commitment to justice and equality for all. But this hardly shows that they lived their whole life, in all domains, guided by that single principle, or, if they did, that it would be a good thing. What exactly does commitment to justice and equality for all do for one when one is trying to attend sensitively to a child who has suffered some interpersonal disappointment, or when one is trying to be responsive to the multifarious needs of one's friends and family? (Flanagan, 1993: 7)

If religious saints do remain focused on certain issues to the exclusion of others, this might be, interestingly enough, a difference between moral saints and religious saints, since religious saints might not always be regarded (especially by those outside of that religion) as moral exemplars. Certainly, the most famous saint of the recent past, Mother Teresa, has been both praised for her work with the poor of Calcutta and strongly criticized for her opposition to contraception, whose use would have reduced the number of poor and increased the resources available to care for those poor who remained.

Perhaps "saint" in the religious case, though, does not mean a *moral* exemplar, but a *religious* exemplar. To be a religious exemplar requires, in general, that one be morally good, but not that one be morally *exemplary*, only morally good enough that one can be religiously exemplary. People may disagree, in particular cases, about whether religious saints are morally exemplary, but the general point is clear: religious saints and moral saints aren't always concerned with the same issues.

It remains true, however, that both religious and secular saints often have a focus—or, pejoratively, a fixation—on just a few key issues. Does that similarity suggest that Scrupulosity and sainthood are similarly motivated? No. The similarity in focus masks an underlying difference in the motivation that causes this focus and, by extension, in whether we can attribute the actions to mental illness or to moral character.

Fixation in Scrupulosity is what we would expect when one is moved by anxiety rather than moved by the relevant religious or moral motivation. A moral or religious concern with a few narrow issues does not make it too difficult to notice or respond to other considerations, even if the person is uninterested in the other issues or finds them to be less worthy of effort or attention. In contrast, the anxiety of a person with Scrupulosity motivates the individual to reduce that anxiety, and, given the disorder, it's difficult for the person to balance reducing that anxiety against other considerations—particularly other considerations that would raise that anxiety. Anxiety commands so much of the person's attention that caring about or sometimes even noticing other considerations becomes impossible. Thus, the anxiety that serves as an underlying motivation in Scrupulosity is what ultimately distinguishes it from strong moral character.

Besides, such intense focus or fixation on a small number of issues might be less common in moral saints than in people with Scrupulosity. In most people whom we think of as very moral, it is rare to find a focus on only one area of morality to the exclusion of other areas. When I call someone "a saint," I mean that the person exemplifies a moral life, is worthy of emulation or, quite often, demonstrates how to be a good person in difficult circumstances. The individual might care about some issues more than others—perhaps the person cares especially about the homeless, or about animal welfare— but this ordinary focus isn't the kind that keeps a person from noticing a large number of other important morally relevant issues. So this focus on only some issues may not be as common in saints as it is in Scrupulosity.

Inflexibility

The second way in which Scrupulosity differs from strong moral character is related to the first. People with Scrupulosity display a kind of rigidity or inflexibility with regard to circumstances. They continue to perform their compulsions even in circumstances where those compulsions make no sense (other than to relieve their anxiety). In contrast, moral saints limit their distinctive acts to situations where those acts will serve their moral goals and values.

To see the difference, consider careful surgeons who wash their hands thoroughly before each operation. They are concerned about cleanliness, because they don't want to risk infecting a patient, and they know how easy it is to spread disease and how difficult it can be to get all germs off their hands. However, this concern can be limited to their professional life. In their ordinary lives, these surgeons interact normally with others, shaking hands at social events with strangers without then scrubbing their hands. They might wash their hands more than the average person, and they might be more careful about what they touch when they know they are sick, but their concerns needn't pervade or become disruptive to their lives. They wash when they need to wash and wash less when it's less important, so their actions correlate with the relevant risks and benefits of different situations. To echo Hume, they can leave their worries in the surgical suite when they finish the operation and re-enter the outside world.

Contrast people with contamination OCD or with Scrupulosity about infecting others—not surgeons, but individuals who scrub their hands continuously out of fear that the remaining germs might infect someone else. They treat every situation in their lives with the same concern about spreading germs, as if every encounter were a medical operation. Unlike the Humean surgeons, they cannot leave their doubts behind. They know that they aren't likely to spread germs if they have already washed their hands, but they can't shake the thought that they *might* spread germs. It's not impossible, so they can't ignore it. And what they are anxious about is harming others by infecting them, so their concerns seem moral.

Some cases of Scrupulosity, like Bridget's, involve anxiety about physical contamination. In most cases of Scrupulosity, however, the dreaded contamination isn't physical but moral, spiritual, or otherwise metaphorical. One patient was so concerned about uttering a racist slur in public that he had trouble ever stepping out into public. Bob and Linda felt contaminated by their bad images and thoughts. Whatever the content of the obsession, the point here is that the obsession invades many areas of the person's life instead of arising only in appropriate circumstances. In that way, people with Scrupulosity often display a kind of inflexibility that is not present (or not as common) in moral saints.

Possibility

The third difference between Scrupulosity, on the one hand, and moral saints and others with strong moral character, on the other, is that people with Scrupulosity are often inhibited in their actions by their obsessions over harms that are merely *possible* but extremely unlikely, whereas moral saints seem more concerned with *probable* or *likely* harms (cf. O'Connor & Robillard, 1995).

Again, recall the careful surgeons who leave their doubts about what is merely possible, but very unlikely, at the wash basin when they enter the surgical suite. Moral saints are similarly not held back by thoughts of possible but improbable harms. Someone like Gandhi could have been held back by the chance that his protests might have led to a backlash by those in power against those he was trying to liberate, and Zell Kravinsky could have avoided donating if he was worried too much about the slim chance that his donations of money and his kidney would somehow harm those he was trying to help. Maybe this is because Gandhi and Kravinsky were unconcerned about what was merely possible but very unlikely, or it might be because, while they were concerned about the merely possible, they didn't let worries about the merely possible interfere with their judgments about what was best to do.

In contrast, Adam's obsession about improbable errors prevented him from doing other things while he checked receipts, and Bridget's obsessions about poisoning her customers prevented her from serving food before checking the containers. But ordinary people of action—including moral saints and morally good people in general—are not stopped by extremely improbable possibilities in the way that many persons with Scrupulosity are.

Personal Responsibility

The fourth way in which Scrupulosity is distinct from strong moral character is that, although people with Scrupulosity are concerned with genuinely moral issues, such as harm to others, what matters to them is often not the occurrence of the harm itself but instead their own perceived personal responsibility for causing the harm. They are more worried about keeping their own hands clean—metaphorically in the case of Scrupulosity—than about preventing harm to others. They feel a great sense of responsibility and think that bad consequences depend uniquely on their own actions.

Contrast yet again surgeons who thoroughly clean their hands before surgery. Their careful attention to scrubbing comes from legitimate concerns, so they are concerned with scrubbing their own hands meticulously. But they also know that other surgeons and attending nurses need to scrub their hands as well. They want the whole operating room to be clean and sterile. They understand that they play an important role in that but that the weight of responsibility is not uniquely on them.

Similarly, moral saints and people with admirable moral characters are usually not motivated because they believe that their actions are uniquely responsible for preventing the harms that they want to prevent. They might believe that they are in a particularly good position to help others. Mother Theresa reported, about her initial call to help the poor, "I was to leave the convent and help the poor while living among them. It was an order. To fail would have been to break the faith" (Clucas, 1988: 35). But a sense that she would be "breaking the faith" to resist helping the poor is not the same as feeling uniquely responsible for the fate of the poor she would live among, and her establishing a religious community to help with her work strongly suggests she did not think her actions were the only ones that could help.

The sense of personal responsibility does not play the same role in morally good character that it does in Scrupulosity.

Wrong Reasons

Finally, people with moral Scrupulosity care about moral issues for the wrong reasons. We'll develop this point further in the next chapter, but here it will help to reflect on difficult cases like Little John's. If I'm a generous person, I help the needy for the reason that it will benefit those whose needs are greater than mine. If I work for a charity because I am forced by a judge to do community service, or because I want to impress my boss, then—while my actions will still be appreciated by those who benefit—it would be inaccurate to say that I'm a generous person or have a generous character.

Similarly, when people with Scrupulosity appear to be extremely concerned with genuinely moral issues, it is unclear that they are concerned for the right reasons. Bridget's repeatedly checking containers is caused in large part by her need to relieve her own bad feelings. Her acts are therefore to soothe herself rather than to protect the health of her customers. To the extent that her actions attempt to relieve her own doubt and anxiety—and relief of one's own doubt and anxiety are not moral reasons—then it is inaccurate and misleading simply to attribute an extremely moral character to her on the basis of her extreme actions.

Of course, even genuinely moral people are sometimes motivated by doubts or anxieties about doing the right thing. I give a little more to charity this year because I doubt that I gave enough last year. Nonetheless, the question is whether the doubt *itself* motivates me or I am motivated instead by an underlying moral concern to do my part in helping the people whom the charity serves. If I doubt that I gave enough last year, and you show me evidence (maybe my receipts) that I gave more than enough, then my doubt will go away. The doubt was only a response to my thought that I didn't give enough.

In contrast, if I am motivated primarily by anxiety, or if my doubt is chronic and not limited to this situation, then these reassurances might not alleviate that anxiety or doubt. To maintain my doubts and explain my anxiety, I might question whether I really gave so much (maybe the receipts are not genuine) or whether I gave with a pure heart. The underlying doubt and anxiety persist regardless of the actions that would normally alleviate it.

This persistence suggests that the doubt is based on anxiety rather than on reasons for doubting.

Conclusion

These reasons all suggest that people with Scrupulosity, even when ego-syntonic, do not have ideal or praiseworthy moral characters or virtues to be imitated or emulated. We argued in the previous chapter that Scrupulosity is a mental illness. These two conclusions together show that Scrupulosity is a mental illness and not an admirable character trait.

If people with Scrupulosity do not generally have strong moral characters, their moral judgments cannot be the expression of a strong moral character. But are their moral judgments nevertheless insightful or are they distorted? Indeed, are they genuine moral judgments at all? This is our next topic.

6

Moral Judgments

The preceding chapters explained why Scrupulosity is a form of OCD and a mental illness rather than just admirable moral character, although some scrupulous traits still occur in non-clinical populations. None of this entails that there is anything wrong with the moral or religious judgments that are central to Scrupulosity. After all, many people without Scrupulosity become quite anxious in the face of tough moral decisions and judgments. Hence, we need to look more closely at judgments by those with Scrupulosity in order to see precisely how their judgments resemble—and how they differ from—ordinary moral judgments. This comparison will help us understand both Scrupulosity and ordinary moral judgments, and, in particular, what role anxiety can play in genuine moral judgments.

Moral judgments those with Scrupulosity make deviate from moral judgments others make in a variety of ways. First, those with Scrupulosity might *care* more than other people about their moral judgments. Their moral judgments might play a larger role in their lives. Second, the *content* of their judgments might be unusual. They might judge some things to be immoral that others see as moral and some things to be moral that others see as immoral. Third, their moral judgments might differ in *formal* respects. People with Scrupulosity might make first-person judgments that differ from their third-person judgments in ways that ordinary moral judgments do not. Fourth, the *motivation* or cause of their moral judgments might be unusual. Their moral judgments might stem from anxiety instead of concern for others. Fifth, as we discussed above, persons with Scrupulosity might get *fixated* on only one aspect of morality or religion so that they undervalue and end up sacrificing other parts of morality that are at least as important. Not every case of a Scrupulous judgment will involve all of these deviations, but the moral judgments of those with Scrupulosity likely differ from ordinary moral judgments in all of these ways. These differences will raise doubts about when and whether Scrupulous judgments should be classified as moral judgments at all.

Caring about Morality

Some people go through their lives without thinking much about morality. When they consider whether to cheat on their taxes, in a game, or on their spouse, they ask whether they will be caught and punished, not whether it is immoral. For at least some people, they care about what they can get away with, not morality.

Most people, though, do at least think about morality, even if they balance moral concerns with what they can get away with. They might know that cheating is wrong and feel bad about it, but they also care—and maybe care more—about the benefits to them if they get away with cheating.

In contrast, some people—those who seem especially morally praiseworthy—care more about being moral and are more careful in thinking about what they are morally required to do. We praise agents for paying close attention to moral requirements. When a small business undercharges someone a dollar, the customer gets some credit for taking morality seriously if she at least considers paying the extra dollar. She gets even more credit if she actually returns the extra dollar.

Conversely, we condemn agents who are thoughtless about or indifferent to what morality requires. People who talk or act without thinking about people around them are denounced as insensitive jerks: the moral thing to do is pay attention to others. People who make promises with no intention of even trying to remember them are rightly criticized for lacking the moral virtue of trustworthiness.

It's hard to imagine condemning someone with Scrupulosity for thinking or caring too little about morality. Adam thinks about whether a store has charged him too little or given him too much change. Big John thinks about his co-workers enough to greet them and about panhandlers enough to help them. Bridget thinks about whether she is inadvertently poisoning her customers. The fact that they think and care about morality when others are thoughtless and careless shows that they avoid some of the most common causes of immorality.

Indeed, people with Scrupulosity seem to pay *too much* attention to moral considerations and care *too much* about morality. Aristotle characterized virtues as means between extremes: people can go too far in either direction. Just as some people eat too much while others eat too little, and some people are too risk-averse while others are too risk-seeking, so some people are too secretive or deceptive while others are too quick to tell the truth, and some people are too selfish while others are too self-abnegating. It might not make sense to say that a person is *too* virtuous in general—a person is too perfectly balanced between all extremes?—but for any particular virtue, it's possible for a person to be too far to one extreme or another.

Is it possible on any view of morality, though, to care *too much* about what morality requires? Many people treat morality as supreme in the sense that it overrides any conflicting non-moral considerations. If you really are morally required not to reveal a secret, then you ought to keep the secret—even if you really, really want to reveal it. If some additional factor (like some harm that could be avoided by telling the secret) is so strong that it is no longer true that you ought to keep the secret, then it is also no longer true that you *morally* ought to keep the secret (cf. Scheffler, 1993).

Of course, not everyone sees morality as supreme in this way. Maybe self-interest or religion override or at least counterbalance moral duties in some cases. It also might not be a good goal to pursue morality above all else (Wolf, 1982). Nevertheless, if morality is supreme, then it's not possible to put *too much* weight on morality.

Caring too much about morality, however, might mean other things. It could mean that one thinks about morality all day long, even when no moral value is at stake; that one spends hours thinking about every moral decision, no matter how minor; that one makes moral judgments about every action by others; or that one talks about moral issues incessantly. It could also mean that one cares too little about non-moral things. Alternatively, it could mean that all moral considerations are equally important, so that one is not only willing to die to prevent a murder but also willing to die to prevent an error in how much change a person is given after a purchase. Or, maybe it means not that someone literally *cares* too much, but that they *do* too much.

All of these ways of "caring too much" could be true of some people with Scrupulosity, but "caring too much" can mean so many different things that we can't start with the assumption that people with Scrupulosity care too much about morality. Indeed, it is not always clear that what they do care about is morality. People with Scrupulosity illustrate how morality-focused judgments can become pathological and might not even be best characterized as genuine moral judgments. But this will take some work to establish.

Content

One feature of Scrupulous moral judgments that seems deviant is their content. We saw that above in discussions of perfectionism and thought-action fusion. Accordingly, we will begin our discussion of Scrupulous moral judgments by focusing in this section on their content.

When we say that a judgment has moral content, what we mean, generally, is that the judgment is about something that is judged to be morally good or bad, right or wrong, or that it morally ought or ought not to be done—or something closely related to or entailing one of these judgments—perhaps in virtue of some harm to other people. A judgment that it's morally wrong to hit someone, or that it's morally bad, or that you morally ought not to do it all have moral content, as would the judgment that it's mean or cruel to hit someone. But the judgment that it's *gross* to hit someone is probably not a moral judgment, though gross things are bad in some way.

You might wonder at this point what it means to say that something "can cause harm," and why being gross doesn't count as causing harm. What about psychological harm? Indeed, many evaluations of good and bad that we would classify as non-moral cause some psychological discomfort: ugly art and poor taste combinations cause discomfort, so am I making a moral judgment when I say that a sculpture is bad or the chef ought not to have combined these flavors? What if I cringe when I see polka dots and plaid together? What if I am annoyed with an author who interminably and unnecessarily uses adverbs?

It is impossible to say succinctly here why some judgments about what is bad and harmful count as moral and others count as aesthetic, or gustatory, or sartorial, or literary. But we will assume, without additional explanation or argument, that the kind of moral judgment at stake here is about harm to other people that is more serious than aesthetic, gustatory, sartorial, and literary harms. This could also include violations of rules (such as "do not lie" or "don't break promises") whose widespread violation would cause morally relevant harms.

More should be said in defense of any position about what makes a judgment moral. But we want to focus initially on comparing this central kind of moral judgment by people with and without Scrupulosity. These comparisons do not require more precision about the distinction between moral and non-moral judgments. We will return to the notion of a moral judgment at the end of this chapter. For now, let's get on with exploring how the content of judgments by people with Scrupulosity are affected by their perfectionism, moral thought-action fusion, and chronic doubt.

Perfectionism

Perfectionism in those with Scrupulosity entails their having very high standards that exaggerate normal standards. Bridget is concerned about the slightest chance of harming people by letting them be exposed to the tiniest amount of poison. The rest of us are also concerned about accidentally harming people and take precautions to avoid doing so, sometimes even when the possibility of harm is so minuscule that precautions are unnecessary. We stop at red lights even when we can see clearly that no car is coming, so the probability of causing an accident by running the light is incredibly low. If you were driving legally and carefully but still hit a child who darted in front of your car without warning, you would feel bad, either because you could have driven even more slowly and carefully or just because you played some role—albeit blameless—in the accident. Such examples suggest that we have some sympathy with the perfectionist standard that we should never kill or harm other people, not just that we should take some reasonable precautions against harming and killing.

Perfectionist standards may also be held by those who share a Scrupulous religious view. Benjamin is careful not to touch his wife when she is menstruating, but so are many other orthodox Jewish men. Religious Muslims and Jews are careful not to consume any pork, taking precautions against even accidentally eating it. The perfectionist content by itself does not seem to be what separates the moral judgments by those who have Scrupulosity from moral judgments by those who do not.

Other differences remain. After all, just because religious Muslims and Scrupulous Muslims will both be careful to avoid accidentally consuming any pork, that does not mean that their relevant beliefs and judgments are the same in all respects. Likewise, if people with Scrupulosity are extremely careful not to hit a pedestrian and so are we, then we can *describe* the actions and beliefs in the same general way (i.e., we all want to avoid causing harm to pedestrians while driving), but this general description can cover up crucial underlying mental differences.

At this point, we run into a general problem of specifying exactly what the content of *any* particular belief or other mental state is, regardless of whether the person has Scrupulosity (Noggle, 2016). Take Bridget. Let's be generous with the word "belief," so we won't worry too much about what counts as a genuine belief and what is only a quasi-belief. Bridget believes that she should be careful not to poison her customers, which is a belief that we all share. But she checks containers of dangerous substances that come nowhere near the food. That's not what most of us would do in her situation, even though we claim to have the same belief. Perhaps, then, her belief is stronger than ours? Does she believe that she has a moral obligation to avoid *any possible way* that her customers could be poisoned, no matter how unlikely? If she believed that, then she would presumably stand next to the plate during its entire preparation. And could she simply assume that the ingredients themselves are untainted? She would need to check the preparation of the ingredients that go onto the plate, even before they arrived at the restaurant, maybe even from before the vegetables are planted in case something dangerous was in the soil. Since Bridget is not guarding each ingredient that ends up on the plate as it moves from the farm, she must not believe that *every possible chance* of poison should be guarded against. So, again, we seem to be in agreement with her that we should be careful, but don't need to rule out every possible chance of poison.

How else can we specify her belief? We could just ask her what she believes, but people do not always know what their beliefs are. We could infer her beliefs from her actions, but people's actions don't always reflect their beliefs. It's especially hard to determine people's moral beliefs from their actions, since we allow that moral beliefs are sometimes aspirational. Moreover, even if actions generally indicated one's beliefs, the actions of someone with a mental illness are less reliable than most. So we cannot assume that Bridget's actions reflect her beliefs any more than we can assume her words reflect her beliefs. Both words and actions must be interpreted against some background assumptions about what individuals are like, including that they are rational and are trying to be consistent with their other beliefs and actions (Davidson, 2004). Bridget might have even less coherent beliefs and motivations than most of us, which makes it very difficult to know precisely which content to attribute to Bridget's beliefs.

On some charitable interpretations of what Bridget believes, though, we probably agree with her. We agree with Bridget that we should check food a *reasonable* amount, especially if there is a *significant* chance that the food could have been poisoned. However, this superficially similar content contains qualifications like "reasonable" and "significant" that can be interpreted very differently. What Bridget thinks of as reasonable and significant is probably very different from what the rest of us think of as reasonable and significant. Or, perhaps Bridget thinks that she is doing what it takes to be a *good* server, which is another belief we share, though we differ as to what is required to be a *good* server. Therefore, if we are charitable in specifying the content of Bridget's beliefs in these qualified ways, her moral judgments share the content of ordinary moral judgments, but only because we have not specified more precisely the content of those qualifications.

In addition to whatever qualified moral principles we may share with persons with Scrupulosity, we also seem to share with them ideals that we both take to be attainable and worth pursuing. We may agree—again, in very general terms—that people *should* be *as close as possible* to the ideal of *minimizing risk* to others, that *perfection* is better than *imperfection*, that it's *wrong* to *settle* for being *flawed*. The difference is that people with Scrupulosity might see these ideals as required, whereas we see these ideals as, well, *ideal*, but not as required.

Again, however, is this agreement merely superficial? Some people who genuinely care about moral requirements care more about moral ideals than others. Those who care more about the ideals feel bad when they fail to achieve the ideal, even when they know that they did everything that they were required to do. They might see little difference between ideals and requirements. In contrast, those who care less about the ideals are satisfied (or feel less bad) even when they fail to achieve an ideal. They seem to see a deeper divide between ideals and requirements. Those who care more about ideals will, accordingly, see the difference between the perfectionist judgments of people with Scrupulosity and non-perfectionist moral judgments as superficial, and those who care less about ideals will find these differences to be deeper.

What explains how much we care about our failure to live up to some ideal will, of course, depend on more than simply how much we care about ideals in general. Our judgments also vary in particular cases and contexts. A person might feel bad about failing to live up to his ideals of what makes for a good parent without being bothered by failing to give an ideal amount to charity. Or she might worry about how much she gives to charity sometimes but not at other times. We should be wary of overgeneralizing about how perfectionist a person is based on limited cases.

Regardless of how broadly we generalize, we recognize both similarities and differences between the contents of moral judgments made by those with and without Scrupulosity. Everyone agrees that we should be careful when there's a risk of harm, that we should take reasonable precautions not to harm others, and that it is ideal to reduce risks of harm to others when there is no overriding cost. On the other hand, people might disagree radically about how careful is careful enough, about which precautions are reasonable, and about whether the ideal to minimize risk to others is morally required.

Moral Thought-Action Fusion

Moral thought-action fusion—treating thoughts as close in moral status to actions—might seem to be an exception to the claim that there is even a superficial similarity between the moral judgments of those with Scrupulosity and those without. After all, most moral judgments are about actions, and some are about intentions ("It's the thought that counts."), but we don't normally conflate the two. There are special cases, of course: failed attempts to do wrong, for example, are evaluated on their underlying intentions since they weren't able to pull off the wrong acts that they intended—although even in those special cases we might be judging them in part because of their acts of preparing to do something wrong (Yaffe, 2011). Even in such special cases, commonsense morality might not seem to condemn mere thoughts unless there is also an action, or at least a clear intention.

Moral judgments of mental states alone, without actions, do occur. In certain moral and religious traditions, they are very important. The Christian Bible, for example, says, "You have heard that it was said, 'You shall not commit adultery'; but I say to you that everyone who looks at a woman with lust for her has already committed adultery with her in his heart." But, even here, what is condemned is not merely having the thought but, instead, lust, which plausibly includes desire or intention.

Similarly, recall Kant's opening to his *Groundwork of the Metaphysics of Morals*: "Nothing can possibly be conceived in the world, or even out of it, which can be called good without qualification, except a good will." In Kant's view, even if the effects of the good will are thwarted, the good will, "like a jewel, . . . would still shine by its own light, as a thing which has its whole value in itself. Its usefulness or fruitfulness can neither add nor take away anything from this value" (1997 [1795]). Again, though, what is good without qualification here is a good will, and a will is not a mere thought.

Both Christian and Kantian systems of morality are open to significant interpretation, but even commonsense morality condemns mere bad thoughts in some cases. Modifying a case from Marcia Baron (2002), imagine that an old man on a public bus sees a young white man holding hands with a young black woman and thinks that this show of affection is inappropriate simply because they are of different races. Or imagine that the old man thinks that the couple is not really in love or that the black woman is his assistant. Such thoughts are racist and, absent some further story, will strike many of us as wrong, bad, or immoral, even if the old man never intends or desires to act on his thought. They're not as wrong, bad, or immoral as acting on those thoughts, but having the thoughts is morally worse than not having the thoughts. Examples like these show that moral judgments of mere thoughts are not totally foreign to commonsense morality.

People with Scrupulosity with moral thought-action fusion similarly worry about the bad thought that occurs to them, even apart from any desire or intention. But they don't recognize limits on just how much we can judge people for their thoughts, particularly for thoughts that they immediately repudiate. We wish the man on the bus hadn't had that thought to begin with, but would we still condemn him if his immediate strong reaction to having that racist thought was to wish that he could stop having such racist reactions? Some might even think he's more praiseworthy precisely *because* he's struggling to be a better person than he would be if he never had any thought at all.

Moral thought-action fusion is more than just the ordinary view that it's wrong to have bad thoughts. It's more expansive in its condemnation and harder to shake. Recall Bob's unprompted image of touching his infant: he never accepted, endorsed, or felt attracted by these thoughts. Instead, he was immediately repelled by them and rejected them wholeheartedly. It's unfortunate that the thoughts occurred—just as it's unfortunate that the man on the bus had the racist thought—but the moral evaluation we make of a person is determined not by a thought the person has, but by the thought together with the way the individual reacts to the thought. In this respect, then, Bob is harder on himself than most of us would be, and he continues to judge himself harshly long after he has repudiated the thought.

What might explain this harshness is a sense of mental contamination. Mental contamination is certainly common in OCD, and there is some evidence that it is characteristic of Scrupulosity, as we mentioned in

Chapter 3. Those with OCD often worry about contamination that cannot be explained just by the transfer of physical contaminants like dirt and microbes. Any contact with something "contaminated" can contaminate the new thing. Something similar seems to happen with thoughts in the case of mental contamination: the immoral thought is enough to "contaminate" one's whole mind, regardless of how one then reacts to it. When the improper thought pops into Bob's mind, the rest of his mind is immediately unclean, including his intentions and desires, at least until he can find a way to "clean" his mind with a compulsive thought or action. Therefore, what seems to be condemnation of a particular thought might in fact be worry about mental contamination. Most people without OCD don't worry much, if at all, about mental contamination. This suggests yet another way in which the content of a Scrupulous judgment differs from a superficially similar non-Scrupulous moral judgment.

Chronic Doubt

A third characteristic of Scrupulosity is chronic doubt and intolerance of uncertainty. What makes such doubts chronic is that they are repeated relentlessly. Intolerance is then the inability to put up with the uncertainty that such doubts introduce or sustain. The differences between such chronic doubts in those with and without Scrupulosity are in part a matter of degree, since how much people doubt, what they have doubts about, and how easily they can handle those doubts vary widely in the general population. But people with Scrupulosity respond to their doubts in distinctive ways.

These differences are not exclusively about moral judgments. One can have chronic doubts about almost any judgment, moral or non-moral. I can doubt that I was kind enough to a stranger who asked me for help and doubt that I packed my computer in my suitcase. Similarly for my tolerance of the doubt. Can I walk away from my house when I have doubts about whether the stove is on? Can I leave without going back inside to apologize again to my spouse when I have doubts about whether my previous apology was adequate? These actions depend on how well I can tolerate my doubts, regardless of whether the content is moral or non-moral.

Although chronic doubt and intolerance of uncertainty can be present for almost any content, the persistence of the doubts can shape the content of those judgments. Imagine that I judge, when thinking about my income and the needs of others, that I should give more to charity. I realize it would be self-defeating to give away so much that I am then a recipient of charity myself, but that limit doesn't tell me how much to give. Is it morally permissible for me to spend some extra money on myself to enjoy a movie or a fine meal? A nice vacation? A new car? A yacht? How about spending money to support art in my community or to elect political candidates? Am I allowed to feel full and avoid malnutrition, or are hunger and health problems the appropriate cost of doing what is right for people who have even less?

Many of us fail to draw any principled line at all regarding how much to give to charity. Instead, we give an amount that *seems* to be enough, or at least enough that we don't feel any immediate pressure to think about how much to give. I could offer a defense of how much I give, as most of us could, but most of us also know that we might not be giving enough. If we're asked to defend how much we give, we're at a loss. We have doubts about how much we should give. But we can also go about our days without that doubt's weighing us down too much. We're not particularly motivated to figure out the correct amount. If we do decide that we've given enough, we likely decide this for a somewhat arbitrary reason: we use the amount a friend gives, or the amount we gave last year anchors what we give this year, or we just to stick to what "feels right," without thinking much about what makes it feel right.

Contrast how this situation looks to people who suffer from chronic doubt regarding charity, about where it's best to give or whether any amount is precisely the right amount. They might, after much reflection, decide to give, say, $100 this week to this particular charity. That's how much the charity asked for, so they starting by thinking that $100 is right. But then they doubt whether that's right, and they can't set those doubts aside. They perseverate on that particular amount: Is $100 too little or too much for this cause here and now? Even if this is the right amount to give, should some of the $100 go instead to a different charity? Is money the best way to give, or should they give their time instead, or in addition? Are they using money to avoid volunteering? Should they persuade their friends to give, or is it wrong to bother them? How can they ever actually settle on a specific decision and stick to it?

One way to settle on a specific amount is to embrace an expansive, perfectionist requirement about how much to give. These chronic doubters could decide that they must give as much as possible, well beyond what most people see as extreme. Only by giving as much as possible—perhaps even at the expense of their own health—could they be sure that they are giving enough. If giving more could reduce harm to others even by a minuscule amount, they will blame themselves for doing less than everything possible. If spending money on a snack instead of donating it to charity could play any role, however slight, in a child's death from lack of adequate nutrition, then buying the snack makes them, by their own lights, entirely responsible for those lethal consequences (never mind their other gifts or the millions of others who could have helped). The perfectionist standard to give away almost everything eases their chronic, intolerable doubts about how much to give by settling the issue in favor of giving the maximum amount possible.

Now, many reasonable people believe that we should ideally give away the maximum amount possible. We don't want to say that this conclusion could only be based on chronic doubts. So, how does embracing an expansive, perfectionist requirement from chronic doubts change the content of a judgment? As mentioned above, there is a difference between believing that something is ideal and believing that it is required. It would be *ideal* for most of us to give significantly more than we give and to forgo luxuries in order to help those who have greater needs than we have. But it doesn't follow that we are *required* to give that much. Maybe we should, but, while it's obvious that most of us should give more, and it's less obvious but still quite arguable that it would be ideal to give most of what we have, it's not obvious that most of us should also feel guilty for failing to achieve that ideal. If people feel guilty for not giving enough and believe that they *should* feel guilty, that is some evidence that they think that they violated a genuine requirement, since feeling guilty is appropriate only for a violation of a requirement (Sinnott-Armstrong, 2005). Thus, chronic doubt can lead one to see a requirement where most people would only see an ideal.

Nonetheless, a person making scrupulous judgments in light of chronic doubt about how much to give is not obviously incorrect in the moral conclusion about what to give: some utilitarians will agree that one (ideally) should give away almost everything, and some (but not all) utilitarians add that one should feel guilty or ashamed for giving less than the ideal (cf. Sinnott-Armstrong, 2005). Many people worry about how effective their charitable giving is, and at least one significant social movement, Effective Altruism, does systematic research about how charitable money is best allocated.[15] And it's not as if the person in this example is making a moral judgment on irrelevant factors. We all agree that the needs of others and the value of giving to those who have less are relevant to making moral decisions.

Further, there is nothing objectionable about having doubts and rethinking our moral decisions from time to time to be sure we're not making mistakes. A key difference from Scrupulous judgments is that, even for important moral decisions, we have to be able to act without first resolving all of our doubts and without having those doubts intrude into every part of our lives. Benjamin says the "thoughts filled his mind all day, although he tried to dismiss them." Linda says, "I am afraid I'm abusing my health by getting so upset about these things." The persistence and intrusiveness of these thoughts about morality, as we discussed in earlier chapters, is key to distinguishing Scrupulosity as a mental disorder. Having doubts is normal and healthy, and even chronic doubts have their place, but some people are unable to leave behind their doubts about the moral or the non-moral when it is time to act. As with perfectionism and moral thought-action fusion, the similarities to non-pathological cases of chronic doubt are clear, while the differences are subtler.

What we would expect, given this view of chronic doubts, is that people with Scrupulosity will have the strongest doubts about distant harms or harms that are not physically observable, since these are easy to legitimate and hard to reassure oneself about, so they can rationalize persistent and otherwise inexplicable anxiety.[16] If you're worried about something that is easily checked, it's hard to stay legitimately worried about it. But a person with Scrupulosity who is worried about harms that are neither physically observable nor easily demonstrated to be false can believe that persistent doubts—which the person would feel regardless—are legitimate.

Purely religious or entirely mental harms are both indemonstrable and are often the person with Scrupulosity's chief concern: How can Benjamin be convinced that his marriage ceremony was indeed said with the proper intention and is therefore valid? No evidence would assuage that doubt. If I feel that I'm deeply sinful and unworthy of divine love, what evidence

[15] Their research, publicized on givewell.org, helps people decide how their charitable money is best used and encourages charities to use their donations more efficiently and effectively.
[16] This view may also predict that anxiety will be exceptionally strong in cases in which all of one's options are bad or of incomparable or indeterminate value. (Thanks to Charlie Kurth for this point.)

will convince me otherwise? Even the attempted reassurance of those who should be in a position to eliminate that doubt fails. When the priest or rabbi reassures them, they believe that the religious authority shows, just in virtue of offering such a reassurance, that he must not have understood (Miller & Hedges, 2008). Likewise, if the poisons that Bridget worries might be in the customers' food are imperceptible and cause harm only later, then what can she do to reassure herself other than check the level of solvents? Therefore, the chronic doubts of a person with Scrupulosity lead her to worry especially about certain kinds of harms that are characteristic of Scrupulosity, namely, harms that are distant or difficult to detect. The content of her moral judgments thus both shapes and is shaped by her chronic anxiety and doubt.

Form

In addition to having certain contents, moral judgments can take various grammatical forms. For example, some moral judgments are expressed in the first person, such as "I should not waste food" or "It would be immoral for me to waste food." Other moral judgments are expressed in the third person, such as "They should not waste food" or "It would be immoral for them to waste food." The form varies to the extent that the judgments are about different persons but forbid the same kind of action, and we express the same judgment when I say "It is wrong for me" and you say to me "It is wrong for you." So we will describe this grammatical difference as formal.

Many theories about morality accept the abstract principle that a moral judgment that an act would be wrong for one person implies that the act would also be wrong for anyone else who is in circumstances that are similar in all morally relevant respects (Hare, 1952; Nagel, 1970; Sidgwick, 1981). In other words, moral judgments must be universalizable to all people in the same circumstances in order to count as genuine moral judgments.

This principle is often violated. For example, young children sometimes seem to make moral judgments about other people that they do not make about themselves. They say, "It's not fair for her to get the biggest piece of cake," but they less often say, "It's not fair for me to get the biggest piece of cake," even when they and the other person are in the same circumstances. Children who speak this way are rightly suspected of not fully appreciating the moral notion of fairness (Kohlberg, 1973). This formal feature of treating themselves differently suggests that their judgments are not yet genuine moral judgments. At most, they are making quasi-moral judgments. We'll say that they are only making judgments that are on the same topic as the moral judgments—here, the topic of how much each person should get.

What such judgments seem to lack is a kind (though not the only kind) of impartiality. Children who talk this way are partial to themselves. In adults, this partiality is clearer in the way we judge other people more harshly than we judge ourselves. You're selfish for taking the larger piece, but I'm just hungry. This partiality raises doubts about whether the judgments are genuine moral judgments, because moral judgments are essentially impartial. Unless there's some morally relevant difference between us that would explain why I should have the larger piece, then my judgment seems more like a judgment of self-interest than of morality.

The same arguments apply when people are harder on themselves than they are on others in morally similar circumstances. They might not be selfish or self-interested, but they still do not treat both parties impartially, since how they judge depends on the particular identities of the parties being judged. It's fine for you to give the larger piece to someone else only if it's ok for *anyone* in your circumstances to give the larger piece to someone else, regardless of which person you are. If you were the recipient, you would judge that it was ok to give the larger piece to you. (Or maybe you think you should politely argue first about who should get the larger piece before you take it: morality is complex.) Favoring oneself and favoring the other party both show partiality and a lack of universalizability, so either form of favoritism lacks the impartiality that moral judgments require.

But who would ever judge themselves more harshly than they judge other people in morally similar circumstances? The depressed, those with low self-esteem, and the very self-critical; and perhaps also some people with Scrupulosity. The cases we have presented so far suggest that many of those with Scrupulosity are very hard on themselves, and, interestingly, there is nothing in the literature to suggest that they are equally hard on others, that they condemn others or focus on others' failings to the same degree to which they focus on their own. Indeed, if they were as focused on others' failings as they are on their own, they likely would be insufferable to be around, whereas those who work regularly with Scrupulosity report that they are generally quite the opposite, often very thoughtful and conscientious about others' feelings though hard on themselves. (Our own experience with people with Scrupulosity confirms this as well.)[17]

Why do they make such different judgments of themselves and others? We can only speculate. One potential explanation is that people with Scrupulosity—like those with other forms of OCD—feel a great deal of personal responsibility for events over which most people would feel little or no responsibility (Nelson et al., 2006). This asymmetry in how much personal responsibility they feel might lead to these differences in moral judgments.

Recall also that Scrupulosity is an anxiety disorder. Those with Scrupulosity have a great deal of anxiety that they attempt to alleviate through their actions, but also, more subtly, that they attempt to understand through their judgments: they judge that something is worthy of their current anxiety, so their judgment makes sense of their anxiety. But their moral judgments are also attempts to make sense of why they continue to feel anxious even after they've done what they would have thought was required. If, for example, people are anxious when praying, they can make sense of that if they remember that they have sins they have not yet prayed about. But if they pray yet remain anxious, then they have to make sense of why they continue to feel anxiety. Maybe there's another sin? Maybe the prayer wasn't heard?

Those who hold perfectionist standards can easily make sense of why they are so anxious, since they are not yet perfect. But the underlying reason they apply these perfectionist standards disproportionately to themselves is itself perhaps an interpretation that their anxiety is evidence that they've done something wrong.

Regardless of how they make sense of their own anxiety, they are not equally anxious about others' behavior, so their anxiety isn't evidence that others have done anything wrong. Their underlying anxiety thus would not lead them to interpret others as having acted badly.

This reasoning, which fits quite well the evidence we have about Scrupulous judgments, helps to answer the question of whether those

[17] In an initial, unpublished survey, we found that those displaying more scrupulous traits did not make the same judgments about others that they made about themselves. When we asked about moral dilemmas, those who were ranked higher on the PIOS-R scale (were more religiously scrupulous) judged others more harshly than themselves. In contrast, those who ranked higher on the secular scrupulosity scale (were more secularly scrupulous) judged themselves more harshly than others. (These two scales are described in Chapter 3.) Further work is needed, but this expands the observations in the clinical literature about those with Scrupulosity.

with Scrupulosity make moral judgments at all. Their perfectionist moral judgments in the first person might not apply in the third person. For the very same actions, they would evaluate themselves as worse than other agents, and they would judge that they ought to do more than others ought to do. This formal asymmetry suggests in turn that the content of their moral judgments is different from ordinary moral judgments and, more strongly, could even suggest that their judgments may not genuinely be *moral* at all.

Source

We have focused so far on the content and form of moral judgments, but the most obvious way in which those with and without Scrupulosity differ is in the source of their moral judgments, what causes or motivates those judgments. The source of Scrupulous moral judgments should come as no surprise. It is persistent and persistently high levels of anxiety.

Some have proposed that morality and religion in general are themselves manifestations of anxiety, so the real distinction is between anxiety-driven morality and religion on the one hand and the clear-headed actions of the *übermensch* who can rise above all such anxiety-driven concerns with morality and religion, on the other (Freud, 1973). Even if true, however, motivation by anxiety in Scrupulosity leads to judgments that are different from ordinary moral and religious judgments.

Looking closely at anxiety will clarify several important differences between the normal and the pathological cases. Anxiety can make a difference to moral judgments in two directions: greater than average anxiety may *result from* moral judgments, or anxiety may *lead to* moral judgments. Of course, in genuine cases of Scrupulosity, these two likely co-occur and reinforce each other, which we will consider briefly below, but we will first consider them individually.

Judgment-driven Scrupulosity

Call the first type, for simplicity, "judgment-driven Scrupulosity." In this type of Scrupulosity, individuals' initial moral judgments might respond to the same features that ordinary moral judgments respond to, but, as a result of those judgments, they suffer from increased anxiety. Perhaps they doubt the correctness of their judgments, hesitating to implement the judgment they've formed in case it is wrong, in case there is a better option, or in case they do not have the purity of mind or intention necessary to make the action moral. Or, perhaps the decision feels weighty, or they feel responsible for all of the possible consequences of the action and are worried that they may not have anticipated some of those consequences. There are many ways in which one's judgment may cause such increased anxiety.

This way of describing cases of Scrupulosity (sometimes called the "cognitive" model) is common. Look carefully at the wording in the opening examples. Little John "has become particularly sensitive about social justice issues," and Big John "believed that loving one's neighbor meant that he was required to greet" everyone. Benjamin "became preoccupied with the thought . . ." and Linda is "troubled with bad thoughts and desires." Bob first had a "thought, idea, or image," and Peter was "tormented by one particular obsessional doubt." In each case, the normative or evaluative thought is presented as prompting the anxiety, and it is an attempt to soothe the anxiety that motivates the subsequent actions.

What is wrong with judgment-driven Scrupulosity? Limited anxiety is an appropriate response to stressful situations and can help a person focus on figuring out what to do, so nothing is wrong with having anxiety per se. It can even be a valuable part of our lives (Kurth, 2015, 2018). If an upcoming test is making you anxious, that might suggest that you haven't studied enough and motivate you to study more. But the anxiety underlying Scrupulosity isn't so limited or constructive.

In cases of judgment-driven Scrupulosity, the judgment to which one anxiously responds is not an ordinary judgment that prompts an appropriate level of anxiety. One might instead begin with perfectionist standards, judgments that one isn't reaching them fully or even adequately, then feel anxious about the difficulty of reaching those standards. The level of anxiety is high in part because the perfectionist judgments are extreme.

The question, though, is why someone would begin with perfectionist standards. Perhaps these judgments are themselves motivated by prior anxiety and are adopted as a way of rationalizing one's own anxiety. But, for the moment, let's assume that a person simply holds such high standards, or that there are other differences in the person's judgments—perhaps differences not yet identified—that explain why those with Scrupulosity react with such strong anxiety.

Even if the initial judgments in cases of judgment-driven Scrupulosity are formed just like ordinary moral judgments, those with Scrupulosity react to their judgments in inappropriate ways. They hesitate to implement the judgments, or they implement them but still have chronic doubts that their action was the right one, or they try to summon up the purest possible intention before acting.

Ordinary moral judgments can be like this as well, of course, especially for morally hard cases. It is sometimes hard to make up one's mind about what to do, and we might doubt and hesitate before implementing our action, and we might continue to wonder if we've done the right thing or have the best of intentions. These reactions all reflect the recognition that we are facing a morally important case, not a case to be taken lightly.

Notice, though, that judgment-driven Scrupulosity is marked by such anxiety even when the cases are not especially morally important, even when the judgments should be easy to make and implement, and even when one's intention should be obvious. Because those with Scrupulosity have an exaggerated sense of responsibility, they might also exaggerate the importance of their own judgments and actions. They might believe their own actions and judgments are more likely to make a difference in the world: everyone agrees that it's good to wash your hands, but those with contamination OCD might feel that they are especially likely to transmit disease if they don't wash. Or they believe that, even if they do wash their hands but not as thoroughly as they could, then any disease that someone subsequently contracted, no matter how improbable or unforeseeable, would be their fault. This exaggerated sense of responsibility makes what should be easy cases much more difficult for the person with Scrupulosity.

On its own, though, this doesn't tell us whether those with Scrupulosity are wrong in their judgments and reactions. Perhaps we should all be more scrupulous and feel more anxiety about our moral decisions. That would show that we're taking them more seriously, not being dismissive of morality. Perhaps we should be more bothered when we realize, as Little John does, that we could do so much more to help those in need. Perhaps the scrupulous are showing us how we can improve morally.

Perhaps. Most of us should be more sensitive to the morally bad situations surrounding us, especially those we could do something about. But there are still many reasons to doubt that judgment-driven anxiety is conducive in general to making good moral decisions and living a moral life, at least when the anxiety is anything beyond the kind of discomfort that most of us feel from time to time. Broadly, the problem with having more serious anxiety as a response to our moral judgments is that the anxiety narrows our attention to what will soothe that anxiety. That feature of anxiety can be helpful when mild anxiety reminds us to revisit a judgment until it's the right one, which soothes the anxiety. But soothing one's anxiety isn't itself a moral goal, and making a better judgment does not always soothe one's anxiety. In fact, not only is soothing one's anxiety distinct from making a better moral judgment, but soothing one's anxiety is likely to lead one away from pursuing other moral goals.

Here are just three ways in which the presence of anxiety can lead an agent astray, even if the person's initial judgment was not itself motivated by anxiety:

First, anxiety *narrows one's attention* to a small, self-focused range of things that will best soothe one's anxiety and make one fail to notice other morally relevant factors. As we said in Chapter 5, this might neutrally be described as "focus" and pejoratively described as "fixation." Bridget checks on solvents to soothe her anxiety about possibly poisoning her customers. Her decisions, taken narrowly (to serve the food, not to harm her customers, etc.) are reasonable, but, looked at more broadly, her actions show that she has focused excessively on the checking that will soothe her own anxiety to the exclusion of the other morally relevant factors, like serving the customers and helping her employer as she agreed to, or even looking out for greater risks to her customers. After all, if her concern were really not to serve her customers things that could incrementally hurt their health, she might want to discourage them from ordering meat, alcohol, and dessert—though that is unlikely to endear her to her employer.

Second, anxiety leads one to focus on features *other* than those that are morally relevant. If one's anxiety does not respond to morally relevant reassurance—to evidence, for example, that no harm is likely to occur—then one may try to reassure the anxiety in morally irrelevant ways instead. Remember the earlier example of the lock-checker: when relocking the door does not reassure the person that the door is locked, then locking it twice with the left hand before touching it twice with the right might feel more reassuring. Similarly, when Adam judges that he might have cheated someone inadvertently, and the attendant anxiety doesn't respond to the evidence that he found nothing in the receipts to confirm that, he might focus instead on features that are reassuring but morally irrelevant, like a belief that saving and rechecking all receipts will prevent dishonesty, though saving and rechecking the receipts will make virtually no moral difference.

Finally, anxiety makes moral judgments *unresponsive to counterevidence.* Imagine a case of everyday anxiety: I worry that my attempt at a joke came off badly and that I actually insulted my friend in the process. I'm anxious as a result, so I offer an apology to my friend, who tells me that he had realized it was a joke and wasn't bothered at all. I am relieved of my anxiety, make a note to be a little more careful before my next joke just in case, and I revise my judgment that I did something seriously wrong in this case.

Imagine, though, a more anxious way this could have gone. My friend tells me he thought nothing of it, but I'm still anxious. I make sense of the anxiety to myself: my friend was wrong to say he wasn't bothered; he was offended and he doesn't even realize it. Or, even worse, he's lying to me to avoid hurting my feelings. He's so offended he can't even discuss it with me! My judgment that I offended my friend becomes even more secure, sustained by the continued anxiety, and now I doubt that I can even trust his reassurances.

If this can happen when reassurance is possible, it's all the more likely in cases in which reassurance is unlikely or impossible. If I worry that the bump I felt while driving could have been my hitting a pedestrian who then quickly stumbled off out of my sight, I'm very unlikely to find the imagined pedestrian to reassure myself. If Benjamin judges that he failed to say his prayers with the appropriate devotion the first time, and this makes him anxious, his continuing anxiety is evidence that he continues not to have the appropriate devotion even on the third or fourth repetition. There's nothing to reassure him that he's said the prayer correctly until he's repeated it enough that the anxiety diminishes. His rabbi cannot tell Benjamin what was going on in his mind while praying, and no divine reassurance lets him know that his prayer was fine the first time. Bridget also worries about powdering food with solvents in such small doses that it's not possible for her to reassure herself by looking at the food itself, but only by checking whether the levels of the solvents in their containers are changing over time.

Scrupulous anxieties tend to focus on such cases where reassurance is difficult or impossible. Focusing on cases that cannot easily be reassured helps an anxious person make sense of that continued anxiety. The anxiety doesn't go away despite attempts at reassurance, so continued anxiety is evidence that the attempted reassurance has failed. This holds, though, only when the reassurance is inconclusive. When there is very clear evidence that I should be reassured, it's hard for me to understand why I still don't feel reassured. I have to find ways to show instead that the supposed reassurance isn't really reassuring—my rabbi misunderstood me, or my friend is lying. If, however, I am reassuring myself about something that has no definitive evidence to cite (divine acceptance of prayer, whether I am acting with a pure heart, or whether there is more I should be doing), then my continued anxiety will provide evidence that something is wrong, and there will be no evidence to the contrary that shows that I should have been reassured.

Anxiety-driven Scrupulosity

This strategy of explaining one's continued anxiety to oneself points to the other way in which anxiety and judgments might be related. The anxiety sometimes underlies the Scrupulous judgments themselves. Call this second type "anxiety-driven Scrupulosity." Instead of moral judgments' causing anxiety, anxiety causes the moral judgments. When people with Scrupulosity have anxiety, they cannot make sense of it, so they then rationalize it by finding some reason that they really should be anxious. They might exaggerate their moral standards so that their standards imply that they really are immoral. Their extreme moral judgments thereby make sense of their antecedent, continuing anxiety.

As with judgment-driven anxiety, there is nothing troubling about anxiety-driven judgments on their own. The fact that anxiety directs one to make judgments needn't make the judgments themselves any less true or less praiseworthy. Anxiety can point us to the morally relevant features of a situation. Indeed, some such piques of anxiety are one's "conscience." It's worth asking why we feel anxious when we do and not just to ignore the anxiety.

Nonetheless, what goes wrong in these judgments is that strong or persistent anxiety, particularly anxiety that is not reassured, tends to distort moral judgments. People with Scrupulosity form, exaggerate, and distort their moral judgments in at least the three ways suggested above in order to soothe their anxiety, rather than in order to determine what really is morally right or best. They narrow their attention to those issues that seem relevant to soothing the anxiety, ignoring other issues, even some that are more important morally. The features that are most relevant to the anxiety might not be the most morally relevant, or, at worst, might not be morally relevant at all, as when a person performs a ritual of her own creation that helps to soothe her anxiety but does not make a moral difference to anyone. Anxiety can prompt the person to form judgments that are not defensible solely on moral grounds, either because the judgments don't account for the most relevant moral factors, or because they don't account for moral factors correctly at all.

Moreover, their anxiety makes those judgments unresponsive to evidence, even after reassurance. I feel anxious about walking through your yard, and the anxiety prompts me to think about what I'm doing in walking through your yard. I realize that, by walking in your yard, I am getting grass on my shoes that I'm then taking with me when I leave your yard. But stealing is wrong! Now I have made sense of why I'm so anxious about walking in your yard. Your reassuring me that you don't mind if I walk through your yard, that you don't think I'm stealing your grass, or even that you don't mind if I *do* steal your grass won't make the anxiety go away, since my anxiety wasn't caused by my reflections about the nature of property but by my anxiety about walking in your yard.

Anxious motivation hardly seems conducive to making reliable moral judgments. Scrupulous moral judgments are formed in an attempt to make sense of anxiety that often does not represent any morally relevant features of the world, so the judgments are epistemically suspect. They are also morally suspect, because they focus on explaining anxiety instead of assessing morally salient features of the world, such as the welfare of others. When those with Scrupulosity are motivated to legitimate or soothe their own anxiety, even if they also have a desire to know and do what really is morally right, their high standards and demanding judgments are less praiseworthy from a moral point of view. They deserve to be pitied, or worse, for the distorted emphasis they place on certain requirements, not praised for their focused adherence to moral standards.

We artificially separated judgment-driven and anxiety-driven forms of Scrupulosity in our discussion, but no clean division exists in practice. Someone feels more anxiety than normal, forms a judgment, and that judgment then reinforces the anxiety, while the anxiety serves as evidence that the judgment was correct. The distorting presence of strong or persistent anxiety leads to distorted judgments, which then reinforce that anxiety, which continues its distorting emphasis. So judgment-driven anxiety and anxiety-driven judgments are mutually reinforcing and difficult or impossible to distinguish in actual cases.

Are Scrupulous Judgments Beliefs?

In our discussion about the content, form, and source of Scrupulous judgments, we avoided taking a stand on whether the judgment is a belief. The question was this. When someone forms a Scrupulous judgment that, say, the receipts are to be checked one more time to ensure that no mistakes were made, is this properly expressed as the person's *belief* that "the receipts ought to be checked," or "it would be good to check the receipts," or even something more sophisticated like "I am a sinner if I do not check the receipts"? Or is someone like Adam merely acting *as if* he has such a belief? Further, if he's only acting *as if* he has the belief, but he does not in fact have that belief, does he falsely believe he has the relevant belief? That is, if you asked Adam if he believes he is a sinner if he doesn't check the receipts, would he say "yes," or would he say "no" and then try to explain why he acts as he does in some other way?

We addressed some of these questions in Chapter 2, where we said that two standard tests for determining if someone has a belief are (1) to see what propositions they assent to and (2) to see how they act. If I say to you "I like peanut butter" and then I eat some peanut butter, those are both good evidence of a belief. But both of those tests are limited and fallible, and OCD demonstrates how such tests fail us in exactly the cases we find most troubling. People with insight into their OCD will deny that their hands are still dirty, while their action of rewashing indicates precisely the opposite, so which belief do we attribute to them? Do they act despite their belief, or are they unaware of their "genuine" belief that is motivating them?

We won't return to this earlier discussion about the nature of belief, but we will note a further complication raised by anxiety-driven Scrupulosity. It is clear enough how the judgments of judgment-driven Scrupulosity could be beliefs, since a genuine belief that I am a sinner in need of constant forgiveness would explain my regular prayer and confession. But what if one's judgments are driven by anxiety? It's clear enough how a person could be so motivated—motivation by anxiety is an ordinary part of life, even for those without anxiety disorders—but does anxiety-driven Scrupulosity preclude having a genuine belief? That is, can anxiety cause genuine beliefs?

It's tempting to dismiss an anxiety-driven judgment as a rationalization, that individuals falsely interpret their anxiety as caused by some judgment, when in fact they form the judgment to explain why they feel anxious. This rationalization therefore wouldn't be a genuine belief, because a belief is responsive to evidence—perhaps even as a matter of definition. Unlike mental states like hopes and fears that can be maintained despite evidence against them, beliefs fall apart in the face of recognized contrary evidence. So judgments that are formed as a way of legitimating one's own anxiety are *ex hypothesi* anxiety-responsive, at least initially, rather than evidence-responsive. In fact, we have just emphasized how *un*responsive to evidence these anxiety-driven judgments can be.

Consider, though, a sketch of how anxiety might prompt one to form a genuine belief. First, anxiety prompts one to look for what might have caused the anxiety. This search is quite legitimate and needn't be thought of pejoratively as an attempt to rationalize one's anxiety, but only to understand it. We might search to understand why we feel any of our emotions, even those that appear to have an obvious cause. The search, however, is not free from bias. One has favored hypotheses about what led to the anxiety, perhaps hypotheses that come from one's religious beliefs, and one therefore first searches for or favors evidence in support of that belief, downplaying opposing evidence. Thus, the beliefs may be supported by weak, selective, and misinterpreted evidence. But weak, selective, and misinterpreted evidence is still evidence, and a disturbing number of our beliefs are probably formed in just this way. They are not formed in total disregard of the evidence.

Indeed, rationalization more generally often has this biased-search structure: an underlying or "real" reason for people's hoping to believe what they end up believing motivates them to engage in something like a search for evidence (D'Cruz, 2015a, 2015b; Mele, 2000; Molden & Higgins, 2005; Schwitzgebel & Ellis, 2017; Summers, 2017; Tsang, 2002). They don't form a belief simply because they want to believe it—nor, in this case, because they are anxious about it. Instead, the motivation explains the way they go about evaluating evidence and forming the belief. But what they end up with is sometimes plausibly a genuine belief. At least, the presence of anxiety as an underlying motivation does not by itself rule out the judgment's being a genuine belief.

Are Scrupulous Judgments Moral?

The source in anxiety also does not immediately rule out the judgment's being genuinely moral, though this is a subtler point to develop. Those with

Scrupulosity persistently worry about doing wrong. What they think they are worried about—like whether a prayer was said correctly or whether someone would be accidentally hurt—might itself be genuinely moral. Their guilt feelings might also be genuine and motivating. However, they are ultimately moved by the need to soothe their anxiety rather than by a concern to do what is moral. This distorts their judgments in systematic and predictable ways, as we have seen. Nevertheless, these anxiety-distorted moral judgments still might count as moral judgments.

Ordinary moral judgments are motivated in many ways. Some result from anxiety, in some sense of that word. But remember that we don't use the word "anxiety" for ordinary discomfort. As we said in Chapter 2, we use the word "anxiety" here to refer to a pathological state in which one's discomfort is unjustified or excessive. Of course, we recognize that the term is also used in a non-pathological sense to mean something like uncomfortable confusion, particularly practical confusion about what to do (Kurth, 2018). Use the word "anxiety" however you like, but keep in mind that the word "anxiety" here refers to pathological cases of anxiety involving unjustified or excessive discomfort.

Nevertheless, even such pathological anxiety is present in the moral judgments of many people without an anxiety disorder. Their anxiety might not be as persistent or acute as Scrupulous anxiety, but it still has distorting effects. What leads to problems and affects whether a judgment is genuinely moral is not the presence of anxiety itself, but those distorting effects of the anxiety.

Anxiety has predictably distorting effects on Scrupulous judgments because these aversive feelings motivate anxious people to soothe their anxiety. For some, like those with Scrupulosity, soothing their anxiety is paramount. Why are those with Scrupulosity motivated primarily to soothe their anxiety? For some, it might be the abnormally strong or persistent quality of the anxiety that is so hard to soothe or tolerate. For others, it might be the way in which they respond to anxiety that makes it such a problem to soothe or tolerate. Anxiety is at the heart of these differences, which is why we can best explain Scrupulous judgments as motivated primarily by anxiety.

Why is this motivation to soothe anxiety a problem? One reason is that soothing such anxiety requires only that one identify what will soothe the anxiety, not what is really morally required. And this leads those with anxiety at least sometimes to exaggerate something's moral significance. Jacob engaged in "meticulous cleaning for half an hour whenever he uses the toilet," when the closest moral obligation he accepts is only to be clean; Big John says hello to everyone at work, but that greatly exaggerates what is morally required to love one's neighbors. In such ways, anxiety can lead good people to distort their moral judgments.

Given such distortions, can we say that these moral judgments are in fact *moral* judgments at all? They do have the same subject matter as moral judgments: obligations to others, wrongdoing, sins, forgiveness, etc. These people are thinking about moral issues. Nonetheless, having a moral subject matter doesn't prove the judgments are moral. One's judgment that it is right or best to leave a large tip because the server needs the money more might be a moral judgment. But someone who judges "I ought to leave a large tip" in order to impress the person's dining companions has different thoughts and intentions even though the subject matter and behavior are the same. One judgment is part of the morally praiseworthy action of helping others; the other is part of the self-serving action of drawing attention to oneself.

Now, if Scrupulous moral judgments were motivated solely by anxiety, and ordinary moral judgments were never motivated by anxiety, then we could point to this difference in motivation to explain why Scrupulous moral judgments are not moral judgments, just as the self-interested tipper is not making a genuine moral judgment. Different motivations result in different moral judgments.

To see why this view is too simple, though, consider how the presence of anxiety affects the narrow content of a moral judgment. Consider a third tipper who calculates 20% for a tip, and then starts worrying about whether the tip should be calculated on the total before or after the tax is added, then worries that 20% isn't right given this particular restaurant and server, then starts worrying about whether it's right to eat at restaurants that don't pay a living wage, and starts calculating what would need to be tipped to bring the server's wage for the previous hour to a living wage. Now, let's posit that this person's anxiety about how much to leave goes away only by leaving a large enough tip. But this tipper's judgment, even though it's motivated by a desire to reduce or eliminate anxiety, isn't necessarily about one's anxiety. This third tipper, like the other two, also judges "I ought to leave a large tip," not "I ought to soothe my anxiety."

In a more obvious case, if you tell Mary that, in order to feel reassured that her prayer was acceptable, she could either say the prayer 18 times or take a pill to calm her anxiety, she might prefer to say the prayer 18 times, even though her *feeling* of reassurance would be the same either way. (As we'll see in the final chapter, one goal of therapy is to make her see that eliminating anxiety was in fact her motivation all along, regardless of how she got there.) What is motivating her is an underlying anxiety, but the content of her various judgments is not "eliminate anxiety." Her judgments have the more specific content that they seem to have (e.g., "I should pray again"). What the motivating anxiety provides is a further explanation of why Mary formed those judgments. Anxiety distorts genuinely praiseworthy moral reasoning, but not in a way that can always be detected by looking narrowly at the content of the judgments.

The conclusions those with Scrupulosity reach therefore might be genuinely moral in their narrow content. This is because the features these individuals pick out to justify their conclusions could be morally relevant features that do justify that narrow conclusion considered in isolation, thus making the conclusion a narrowly moral one. If you ask me for a hammer and I lend it to you because you want it and I can help you get what you want with little cost to myself, then I am making a narrow moral judgment about what I ought to do based on this one factor.

The question is whether a narrow judgment with some moral content like this one remains a genuinely moral judgment when considered more broadly. Suppose I know the reason you want a hammer is to break into a stranger's car, yet I still judge that I should lend you a hammer because you asked. I know you shouldn't break into the car, so I'm deliberately ignoring that crucial, morally relevant feature in my judgment of what I ought to do. My judgment to lend you the hammer that you want *because you want it* hardly seems moral now, because practical moral judgments are judgments about what is right or best (or wrong or worse) to do—what some would call "all-things-considered" judgments. We're not going as far as to say that moral judgments are necessarily all-things-considered judgments, but we are at least saying that you can't make a judgment about what is right or best to do without incorporating and balancing the features that you recognize as clearly relevant to whether something is right or best. Moral judgments are not just stimulus-response reactions to one isolated morally relevant feature, ignoring others.

For people with Scrupulosity, what motivates their search for morally relevant features suggests that they might not be trying to make such an overall moral judgment. Mary believes that she should pray because prayer is obligatory (the narrow content), but she also prioritizes prayer over important family and health obligations because those other obligations won't soothe her anxiety (the broader content). She recognizes the moral value of family and health. So, if she were making a genuine moral judgment, it would have to respond to more than the narrowest relevant feature of a situation, which in this case is the feeling that the prayer has not been said successfully. A genuinely moral judgment responds to all the morally relevant features together.[18]

Another problem with taking Scrupulous judgments to be moral is suggested by the way in which people with Scrupulosity soothe their anxiety. We have suggested that one way they might do this is by looking for specific, principled answers to moral or practical questions, not comfortable with the uncertainty of acting without a clear and precise practical directive. This recalls Aristotle's prescription that we should demand precision only as far as is appropriate for a subject (NE, Book I, 1094.b24). If we demand more precision than a subject admits, we may not be able to find any answer to our questions; or, if we do find a more precise answer, it is an answer that is orthogonal to the original subject matter. For example, a baker needs to know how much flour she needs for a loaf of bread. She may ask how many cups to use; if she's a more serious baker, she may ask more precisely how many grams to use and account for how much moisture is in the air when weighing the flour. She could ask for an even more precise answer: she could ask how many nanograms to put in, even how many molecules to put in. If she asks these more precise questions, however, she runs two risks: first, she may not be able to come up with any answer that is better for baking a loaf of bread than her original answer was; or, if she does come up with an answer, there is nothing about the baking project itself that determines how many molecules she should use. The baking answers reached their end well before determining the number of molecules.

Morality as a subject also seems not to admit of very precise prescriptions: we should be *careful* not to *harm* others, or not to *harm* them *significantly* or *unnecessarily*, give a *reasonable* amount to *charity* to help those *worse off*, and so on. It is very difficult to give a moral prescription with enough

---

[18] Some single moral features, when present, might trump all else. Perhaps the moral requirement not to torture or kill innocent children requires one to ignore anything else. We won't take a stand on this. If there are such trumping features, then a moral judgment might deliberately ignore features that otherwise would have been morally relevant. But these are not the kinds of features at stake here. Mary might treat her decision as having life-or-death importance that trumps everything else, but that's precisely the problem: genuine moral judgments do not, or at least do not in general, treat every morally relevant feature as a trumping one. They must instead be balanced in any moral judgment of what's best to do.

specificity that it can be applied without any further practical judgment in particular cases. More precise answers often cannot be determined; if they can be determined, it is unlikely that morality is what determines those precise answers. It is morally irrelevant how precisely we move our fingers when typing a credit card number into a charity website. If we do decide how best to move our fingers, it is not because morality required those movements. Even if moral prescriptions were in principle specifiable down to those smallest finger movements, such precision is practically irrelevant to us: we cannot determine our moral obligations so precisely. Finally, even if we could in principle determine them, actually doing so would take time and effort that, morally speaking, would almost certainly be better spent in other ways.

Scrupulous moral thought, however, demands precision beyond what is appropriate for the subject, and it focuses on features that soothe or rationalize one's anxiety. This aversion to vagueness is a sign that such thoughts are not driven by an appreciation of what morality requires. The overly precise answers that one reaches are morally no better than many alternative answers one could have reached. Or, at best, morality would have required doing something else with the time spent reaching those precise conclusions.

This insight about what drives Scrupulosity might in turn make us all question whether seeking precise moral answers in all practical contexts is always driven by moral considerations. At least in the case of Scrupulous judgments, it seems to be motivated by anxiety or other attitudes that are, perhaps, less morally praiseworthy. Our own ethical reflections should be careful to keep this in mind. It might be impossible to be too moral, but it's possible to demand too much precision about what morality requires. This is another way in which Scrupulous judgments differ from genuine moral judgments.

7

Responsibility

People with scrupulous traits look in some cases like moral exemplars, but they are also likely to be annoying to anyone who has to interact with them on a regular basis. Working with a perfectionist annoyingly reminds us of our own lack of perfection and can keep us from making progress. Chronic doubt about what is morally permitted makes trivial decisions difficult and slow. Imagine what it's like to sit with individuals who can never make up their minds about what to order in a restaurant, but the menu is for everything they do. As these traits become extreme and persistent, the annoyance can grow.

More than just annoyance, people with Scrupulosity can cause or risk serious harm to other people. Ezekiel's wife was so unhappy that she contemplated divorce. This divorce (and the tension in their marriage) could cause serious harm to Ezekiel's wife as well as their children. Peter stalked his former girlfriend, which can cause serious harm to the victim of his stalking. Jennifer deceived her parents, which could undermine their trust. And Bob could not take on his share of childcare responsibilities, burdening his spouse. Moreover, people with Scrupulosity damage their own life prospects and even health, particularly by losing sleep or otherwise engaging in stressful ruminations in order to try to reassure themselves. Mary "was experiencing difficulty staying awake during the day," which was bound to annoy or disappoint her family, friends, and coworkers. The harm that Scrupulosity sufferers inflict on themselves can in turn harm all of those who interact with or depend on them. No person is an island.

The central question in this chapter is whether people with Scrupulosity or scrupulous traits are morally responsible for the harms—serious or minor—that they cause as a result of their distinctive traits. Along the way, we'll show how this issue is more complex than it might appear at first glance.

Intention

The answer to our central question seems simple if agents are responsible only when they cause harms intentionally. People with Scrupulosity and scrupulous traits almost never intend to cause harms. The harms that they do cause are unintentional and sometimes even unknown. If they know that they are causing harms, those harms are not essential to their goals or plans but are only side effects or byproducts of their doing what they think is morally right. They seem more likely to injure someone as they try to avoid hurting someone else than as a premeditated aggression. As a result, Scrupulosity, like OCD, is rare in the criminal justice system. Nonetheless, there are many ways that we can harm each other, only some of which are criminal.

For example, serious harms can result from negligence or recklessness without any intention to harm. Legally, agents act recklessly when they are aware that their acts create a risk, but they disregard that risk for no adequate reason. Agents act negligently when they are not aware that their acts create a risk, but they should be aware because a reasonable person would be aware. In either case, an agent can be morally and legally responsible for a harm. For example, drunk or distracted drivers do not intend to hurt anyone on the way home but are still responsible if they kill a pedestrian, because their driving was reckless. One can be morally and at least civilly responsible for a harm by leaving a loaded gun unlocked at home where a child picks it up and kills someone by mistake, even if the person did not know that the child was at home and so was not aware of the risk. Various cases of these kinds show that agents can be morally and legally responsible without an intention to do any harm. That shows why the fact that agents with Scrupulosity do not intend harm is not enough to show that they are not morally responsible.

Negligence and recklessness are sometimes understood as carelessness. In contrast, agents with Scrupulosity are usually very careful—sometimes too careful—about what they do. Look, however, at what they do and do not care about. If Bridget leaves her customers waiting while she checks the containers, she does not care for their schedules even if she does care about poisoning them. When Big John spends his work time circling back to make sure he's greeted everyone, he does not care about his employer's demands or whether he annoys his colleagues. In at least some ways, then, agents with Scrupulosity do seem to care less than they should and therefore resemble agents who are negligent or reckless.

We're not concluding that those with Scrupulosity are negligent and reckless in general, only that lack of intentionality is not enough by itself to remove responsibility. Agents with Scrupulosity still might lack responsibility for some other reason, but not simply because they do not cause harms intentionally.

Mental Illness

Another argument that is too quick and simple cites our conclusion in Chapter 4 that Scrupulosity is a mental illness. Most people assume that people with mental illnesses are not responsible in the same ways and to the same degrees as people without mental illnesses. This can't be right. People with mental illnesses sometimes do horrible acts that have nothing to do with their mental illnesses. Someone with kleptomania who murders is fully responsible for the murder, despite the person's irrelevant mental illness.

Moreover, some mental illnesses do not remove or reduce responsibility even for acts that do stem from mental illnesses. Someone with pedophilia is responsible for taking advantage of children, which stems directly from the mental illness. An agent with narcissistic personality disorder who treats others as if they are not worthy of concern is responsible for treating others in this immoral way, though it's caused by the mental illness. Finally, some mental illnesses do not rob the agent of all control even in the area of their mental illness. As Kozuch and McKenna (2016) argue in detail, agents with mild cases of depression, generalized anxiety disorder, or attention deficit disorder can be at least partly responsible for acts that they would not have done if not for their mental illnesses. For these reasons, the mere fact that Scrupulosity is a mental illness is not enough by itself to show that or explain why agents with Scrupulosity are not responsible.

In order to think about why Scrupulosity still might reduce or remove responsibility, it is useful to start by thinking about cases of OCD. Imagine that your friend shows up late to an important meeting because he has a lock-checking form of OCD, so he went back to check the locks on his doors several times before he finally got into his car and drove to the meeting. Your friend's extensive lock checking is part of a larger collection of OCD symptoms and does not show that he cared very little about you. In this case, you may be annoyed, but you would not hold him responsible to the same degree as you would another friend who showed up late to your meeting simply because she took a nap without setting an alarm or went to a sale for something she didn't need and ran into a long line at the store. These acts would show that this friend considers you less important than naps or sales, unlike your OCD friend. That is why you would hold your OCD friend less responsible, at least if he apologized and displayed remorse for showing up late.

On the other hand, you would probably hold your friend with OCD more responsible than a person who showed up late to the same meeting because a drunk driver rammed his car while he was driving to the meeting—assuming that he was not already running late when he encountered the drunk driver. This third person is not responsible at all, whereas your friend with OCD is at least a little responsible.

Thus, your friend with lock-checking OCD seems to lie somewhere between your other two friends. He is less responsible than one and more responsible than the other. This comparison causes trouble for some theories of responsibility, because they assume that responsibility is dichotomous: a person is either fully responsible or not responsible at all. In contrast, common sense allows intermediate degrees of responsibility. Indeed, most wrongdoers seem partly but not fully responsible, lying somewhere between acting with complete intention and control and being pushed or having a seizure. Thus, the case of OCD already teaches a valuable lesson: theories of responsibility need to allow at least some intermediate degrees of responsibility.

The same point applies to people with Scrupulosity. Imagine that Big John showed up late for the meeting because he had to greet everyone on the way, and he missed a few, so he had to circle back to greet the ones he missed. Big John is less responsible than the person who was late because he was napping and more responsible than the person who was hit by a drunk driver. Big John seems to have this intermediate degree of responsibility for the same reason that your friend with lock-checking OCD does.

To say simply this and no more is, admittedly, not very illuminating. What we really want to know is how and why the person with Scrupulosity is less responsible than the one and more responsible than the other. As we saw, the bare fact that Scrupulosity is a mental illness by itself cannot answer this question.

One possible answer is that there are different kinds of responsibility, and people with Scrupulosity have some of these kinds of responsibility but not others, so they lie between people who are responsible in all ways and people who are responsible in no ways. An alternative answer is that responsibility varies in degrees along a continuum of something else that explains the responsibility (other attitudes or responsiveness to reasons), and people with Scrupulosity have an intermediate degree of these factors that track responsibility. These possible answers are compatible, and we will argue for them both, starting with the first claim that people with Scrupulosity are responsible in some ways but not others.

Kinds of Responsibility

Responsibility can be distinguished into many types. For example, H. L. A. Hart famously distinguished responsibility into five types: causal, role, legal, moral, and capacity (Hart, 1968). Something is *causally* responsible for an effect when it is part of the cause of that effect, such as when a drought is responsible for a famine. Someone has *role* responsibility simply in virtue of a certain role or position, such as a father's responsibility or duty to help take care of his children. *Legal liability* responsibility is the responsibility that the law assigns when it holds someone liable for something, such as when a car manufacturer is held civilly or criminally liable for defects in its products that cause harms. *Moral liability* responsibility is the moral analogue of legal liability responsibility, when it is morality and not the law that assigns the liability, such as when a child is liable to a punishment (such as criticism or a loss of privileges or of weekly allowance) for lying, even though the law would not get involved in such a small family matter. And people have *capacity* responsibility when they meet the minimum standards that anyone must meet in order to be liable for any act, such as when a sane adult is responsible in general for acts, but a very young child is not. *Capacity* responsibility can also be subdivided into moral or legal capacity responsibility on the basis of whether the relevant liability is moral or legal. These distinctions, while widely used, are far from exhausting the many ways that we can distinguish types of responsibility.

In Hart's terminology, our topic here is moral liability responsibility. There is no question that people with Scrupulosity cause and, hence, are causally responsible for some harms, as the examples above show. There is also no question that Scrupulosity does not generally affect one's role responsibilities, for example, the role responsibilities of parents toward their children, because it does not directly affect what roles one has. There might be some question about whether or not people with Scrupulosity would (or should) be held legally liable for harms they cause, but legal liability does (and probably should) vary by jurisdiction, and it's impossible for us to consider legal responsibility here generally—though our reflections on other forms of responsibility certainly could inform assessments of legal responsibility.

Scrupulosity might seem to raise questions about capacity responsibility. For example, could Scrupulosity remove responsibility for a wide range of actions in the way that childhood does, by showing the person lacks some fundamental capacity? Young children—younger than five, say—are not liable for much of what they do because they lack the mental, emotional, and self-regulative capacities necessary for a person to be morally (or legally) responsible. Similarly, in some adults, extreme dementia removes or reduces moral responsibility for a very wide range of actions. Childhood and extreme dementia are exemptions, not excuses. Exemptions remove a general capacity to be morally responsible, so the exempt are not even candidates for moral responsibility. (A similar point can be made for legal responsibility.)

In contrast, Scrupulosity does not exempt from responsibility. Whatever impairments come from Scrupulosity are not general enough to reduce or remove moral responsibility for all or even most acts. Even if Bridget is not morally responsible for checking the solvents yet again, she is still responsible if she is surly with customers or steals tips from other servers. Even if Bob is not morally responsible for failing to do his share of childcare, he is still morally responsible if he also fails to do his share of cooking or shopping. Perhaps Scrupulosity could in rare cases become so pervasive as to count as an exemption. In general, though, it does not diminish capacities like the capacity to make genuine moral judgments as much or as generally as in childhood or dementia. Accordingly, our main issue here is not whether Scrupulosity provides an exemption that reduces moral capacity responsibility. Instead, our question is whether, when, and why Scrupulosity provides an excuse that reduces moral liability responsibility.

It is also important to distinguish excuses from justifications. If you will be hit by a baseball flying toward you unless I shove you out of the way, then I am justified in shoving you. I did the right thing, so I do not need any excuse. (I still need to say "I'm sorry" for shoving you: apologies serve social functions beyond acknowledging that one has done something wrong.) In contrast, if I mistakenly believe that the ball is coming toward you, but my belief is reasonable, then I mistakenly believe I am justified. I did not need to shove you, but I might be excused if my mistake was a reasonable one—the ball was going to miss you, but it was coming too fast for me to realize this quickly—so I am not morally responsible in these special circumstances.

Given this distinction, are people with Scrupulosity justified or excused? They are usually only excused. Bridget claims she believes that the people in the ambulances that pass her will die unless she pulls over to pray for them. If her belief were true, then she would be justified in pulling over to pray. Presumably, however, her prayer will not really have any effect on their survival. Thus, Bridget's action of pulling over could be excused, like the mistaken shove, but it is not justified.

Whether the action is *in fact* excused is more complicated to assess, since it's possible to act on a sincere belief yet not be excused. For example, if one sincerely believes that short people can't do mathematics and therefore refuses to hire someone short for a job that requires mathematics, this discrimination is not excused just because the belief is sincere. We would have to know a lot more about the person's other beliefs, sources of evidence, environment, and so on before knowing whether this action is excused. Similarly, for Bridget, we need to know what (else) Bridget believes, how she formed those beliefs and how reasonable they are, or at least what makes them seem reasonable to her, before we can conclude that her action is excused. But it might be excused, even if unjustified.[19] In any case, the question here is whether agents like Bridget, who cause harm as a result of their Scrupulosity, are excused.

---

[19] Since our interest is to assess responsibility, which requires some assessment of an actor's mindset, we're not interested in cases of coincidental justification, e.g., if, all evidence to the contrary, Bridget's roadside prayers actually do save lives. (For what it's worth, this needn't be a supernatural explanation. Imagine: Bridget pulls over to the side of the road to pray whenever there's an ambulance, which has the side effect of slowing traffic behind her for longer, which gives the ambulance more room to maneuver, making it easier for the ambulance to get to the hospital.) We're also not interested in justifications that have nothing to do with the agent's motivation. For example, if a person is motivated by fear to buy a gun, he may subsequently develop a justification for gun ownership that hypothesizes that his gun ownership will deter a government tyranny—but such a justification is a post-hoc rationalization, not what actually motivated the person to begin with. We are not including as justifications post-hoc rationalizations or coincidental justifications, only cases in which the actions are in fact justified and the actor's mindset reflects that justification. It won't be useful to us if we can now construct some elaborate justification for a Scrupulous action that in fact played no role in motivating the person.

One final clarification might be helpful: we consider responsibility for harms, but we are also responsible for benefits and good results. We can ask who is responsible for cleaning up the kitchen or for bringing peace to the region. When we ascribe responsibility for something good, we give credit; when we ascribe responsibility for a bad act or result, we blame. Now, it would be interesting to ask whether and when people with Scrupulosity deserve credit for the good things they do, like helping the needy. We might justify credit and blame differently. However, almost all discussions and theories of responsibility aim at determining responsibility for bad acts and results, so we will also focus here on responsibility for bad acts and effects.

We can now draw one further distinction between being responsible and being blameworthy. An agent who is justified in causing harm is responsible for the harm but not blameworthy, because a justified agent does not do anything wrong. Similarly, an agent who does good is also responsible but not blameworthy. These cases show why being responsible is not the same as being blameworthy. An agent is blameworthy only if the agent is responsible for doing wrong, such as causing harm without justification. Nonetheless, since agents with Scrupulosity are rarely justified, and we are interested in cases where they cause harm rather than doing good, we will usually not need to distinguish being responsible from being blameworthy.[20]

Overall, then, our questions are whether, when, and why Scrupulosity provides an excuse that reduces or removes moral liability responsibility for bad acts or consequences. In the following discussion, we will have in mind moral liability responsibility for bad things unless otherwise noted.

Finer Distinctions

This issue is, we're sorry to say, still not precise enough. Even within moral liability responsibility for bad things, we need to draw finer distinctions. In particular, we follow David Shoemaker in distinguishing three kinds of moral responsibility. Shoemaker's account is complex and subtle, but we will present only the most basic ideas. (For details, see Shoemaker 2011 and 2015.) Roughly, to hold that a person is responsible is to hold that a certain response is fitting or, to go beyond Shoemaker's notion of fitting, that

---

[20] The relation between responsibility and blame or blameworthiness can be complicated (Scanlon, 2008). For simplicity, we will focus our discussion on responsibility.

the person is liable to a certain response in the sense that the person has no legitimate complaint if others respond in that way, and others are justified in responding in that way as long as their responses do not impose any incidental costs or side effects. Within this general framework, different responses distinguish different kinds of responsibility.

Attributability

The first kind of responsibility is attributability-responsibility or simply attributability.

The response that is appropriate for attributability is primarily disdain for bad qualities (or admiration for good qualities). Disdain is appropriate only when the bad quality expresses the agent's so-called deep self or when that quality is caused by and expresses (or corresponds appropriately to) the content of the agent's cares and commitments (cf. Sripada, 2016). Thus, an agent is attributability-responsible for a bad action if and only if that action is caused by and reflects the content of the agent's cares and commitments. Conversely, an agent is not attributability-responsible for an action when the act results from something external to the agent's deep self, such as disease, coercion, or reasonable mistake.

The crucial question here is then whether the distinctive attitudes and acts of people with Scrupulosity are caused by and express the content of their cares and commitments. It seems so. Ezekiel, Benjamin, Mary, and Big John are all clearly committed to their religions, and these religious commitments are what lead them to perform their prayers and rituals, which fulfill the content of their commitments. In a secular case, Bridget is committed to not harming her customers and to preventing harm to her brother and to people in ambulances, and these commitments cause her to perform acts that fit well with the content of her practical commitments. Even those who express conflicts, like Adam, are not necessarily opposed to their acts but only to the force with which they feel compelled to perform them. Adam is committed to honesty, and that practical commitment causes him to check and recheck his receipts, which makes sense in light of the content of his commitment. As a result, their acts thus do seem attributable to these agents, because their acts do seem to express their cares, commitments, and hence deep selves. Thus, these agents seem to have attributability-responsibility.

Admittedly, the distinctive acts of Scrupulosity result from their anxiety, but this anxiety is inseparable from the content of their cares and commitments. Ezekiel and Benjamin care so much about religious rituals that they get anxious when they doubt that they have performed those rituals correctly. This is true even if they are first anxious and then express that anxiety through distinctively religious cares and commitments. In other words, just as anxiety might cause people to form genuine beliefs, so anxiety can cause people to develop genuine cares and commitments. The anxiety by itself does not express their cares and commitments, but the particular targets of their anxiety and the particular actions that it produces still do reflect their cares and commitments. That seems enough for attributability.[21]

In addition to the theoretical reasons to attribute their acts to agents with Scrupulosity, their self-reports also often imply that their distinctive actions reflect their attitudes, cares, and commitments. This is especially clear in ego-syntonic cases when they endorse the standards that require their attitudes and actions. When the agent's endorsement of those standards causes the agent to act, and the resulting act is consistent or in line with those standards, the act clearly does express the agent's cares and commitments. That makes these agents attributability-responsible.

To be clear, we are not saying that intrusive thoughts are attributable to people with Scrupulosity in the same way that their actions are. Bob is not attributability-responsible for the thought or image of touching his daughter's private parts that flashes through his mind. He is not attributability-responsible because this intrusive image is strongly contrary to everything he wants. Indeed, he is probably so disturbed by the image precisely because of how dramatically contrary it is to what he wants.[22] (If he'd instead had an image of putting the diaper on too loosely, which was also opposed to what he wanted, he just would have checked it again without much distress.)

---

[21] A related concern is whether the action should be attributed to the Scrupulosity instead of the agent. This metaphor that it is the disease, not the person, that acts might make sense in some cases (such as epileptic seizures), and it is controversial in others (such as alcoholism), but it is not a clear and stable enough metaphor to build on in cases like Scrupulosity.

[22] An astute psychoanalyst will no doubt chime in here to ask whether Bob's objectionable thought isn't in fact what Bob *really* wants, and maybe his distress comes about in part by his realizing that what he really wants is also something he deeply wants not to want. This line of thought is worth exploring, but we'll stick with the more straightforward understanding of the case: Bob's intrusive thought is something he doesn't want, not a manifestation of what he does want.

Another reason that Bob is not attributability-responsible for an intrusive thought or image is that it is not an action or attitude, so it is not the right kind of thing for Bob to be responsible for, at least under normal circumstances. He could be responsible for doing things to bring about such thoughts—and we will return to this point when we discuss the tracing principle below—but, as described, the thought occurred to Bob without his doing anything to prompt it. The only things that Bob can be responsible for are the actions that he performs in response to the intrusive thought, such as his refusal to change his daughter's diapers, not for the intrusive thought itself. When these subsequent actions express his cares and commitments, they are attributable to him.

Answerability

Shoemaker's second kind of responsibility is answerability-responsibility or simply answerability. Whereas the response that characterized attributability was disdain, the response that characterizes answerability is regret (Shoemaker, 2015). The basic idea is that it is fitting for us to regret doing an action when, but only when, we can cite reasons why it was less worthy than some alternative we had.[23] If we cannot give any reason not to have done what we did, then it is inappropriate to regret doing it.

In contrast with attributability, which requires only that the act express certain cares and commitments, answerability requires that the agent has the ability to cite reasons based in the agent's cares and commitments. We need the ability to cite reasons in order to be able to answer the question, "Why did you do it?" Still, what is needed is only the ability in principle, not in practice. The agent might not have the intelligence or reflective capacity actually to specify what the justifying reasons are, but the agent is still not answerable unless the agent would cite those reasons at least conditionally: if the agent were intelligent and reflective enough, had no external obstruction or manipulation, and had enough time, incentive, and so on.

---

[23] A somewhat different view of answerability is developed by Angela Smith, who sees agents as answerable when and only when they are apt targets for requests for justification (Smith, 2015; cf. Scanlon, 2008). It is not apt or appropriate (in Smith's terms) to ask young children or seniors with serious dementia to justify their actions because they are not able to cite the reasons that they took to justify their actions. The differences between these views do not matter for our purposes here.

Whose reasons matter for answerability? Only the agent's. On Shoemaker's view, what agents need to be able to cite are not reasons that objectively justify their act. The reasons that the agents accepted as their own and took to justify their action might not really justify anything if the agents are mistaken. Nonetheless, they are answerable in Shoemaker's sense if they are able to cite what they subjectively took to be reasons for their action as well as reasons against their action or for alternatives. The agents are able to answer the question of why they did something and did not do something else, even if the answer does not really justify their act at all.

On this subjective or personal understanding of answerability, those with Scrupulosity seem answerable. Bridget can cite some of her reasons for checking the containers—namely, the containers hold poisons that would harm her customers if they got into the food she is serving, and it would be bad or wrong for her to harm her customers. She is even able to cite a reason to check the containers a second time, because there is some possibility that she missed something when she checked before. Admittedly, Bridget cannot say why or how the poison could have gotten into the food she is serving, but it is still the reason that she subjectively *took* to justify checking the containers. (Her doubts presumably do not *in fact* justify checking the containers.) That is enough for answerability of the subjective kind.

A similar argument shows that Bridget is also answerable for the acts that she performs in order to prevent harms to her brother and to people in ambulances, even though her reasons do not really justify those acts. Other examples, too, can offer what they take to be reasons and thus seem answerable in the subjective sense.

We could demand more for answerability than the ability to cite what the agent *took* to be reasons. We could require that the agent be able to cite reasons that *really do* justify. Even on this revised account, however, most agents with Scrupulosity are still answerable. At least when the reasons are narrowly specified, the reasons are good ones. Bridget does what she does in order to avoid harming her customers and to help the people in ambulances, and we should help and avoid harming others. Many of those with Scrupulosity act on perfectly ordinary and defensible reasons, at least when specified narrowly, even if they tend to fixate on those reasons to the exclusion of other good reasons. Like Bridget, then, such agents might be answerable even on a revised account that requires their subjective reasons to be genuine reasons, as long as we specify their reasons narrowly.

Might people with Scrupulosity lack answerability because they have little insight into their condition, so they don't understand that they are ultimately motivated by their anxiety? *DSM-5* reports that persons with OCD, including Scrupulosity, can vary widely in insight. However, the kind of insight that *DSM-5* describes is insight into the irrationality of their beliefs. Complete lack of insight about the irrationality of their beliefs, though, doesn't rule out that they do act on good reasons. One *does* have a reason to avoid causing harm. Moreover, it's too demanding for any plausible conception of answerability to require that we have insight into why we find our reasons to be good reasons. None of us understand our underlying reasons or motivations well enough to meet that standard. On most any plausible account of answerability, then, Scrupulosity is compatible with being answerability-responsible.

There is much more to say about these first two kinds of responsibility: attributability and answerability. They do not, however, clearly distinguish those with Scrupulosity from those without Scrupulosity. Hence, our primary concern is instead a third kind of responsibility, which will be our primary topic for the remainder of this chapter.

Accountability

Shoemaker's third kind of responsibility is accountability-responsibility or simply accountability. As with attributability and answerability, accountability is defined by the fittingness of a particular emotional response. This time the relevant responses are anger (2015) or resentment and indignation (2011)—and their positive counterparts, which we will ignore here. To hold people responsible in this sense—that is, to hold them to account—is to respond appropriately to their acts with anger, resentment, or indignation. Thus, people are accountable when and only when it is appropriate or fitting to feel anger, resentment, or indignation toward them for their acts.

There are many kinds of anger. People naturally get angry at pets for spoiling carpets and at the weather for spoiling an outing. Shoemaker is referring more specifically only to anger at agents (so not the weather) not just for causing trouble, but for failing to have proper regard for others who are affected by their actions (so not pets). Proper regard involves both emotional empathy (sharing what others feel) and also what Shoemaker calls "evaluational empathy" (seeing other people's interests as reasons for oneself). This anger at lack of proper regard is called "moral anger." It is also sometimes described as "resentment and indignation" (Shoemaker, 2011). It is moral anger, or resentment and indignation, that we don't feel at pets or the weather (unless we anthropomorphize them).

Indignation and resentment are also inappropriate reactions when people have overwhelming justification for the harm they cause. You may feel anger at someone who pushes you, but if the person was pushing you out of the way of an oncoming car, then your anger is inappropriate. (Inappropriateness does not entail that the anger will disappear, even if you realize it's inappropriate.) Thus, our focus, following Shoemaker, is on cases where the agent is both responsible and blameworthy, as the two were distinguished above.

An agent is then accountable for an act or a harm if and only if the fact that the agent did the act or caused the harm makes it appropriate to blame the agent and to feel resentment, indignation, or moral anger at the agent because the act shows a lack of proper regard for others. These reactions are appropriate only when the agent is capable of having that proper regard, so they are appropriate only when agents are able to recognize other people's interests as reasons for them. Thus, whereas answerability requires only that the agent is able to cite *her own* reasons for action, accountability requires that the agent is able to see *other people's* concerns as reasons for the agent herself.

Who should feel the resentment, indignation, and moral anger that are appropriate? The most obvious people to have these reactions are the victims, the people who are wronged. However, murder victims cannot feel anything, yet murderers are still responsible. And many victims of injustice falsely believe that their harms are deserved, blame themselves or refuse to blame others, so they may not feel moral anger toward the perpetrators of those injustices, yet the perpetrators are still responsible. Thus, to say that the moral anger is appropriate only means that it would be appropriate for someone—the victim or someone on the victim's behalf—to feel these reactive attitudes, not that someone actually has these reactions.

An alternative to focusing on reactions is to focus on adverse treatment. People are responsible, on this view, if it's appropriate to treat them adversely, e.g., publicly condemn, ostracize, or punish them. One advantage of focusing on the appropriateness of moral emotions as reactions instead of on the appropriateness of adverse treatment, however, is that it's not always appropriate to treat someone adversely even when that person is responsible.[24] For example, I might be responsible for breaking a promise to someone deceased, where considerations of privacy make it inappropriate for anyone to publicly condemn, ostracize, or punish me. Others could still legitimately feel resentment or indignation toward me, and I can feel it toward myself, but it would not be appropriate for someone to treat me adversely. Such cases then show why accountability depends on liability to reactive attitudes or emotions instead of adverse treatment (McKenna, 2012).[25]

Applied to our cases, agents with Scrupulosity or with scrupulous traits are then accountable if and only if it is legitimate for someone (including but not restricted to people harmed by them) to hold them to account by feeling resentment, indignation, or moral anger toward them for their lack of regard for others. For example, if Peter's ex-girlfriend, Sue, were to discover his stalking, she would feel angry, indignant, and resentful, not to mention worried and threatened, even if she knew of Peter's Scrupulosity. Those imagined responses are certainly understandable; the question is whether those responses would be justified.[26] Her privacy was being invaded. She would at least be uncomfortable, perhaps feel genuinely threatened. And there is no question that we should do what we can to keep her from feeling threatened. But, for our discussion here, let's look at Peter's responsibility, and, as a proxy for that, whether Sue ought to feel indignation and resentment toward Peter for his lack of regard or only pity Peter for his condition and feel sad about the whole situation. Similarly, in order to determine whether Bob is accountable for failing to help his wife with childcare, we need to ask whether it would be appropriate for his wife (or others) to feel resentment, indignation, or moral anger toward Bob. In order to determine

---

[24] Indeed, it can be therapeutically useful to tell patients that they are responsible, while still refusing to blame them or administer an adverse treatment (Pickard 2011).

[25] Defenders of adverse treatment as a test of responsibility could respond by specifying that "appropriate" only refers to ideal circumstances, e.g., when adverse treatment would not be too costly and would not violate independent rights. Alternatively, it may not be the appropriateness of the treatment that matters but the fact that an agent would have no legitimate complaint against adverse treatment were it to occur. We don't believe that these differences matter here, so we will talk only of appropriate emotional reactions instead of justified adverse treatment.

[26] There is something uncomfortable in this example: we don't want to suggest that anyone should actually challenge Sue on how she *should* feel about being stalked, particularly given the objectionable history of people telling women what is appropriate for them to feel (cf. Manne, 2017). The appropriateness of one's moral reaction is a proxy here for whether people are responsible for their actions, not a comment on whether there are any good reasons at all for them to feel as they do: we don't need to take more of a stance than that on what it means for a person to have an "appropriate" reaction.

whether Jennifer is accountable for disobeying and deceiving her parents, we need to ask whether her parents (or others) could legitimately feel resentment, indignation, or moral anger toward her. Such questions about accountability will occupy us for the rest of this chapter.

Theories of Responsibility

How can we answer these questions about what kind of emotional reaction would be appropriate for someone to have in any particular case? Isn't this the worst kind of philosophical armchair pronouncement, judging people for having the wrong emotions? Indeed, if we simply declared which reactions are appropriate or inappropriate then deduced whether those with Scrupulosity were responsible, that would be obnoxious and not very philosophical.

We could instead do something more philosophical, and less obnoxious, and appeal to our bare intuitions about cases. What this would mean is that, having spent time thinking about responsibility and various cases with the hopes that this will shape how we think about future cases, we will then "intuit" what to say about future cases. The first problem with this method is that there's no reason to assume that we have reliable intuitions about accountability in rare cases like Scrupulosity. Even if we do and should trust our intuitions, and even if they are correct, the second problem is that bare appeals to isolated intuition still fail to provide any explanation. Appeals to intuition claim *that* something is true without giving any reason *why* it is true. But we want to understand why agents with Scrupulosity are or are not accountable.

That is why we need theories. One way to determine whether people with Scrupulosity are accountable is to apply a general theory that captures some necessary or sufficient condition of accountability that works in other cases. If that theory holds that people are generally accountable for certain acts whenever they or their acts have certain features, then the theory implies that individuals with Scrupulosity are also accountable when they or their acts have those same features. Conversely, if the theory holds that people are never accountable for acts when they or their acts lack certain features, then the theory implies that the agents with Scrupulosity are not accountable when they or their acts lack those features. The theory also helps us understand *why* people with Scrupulosity do or do not have accountability by specifying the features that make them accountable or not and by drawing analogies between Scrupulous agents and other cases that we understand better.

Incompatibilisms

Some theories of responsibility—like so-called hard determinism, hard-incompatibilism, and responsibility skepticism (Pereboom, 2001; Rosen, 2004)—deny responsibility generally, so those theories won't see any significant difference in accountability between Scrupulous and non-Scrupulous actions. We will instead consider only theories that allow that some people are accountable in the ways we think they are so that we can ask whether Scrupulosity is different.

Other theories that hold people responsible only to the extent that they are "agent causes" of their own actions or only when their actions result from prior self-forming actions (see Kane, 2011: part VI) will be similarly unhelpful in our discussion. Even if we have a clear theoretical idea of what it means for an agent—as opposed to some other event—to cause an action, what we need to know is whether it is true of any particular case that the agent was the cause as well as how that causal difference matters for accountability. Even when the agent in question has Scrupulosity and the Scrupulosity plays some role in subsequent actions, we still need to determine whether the agent is accountable for those actions and subsequent harms. As an example, on the agent-causal theory that a person is responsible when and only when she acts *on her own reasons*, this leaves open that she might have acted on reasons that she endorsed only because of underlying Scrupulous anxiety. The question for us isn't whether she acted as an agent as opposed to as a physical being, but whether there was something about the way she made her decision or judgment that affects her responsibility. Therefore, agent-causal theories will also be generally unhelpful to our discussion.

We will restrict our discussion to theories that are called "compatibilist" because they allow that responsibility is compatible with determinism. Compatibilist theories pick out features that Scrupulous agents share with some agents but not others. They also pick out features that vary in degree (unlike determinism). Hence, these theories might be able to help us understand why Scrupulous agents are less responsible than some agents and more responsible than others, as well as why they are not fully responsible and yet also not fully lacking in responsibility.

We will focus on the two most popular compatibilist theories of responsibility: deep-self theories and reasons-responsiveness theories.[27] Each group includes many varieties, and we will mention some variations, but we will focus on the kind of deep-self theory championed by Harry Frankfurt and the kind of reasons-responsiveness theory developed by John Fischer and Mark Ravizza. Of course, there are also alternatives that do not fall neatly under the general classifications of deep-self or reasons-responsiveness theories. However, we will ignore these complications for the sake of simplicity and brevity. Our goal is not to be comprehensive but only to bring out some of the most important ways in which we might determine whether someone with Scrupulosity is responsible, using these popular accounts of responsibility.[28]

Deep-Self Theories

A deep-self theory holds, in general, that an agent is responsible when the agent's actions express the agent's "deep self." One common version of this deep-self theory holds that agents' actions reflect this deep self when the actions reflect what agents both want to do and want to want to do—when there is a "mesh" between their first-order desires about actions and second-order desires about desires (Frankfurt, 1988). A primary motivation for such theories is that some first-order desires about actions are transient or unrepresentative of what a person is really like "deep down" or "inside," so the mere presence of desires does not express what the agent's deep self really wants or values unless those desires are backed up by something "deeper," such as a second-order desire.[29] The relevant mesh between

---

[27] It is possible that both deep-self and reasons-responsiveness are necessary for accountability-responsibility or that each is sufficient, so a complete account would also need to consider various combined views.

[28] Deep-self and reasons-responsiveness theories have not traditionally drawn Shoemaker's distinctions between accountability and other kinds of responsibility. Nonetheless, we will consider these theories as theories of moral accountability for bad actions.

[29] The distinction between what we do and do not attribute to the deep self does not depend on any controversial metaphysics of the self. The point is simpler: some of a person's behavior doesn't reflect what the individual most wants, values, or cares about or the person's character. Particular explanations of this fact may depend on controversial metaphysics of the self, but the fact itself is not controversial.

levels is therefore evidence that the act springs not from a mere desire about action but from a desire about desires and, hence, from a deep self.

This deeper source of action—whether second-order desires, values, cares, or something else—matters to responsibility because it is more distinctive of humans (Frankfurt, 1988), or because this deep self expresses the "real" person (Wolf, 2003; Sripada 2016), or perhaps because it reflects more stable values (Watson 1975). On this general approach, what makes it legitimate for other people to feel resentment, indignation, moral anger, or similar negative reactive attitudes toward an agent for an act (and, hence, what makes that agent accountable for that act) is the fact that the act was caused by a desire or attitude that meshes appropriately with the agent's second-order desires, values, or cares.

This approach has in its favor that it can distinguish otherwise similar cases, like willing and unwilling addicts (Frankfurt, 1988). All addicts have a first-order desire to use drugs. Unwilling addicts also have a second-order desire not to have that first-order desire to use drugs. They wish that they were not addicted. In contrast, willing addicts have a second-order desire to have their first-order desire to use drugs. For example, a doctor who steals painkillers to feed his addiction, has tried several times to quit, and still wishes that he could quit is an unwilling addict. In contrast, a doctor who steals painkillers to feed his addiction, has never tried to quit, and has no desire to quit because he thinks he can safely continue to obtain and use drugs is a willing addict.

On this deep-self theory, willing addicts are responsible for the harm that their addictive behavior causes another, because their desires and behaviors mesh appropriately with their other beliefs and desires, including their second-order desire to continue to desire drugs (or at least the absence of any second-order desire not to desire drugs). They desire to desire what they desire, and that makes them responsible. In contrast, unwilling addicts are not responsible, because, although they do what they desire to do, they do not desire what they desire to desire. This lack of mesh shows that the desire that causes them to take drugs is not part of their deep selves. Whether the addicts *themselves* are responsible for taking drugs depends not just on their addictive desires but on whether they endorse those desires, which endorsement justifies us in attributing those desires to *them* at a deep level.

This theory of responsibility matches some common judgments about cases of OCD. The theory can distinguish OCD lock checking from ordinary lock checking. As we discussed in Chapter 3, ordinary lock checkers act on their desires to check their locks. They do so willingly because they want to have a desire to check locks, since that first-order desire to check locks keeps them safe. They experience those desires as ego-syntonic because their first-order and second-order desires mesh properly. In contrast, people with lock-checking OCD, like unwilling addicts, experience their urges as intrusive and unwelcome, so they have a second-order desire not to desire to check locks, or at least a second-order desire not to have such a strong first-order desire to check locks so often. Their condition is ego-dystonic. Because of this lack of mesh between first-order and second-order desires, people with OCD aren't *themselves* responsible for their lock checking. Their acts do not spring from their deep selves, because they do not endorse the lock-checking desires that they nevertheless act on. As a result, they are not responsible for the actions caused by their lock-checking OCD, on this view.

It counts in favor of deep-self accounts that they explain why we more often pity an unwilling addict who is struggling to quit, but blame, resent, and feel indignant toward a willing addict who refuses to try to quit. Likewise, deep-self accounts explain why we are disinclined to hold the person with OCD responsible for the same actions for which we would hold a person without OCD responsible, if, for example, the person were to check the lock repeatedly.

The explanation in both cases is that the unwilling addict and the person with OCD are somehow not *themselves* performing the action, so they are not attributability-responsible. If actions are not attributable to an agent, then that person would not (ordinarily) be accountable. If we do not see an agent's behavior as reflecting what the agent most wants, or values, or cares about, then we will not feel that any resentment and indignation toward that agent is merited or justified, which is to say that we will not see that agent as accountability-responsible.

This theory can be tested by applying it to Scrupulosity. We doubt that agents with Scrupulosity are responsible to the same degree as non-Scrupulous agents. The question here is whether deep-self theories can explain this comparison. The reason that deep-self theories might have trouble explaining this ranking is that Scrupulous motivations, unlike most OCD motivations, are often ego-syntonic (Tolin et al., 2001). People with ego-syntonic Scrupulosity explicitly or tacitly endorse their desires. For example, Ezekiel "considered his rituals to be excessive, but experienced no resistance to carrying them out, and said that he would have put up with them were it not for his wife, who was contemplating divorce." His lack of resistance suggests the lack of a conflicting second-order desire. He does admit that his rituals are excessive, but his point here seems to be that they exceed community standards, not that they exceed what he thought was appropriate for him to do. His wife's reaction gives him some reason not to put up with his desires, but he would prefer that his wife agreed with him that his implementation of the rituals is appropriate. It is easy to imagine Ezekiel with almost perfect mesh between his first-order and second-order desires. And yet, as with others who have Scrupulosity, he does not seem fully responsible in that situation: contrast him with those who also endorse their desire for such "excessive" rituals but who do not have Scrupulosity. Aren't these people more responsible for the resulting harms?

Some caveats are needed. Ezekiel's first- and second-order desires might mesh with each other but not mesh with his other desires, e.g., his desire to get along with his wife, to be religious, to have enough time to eat breakfast. As we will see, different deep-self theories will take these other desires or values more seriously than the Frankfurtian theory we are discussing here, and it's worth thinking more about which desires, values, etc. need to mesh for us to attribute an act to a person.

Likewise, to be sure that there is a mesh between desires, we need to know how to specify the desire that Ezekiel endorses. Does he endorse a desire *to pray as much as* (he feels) *is necessary* or even a desire *to pray as much as will make his wife angry*? Presumably he now foresees that his excessive prayer will make his wife angry, but it would be a mistake to think her anger is part of the content of the desire he endorses. This is because, should it turn out his wife will no longer be angry, he would still desire to pray the same amount. Therefore, the desire he actually endorses is the desire to pray as much as he feels is necessary.

Scrupulosity is a clearer case in this way than other forms of OCD, though they too will require us to specify the desire that the person endorses (or refuses to endorse). Is the right way to specify the desire of compulsive hand-washers as a desire *to wash their hands until the skin peels away*? Surely not, since they would prefer to wash their hands clean without the skin's peeling. But if we specify their desire as a desire *to clean their hands*, then they will endorse that desire. Does this suggest that those with OCD endorse their own desires generally like individuals with Scrupulosity?

Perhaps it does. We leave it to more general explorations of OCD to determine whether, when, and in what sense OCD is ego-dystonic despite such possible endorsement. But one difference likely remains between Scrupulosity and the other OCD cases: the endorsement for those with Scrupulosity runs much deeper. The compulsive hand-washers might endorse the desire to have hands that are entirely free of germs, but might also wish that they could be happy with hands that had a few (relatively unthreatening) germs on them. People with Scrupulosity will not feel the same way about having committed just a few (unthreatening?) sins or hurting people (just a little?). So they endorse not just their first-order desire but many related desires.

A defender of deep-self theories might respond that Ezekiel endorses his first-order desires only because he has poor insight into his condition. That lack of insight might then explain why he is not fully responsible. However, this reply abandons this deep-self theory. Whether or not Ezekiel and others with Scrupulosity have poor insight into their condition is irrelevant to whether their second-order desires mesh with their first-order desires. Hence, this lack of insight provides no defense for this deep-self theory.[30]

A deep-self theorist also might try to reclassify such cases of Scrupulosity into a third category. In addition to the willing and the unwilling, there is also the "wanton": this group has no second-order attitudes at all with regard to their first-order attitudes. Perhaps people with Scrupulosity do not actively endorse their first-order desires but are merely wanton toward them, neither endorsing nor failing to endorse. This is possible in some cases. However, based on available case descriptions, many people with Scrupulosity *do* endorse their first-order desires. We see no good reason to deny or reinterpret those case descriptions. According to their reports by patients and therapists alike, people with Scrupulosity tend to be very reflective about not only their actions but also their thoughts and desires, possibly because they generally take their thoughts to be important (as illustrated in thought-action fusion). They think too much, not too little, about what kinds of people they should be. This characteristic makes it hard to interpret them as wantons.

Another analogy assimilates Scrupulosity to resigned addicts (Kennett, 2014; Graham, 2015). Consider addicts who give up the fight against

---

[30] One further response would be to claim that mesh and adequate insight are separately necessary and jointly sufficient for deep self and responsibility. This conjunctive theory would explain why Ezekiel and Little John are not responsible. However, the insight condition likely does all the work here without the mesh condition.

addiction, become resigned to their addiction, and then even endorse their addiction. Why? Perhaps because they are living on the streets with no chance of a job, because they have no training, no skills, no experience, and no references. They know that they will remain addicts if they continue to take drugs, so their only realistic options are living on the streets as addicts and living on the streets without taking drugs often. They have lived on the streets long enough to know how horrible it would be without taking drugs regularly. Living on the streets as addicts seems more bearable. To that extent, they endorse their addiction in their present circumstances, meaning that they have a second-order desire to maintain their first-order desire to take drugs.[31] Most people pity the resigned addicts rather than resenting them or holding them responsible.

Are people with Scrupulosity analogous to this type of resigned addict? Partly, insofar as people with Scrupulosity are resigned to fulfilling their moral obligations, no matter how stringent. For example, Mary was described as feeling "hopeless," apparently resigned to her lengthy nightly prayers and the resulting lack of sleep. Still, even if Mary is resigned to losing sleep in order to complete her prayers, she may still endorse the necessity of completing her prayers. She believes that her only choice is to fulfill her moral and religious obligation to pray as much as she does or to live a life that is even worse, both in the sense that she will be acting immorally and also in the sense that she will—or at least believes she will—feel a lot more anxiety. Mary endorses her moral and religious obligations as well as her prayers that fulfill those obligations: she sees her obligations and actions as more justified than the alternatives, given her situation, though she might—like the resigned addict—also wish she had better options.

Can this analogy be used to defend deep-self theories of responsibility? We do not see how. After all, people with Scrupulosity like Mary as well as the resigned addict both have second-order desires that mesh well enough with their first-order desires. In addition, resigned addicts do not seem as responsible for their actions as someone who was in better circumstances and was nevertheless resigned. Neither do Mary and others with Scrupulosity. Thus, if the person with Scrupulosity is a counterexample to deep-self

---

[31] To avoid a possible misreading, note that one can endorse one's *desire* to take drugs without endorsing one's *addiction* to drugs. Even addicts who don't try to quit may not endorse having an addiction, though they continue to endorse their drug use, and though they may see that the regular use entails that their addiction will continue.

theories, so is the resigned addict. Instead of helping deep-self theories, the resigned addict actually creates more problems for the deep-self approach.

Admittedly, people with Scrupulosity probably feel frustrated at what they see as their moral obligations. However, they still endorse them as their moral obligations. Many people with ego-syntonic Scrupulosity do not see themselves as misdirected or conflicted. Instead, they see themselves as moral people in immoral or slack societies. They are not merely resigned to living with higher moral standards, so they are different from resigned addicts. They are also reflective about their desires and thoughts, so they are not wantons. Their values and second-order desires mesh with their first-order desires, at least as well as the second-order and first-order desires of most people. The conflicts they feel—and they do feel conflicts—aren't between their first-order desires to fulfill some obligation and their second-order endorsement of that obligation. They might wish that things were different, and they might even wish they didn't have that obligation, but the mesh between first-order and second-order desires is clear. Thus, a deep-self account of responsibility seems to imply that people with Scrupulosity are responsible for their actions and the harms they predictably cause.

This implication is at odds with most people's judgments of mental illnesses, including OCD. As we suggested above, people with Scrupulosity are probably not as responsible for harms as a result of their condition as those without Scrupulosity would be, and it's hard to see how the deep-self theory would explain that.

Our argument so far has been aimed most directly against Frankfurt's second-order desire version of a deep-self theory. Other deep-self theories might seem to escape these problems. Gary Watson's view that an agent is responsible when the agent's actions and desires mesh with the agent's values or beliefs about what is good or best (Watson, 1975) also captures the idea that, when one acts on a desire that is unendorsed—in this case, unendorsed by one's values—then one's action does not express who one "really" is. Mary desires to finish saying prayers, but she presumably does not think that saying extra prayers is the most valuable way for her to spend her life, so this first-order desire isn't endorsed by her values, even if she does believe that, given her circumstances, she is obligated to finish her prayers after her kids go to sleep.

This interpretation, however, takes a selective view of Mary's values. She values her religious life and believes that it should be taken seriously, even when it's inconvenient. Whatever we think about the status of her

Scrupulous beliefs and values—whether they are genuine beliefs or just quasi-beliefs—her view of the best possible life doesn't involve staying up late saying prayers to ensure they're said correctly. Her conflict is only because her life can't perfectly live up to her values and beliefs about what would be best. There will always be some sense in which her actions are not entirely endorsed by her values—she doesn't value staying up late to finish prayers—though the actions are endorsed by other of her values, such as that she values her religious life. Similarly, Bridget really does value her customers' lives and safety and that is why she checks the containers, but she also would value a life that doesn't require so much checking and reassurance.

This kind of practical conflict between desires and multiple values cannot be enough on its own to reduce responsibility. When my values conflict in some particular case, I am no less responsible just because some of my values are in conflict. If I value privacy but also value sociability, then I will sometimes be in a conflicted situation: I have to host an event for my friends at my house, though I would prefer that my house remain entirely private. Either I host my friends at my house, giving up some privacy, or I do not host them, giving up some sociability. I am no less responsible for my action (and any resultant harms) just because some of my values would endorse one action and some would endorse its contrary.

Similarly, we cannot hope to understand the diminished responsibility of Scrupulosity as a result of conflicting values or beliefs about what is best, even on the assumption that there is no mesh between their actions and their values. We would have to know *which* of their values are important, and, since a person's moral and religious values are often very deep and central ones, it seems that any deep-self theory will conclude that a person's actions mesh with those core values in many cases of Scrupulosity.

This same objection applies to the version of a mesh theory that appeals not just to one's values but to "cares" that make up one's deep self. As Sripada (2016) puts the position:

> one's self consists of one's cares [that] exhibit distinctive motivational, commitmental, evaluative, and affective dispositions. (1230)

On this view, an action expresses one's deep self when the person's self or cares include a motive that is sufficiently involved in the causation of the action (Sripada 2016: 1216). Scrupulous actions do align with the content of one's cares and motives, as just discussed, but do those attitudes *cause* the action? The answer has to be that the person's cares, especially moral and religious concerns, do at least partially cause the action. Big John's actions of greeting everyone at work express, according to him, his desire to treat his neighbor as he would want to be treated himself. His expression of the Golden Rule certainly doesn't match most interpretations of it, but in the absence of his religious or moral concern would he still greet everyone? It seems unlikely.

This is not to deny the importance of anxiety in explaining his motivation and actions. But we should not assume that the anxiety explains actions independently of his cares, beliefs, and values. Anxiety does not move a person the way a seizure moves a person. Anxiety instead affects which of one's concerns one fixates on and whether a person is reassured by or can even consider counterevidence. Big John's actions are motivated by his anxiety, but they are also motivated by his religious or moral values, which are central to his deep self. Sripada's deep-self theory based on cares, then, still fails to explain why agents with Scrupulosity could lack or have reduced responsibility, since their actions do express their cares.

There are other deep-self theories, but the case of Scrupulosity raises challenges that cannot clearly be remedied within any deep-self framework that we know of. The problem is that Scrupulosity is not just a disorder of unwanted desires. Scrupulous motivations and actions also draw on and mesh with people's second-order desires, their values, their cares, and their deep selves. If they are less than fully responsible, it cannot be from a lack of mesh.

Admittedly, we are assuming that people with Scrupulosity are less than fully responsible for the relevant actions. If one denies this assumption and believes instead that those with Scrupulosity are fully responsible, then a deep-self theory might explain why. Regardless of whether those with Scrupulosity are fully responsible, though, it should at least be clear now what the deep-self theory is committed to in the case of Scrupulosity.

Even on our assumptions, deep-self theories can still successfully capture a different notion of responsibility. Although we're focusing here on accountability, deep-self theories might instead capture the conditions that need to be met for attributability. Indeed, Shoemaker's discussion of attributability (2011) refers to cares and commitments as parts of a deep self, much like Sripada's deep-self theory. So we needn't deny the value of deep self for other important kinds of responsibility.

Despite this value of deep-self theories, our conclusion is that they fail to provide a sufficient condition for accountability. Deep-self theories still might identify a necessary condition for accountability (or a sufficient condition of some other form of responsibility), but in order to determine what is sufficient for accountability, we must turn to other theories.

Reasons-Responsiveness Theories

The main competitor to deep-self theories claims that responsibility hinges on an ability to respond to reasons (e.g., Gert & Duggan, 1979; Fischer & Ravizza, 1998). My responsibility is dependent not only on my ability to act but, more important, on the degree to which I am able to recognize and react to reasons for and against that act.

The ability to respond to reasons (or reasons-responsiveness) is the ability to recognize reasons plus the ability to act on reasons after they are recognized. The former is called "receptivity" to reasons, the latter is called "reactivity" to reasons, and both are required for "responsiveness" to reasons. An agent needs to be able both to detect the reasons for and against acting in a particular way and then to act accordingly in order to be responsive to reasons.

How can we tell whether someone can receive and react to reasons, but just doesn't? An agent's abilities can be determined by what the agent does in ideal circumstances. I lack the ability to run a mile in six minutes if I would never do so even when I knew I had strong incentive (such as when you would pay me a million dollars for doing so) and nothing external prevented me (such as shackles on my legs). Of course, I might sometimes try but fail to do what I have the ability to do, such as when I can hit a target but miss. If I succeed usually or a reasonable number of times, even if not always, then I still have this ability.[32]

We can use this kind of account of abilities to explain reasons-responsiveness. Let's begin with reactivity to reasons. An agent is *reactive* to reasons regarding a kind of act if and only if both of the following two conditions are met:

(p*) If the agent recognizes overall reason to perform an act of that kind, then the agent usually will perform an act of that kind.

---

[32] There are technical problems with this brief account that we ignore, since those problems do not affect the particular issues that we are discussing here.

(n*) If the agent recognizes overall reason *not* to perform an act of that kind, then the agent usually will *not* perform an act of that kind.[33]

On this account, Adam is able to react to reasons regarding checking his receipts if he usually—all else equal—checks his receipts when he recognizes overall reason to check them and also usually—all else equal—does not check them when he recognizes overall reason not to check them. Thus, if Adam finds no reason to check the receipts again and good reasons not to check the receipts again, yet he checks them again anyway, then Adam would not be reactive to reasons regarding checking receipts.

Sometimes compulsions result from a lack of reactivity to reasons, but they may also result from a lack of receptivity to reasons. An agent is *receptive* to reasons regarding a kind of act if and only if both of the following two conditions are met:

(p*) If there is a reason for the agent to perform an act of that kind, then the agent usually will recognize that reason to perform an act of that kind.

(n*) If there is a reason for the agent *not* to perform an act of that kind, then the agent usually will recognize that reason *not* to perform an act of that kind.

Agents lack receptivity to reasons when they are distracted from or otherwise blind to the reasons for or against their actions. If Adam isn't receptive to reasons, then he can't even see the reasons not to keep checking. Perhaps he's too anxious to notice reasons against his action; perhaps he's so focused on the likelihood that he'll sin by not checking them that that's all he can attend to. He can't act on other reasons because he doesn't see the relevant issues or recognize them as reasons not to act.

Notice that receptivity and reactivity are independent and one may lack one without lacking the other. Nevertheless, in many cases of mental illness, both reactivity and receptivity to reasons are reduced. And both are required for full responsibility. Therefore, we include both together when

---

[33] This account needs both a positive clause (p) and a negative cause (n), because conditionals can be true by falsity of antecedent. If the account included only (p), then any agent who never recognized overall reason to perform an act of that kind would make (p) true so the account would imply that he has the ability to react to reasons, which is implausible. The negative clause (n) avoids this result.

talking about the kind of "responsiveness" to reasons that is necessary for responsibility:

> An agent is *responsive* to reasons regarding a particular act or kind of act if and only if that agent is both reactive and receptive to reasons regarding that particular act or that kind of act.

If Adam lacks reasons-reactivity, then that would explain why he is not fully responsible, since he cannot act on reasons even when he recognizes them. And if Adam lacks reasons-receptivity, that would also explain why he is not fully responsible, because he cannot recognize when there is a reason for him to do something, even if he would be able to act on reasons if he saw them. Thus, Adam would not be fully responsible when he lacks reasons-responsiveness in either of these required ways.

Readers who know the philosophical literature on this topic might worry that we describe agents as reasons-responsive, whereas Fischer and Ravizza (1998) instead describe mechanisms or processes that produce actions as reasons-responsive. By talking about mechanisms or processes, Fischer and Ravizza hope to point not only to the person's responding (or not) to reasons but also to an explanation about why they respond (or don't). If the mechanism works fine in general but doesn't work in this case, then we can say that the person *can* but *does not* respond to reasons; if the mechanism fails more generally, then we say that the person *cannot* respond to reasons.

The notion of a mechanism that responds to reasons does not work well in our discussion for three reasons. First, there might be many such "mechanisms" in an OCD or Scrupulosity case, and we don't want to rest too much on the failure or success of any one mechanism. Second, it is not clear how to individuate mechanisms. Suppose Adam does not respond to reasons when it comes to checking his receipts, but he responds to reasons when it comes to paying his taxes. Is this because the mechanism or process that leads him to check receipts is distinct from the mechanism or process when he pays his taxes? Or is it because there is one more general mechanism and its operation is impeded only when, say, special kinds of anxiety are involved? Third, there may be no problem with the mechanism(s) more generally, but only a problem in certain cases that keeps the *person* from responding to reasons. Consider a pasta maker that works perfectly fine unless there is too much moisture in the dough. The easiest way to fix it is not to adjust the machine but to dry the dough. Similarly, the reasons-responsive mental mechanism(s) might work well in general, but not when gummed up by anxiety. Is that a problem with a mechanism or a problem with the person more generally? Is it something that can be fixed by adjusting the mechanism so it's not bothered by the anxiety or by reducing the anxiety, perhaps by changing the circumstances?

If our account of reasons-responsiveness focused on mechanisms, then we would need to solve these problems in order to know what to say about Scrupulosity. For example, we've already explained how those with Scrupulosity fixate on particular reasons to the exclusion of other reasons. Such a focus is certainly a failure of the person to respond to reasons more generally, but is it a failure of some particular mechanism? If so, which mechanism? Another problem is that, when the anxiety of a person with Scrupulosity makes that person fail to respond to reasons, some coping strategy might (over time) neutralize the anxiety or enable the individual to compensate for it. If that strategy is effective, then even before adopting this coping strategy, the person was capable of developing this new mechanism to keep the old one from failing to respond to reasons. But then does the availability of that coping mechanism mean that the person was *able* to respond to reasons all along?

We pose rather than answer these questions because our focus here is not in defending a particular theory of responsibility, but only in showing how some prominent theories would deal with Scrupulosity. To say more about whether anxiety or Scrupulosity makes one incapable of responding to reasons requires saying much more about *what* is incapable of responding to reasons—persons, mechanisms, or something else. That is a worthwhile project, but it's not ours. So, to avoid all of the complications about mechanisms, we will continue to talk crudely about people being reasons-responsive or not.

Our question is whether reasons-responsiveness of some kind is necessary or sufficient for accountability. Even if Adam is not accountable for the acts distinctive of his Scrupulosity because he lacks reasons-responsivity regarding those acts, those acts still might be attributable to him, his deep self, and his character, and they might reveal that he lacks virtue or has a vice. What is denied when reasons-responsiveness theories deny that Adam is responsible is only that he is an appropriate target of indignation, resentment, moral anger, and related reactive attitudes (or perhaps adverse treatment). His lack of responsiveness to reasons is the feature that is supposed to explain why he is not accountable, according to reasons-responsiveness theories.

One major advantage of a reasons-responsiveness account of responsibility is supposed to be that it can explain why many people suffering from mental disorders are less than fully responsible. When paranoia directs someone to interpret ordinary human interactions as evidence of a large conspiracy against her, she fails to recognize legitimate reasons against her conclusion. When someone's arachnophobia causes her to avoid areas where spiders may be found, she responds too strongly to the small danger of spiders and fails to respond to the many reasons she has to be in those places. And when someone with OCD has a compulsion to check locks, she responds to what is not really a strong reason to check locks and fails to respond to reasons not to check the locks yet again.

The Lack of Reasons-Responsiveness in Scrupulosity

The story of responsibility is not so clear with Scrupulosity. At first blush, people with Scrupulosity respond to reasons that are not abnormal. People with Scrupulosity are worried about violating commands, being sinners, harming other people, and deceiving or breaking promises. Most people worry about these same things. People with Scrupulosity worry more and do more in response to their worries than most people would, but many people go beyond in some areas, and moral saints go above and beyond in many areas. Many people hold themselves to higher standards than others on some issues (perfectionism), ruminate on some possible moral failure (chronic doubt), and even judge that sometimes thoughts are almost as bad as actions (moral thought-action fusion), as we saw in previous chapters. Are those with Scrupulosity then any less responsive to reasons?

To dig beneath superficial appearances, consider again the following questions we considered in our earlier discussion. First, do people with Scrupulosity really respond to reasons or do they respond only to their own anxiety? Second, even if they do respond to reasons, do they respond proportionately to the strength of the reasons or do they overreact? Third, do they react to the entire range of relevant reasons or only to a small subset of relevant reasons? The answers to these questions show how people with

Scrupulosity differ in the ways in which they are responsive and unresponsive to reasons.

First, do people with Scrupulosity respond only to their anxiety? We gave examples in previous chapters of the motives behind donating to a charity or leaving a large tip to illustrate various motivations for the same action. Someone might give money to help the needy, but the donor also has a desire for good publicity. What was her reason for giving? The donor herself might not even know why she gave. We can ask her why she gave, and we can check patterns of her action to see what generally motivates her. If a rich business leader gives only when a donation will help the needy *and* he will also gain good publicity, but never when the publicity is lacking, then this suggests that the publicity is likely a reason he responded to in his giving. In principle, we can use such test cases to determine which reasons a person responds to.

Similar patterns could reveal whether people with Scrupulosity respond to moral or religious reasons or, instead, act solely to reduce their own anxiety.

We have emphasized that people with Scrupulosity respond primarily to their own anxiety. In what sense are they not responding to reasons, though? This is ambiguous. Anxiety might be the explanation of why a person worries about something, but what the individual is worried about isn't any less legitimate as a result. If I'm worried as I leave the house, and I rationalize that as a worry that I might have left the stove on, I still might have left the stove on. So, when we ask about responding to these rationalized reasons, we are not asking about what brings about the reasons but about whether the person is responding to the content of the reasons, whatever motivated them to begin with.

One can also respond to anxiety itself as a reason. Anxiety, in non-pathological cases, can be evidence that something is not right. If I'm anxious when I leave the house, I take that feeling itself as evidence that I forgot something, that my "subconscious" memory is manifesting itself in the anxiety, so I need to take a minute to think about what I might have forgotten.

When is responding to anxiety, or to the rationalized reasons that it prompts, not responding to reasons? At a minimum, one should at least not have evidence that the anxiety is unreliable: if I feel anxious *every* time I leave the house, regardless of whether I leave anything, then the anxiety is no longer evidence that I've left something, so it cannot be a reason to check the house again. Similarly, if I find myself thinking that I've left the stove on every time I leave the house, yet it never is, then the thought cannot serve as a reliable reason to go back inside. If I cannot be reassured and instead find problems with each attempted reassurance, then I should suspect that I'm rationalizing my anxiety and not responding to features of the situation itself. What suggests that those with Scrupulosity are not responding to reasons, then, is not that they're wrong, but that their anxiety and the corresponding thoughts do not fit the facts. Anxiety leads the person with Scrupulosity to be responsive to anxiety when that anxiety provides no reason.

Responsiveness to anxiety can also make people less responsive to other, better reasons. In cases of OCD and Scrupulosity, people often take as reasons features of a situation that are indeed good reasons. However, they recognize them as reasons and respond to them only for as long as the anxiety persists and only to a degree matched by the intensity of the anxiety, rather than by the seriousness of the considered feature. That pattern suggests they are not responding to the reason *as* a reason.

Consider the difference between an OCD lock checker and an ordinary lock checker. Both respond to real reasons, i.e., the possibility that one's lock wasn't correctly locked, thus leaving the house vulnerable to a break-in. OCD lock checkers, however, continue to feel anxiety and to check the lock despite recognizing reasons not to worry and not to check—perhaps because they just checked a minute ago—whereas ordinary lock checkers cease to feel anxiety, feels less anxiety, or at least stop checking after recognizing adequate reasons not to worry or check. Because of underlying anxiety, a person with OCD takes as a reason for acting something that is only a minimal reason or a reason that is strongly outweighed by other reasons. For the lock checker with OCD, anxiety can even have effects on beliefs, such as the person's belief that the house is vulnerable to burglary if not ritually locked in a particular way.

Likewise for Scrupulosity. Big John's extreme and persistent anxiety causes him to focus on being kind to those in need—which is a perfectly good reason to act—but he may conflate the severity of his anxiety with the weightiness of the reason, thinking that he *has* to greet everyone, instead of thinking that it would just be ideal if he did. Moreover, he may continue to act on that reason (perhaps ignoring other reasons as he does so) for as long as the anxiety persists, seeking to reassure himself for far too long that he has been kind to everyone.

Because people with Scrupulosity are motivated primarily by soothing their anxiety, they will often be wrong about which reasons they have or how strong those reasons are. The anxieties of those with Scrupulosity often do not arise in response to genuinely threatening features of the situation. They will not realize this if they lack insight—or the realization might arise only later, through therapy (Salkovskis, 1999). So, this distinction between persons with OCD, including those with Scrupulosity, and regular worriers will explain why those with OCD are sometimes less responsive to reasons and, when they are responsive to genuine reasons, they are less responsive to them *to the extent* that they are reasons. They are instead responsive to the reasons to the extent that they legitimate and provide a path to soothe their anxiety.

Reasons-responsiveness theories can therefore explain why those with Scrupulosity will have less responsibility than those without—not in all matters, but in cases in which their anxiety diminishes their reasons-receptivity or reasons-reactivity. On reasons-responsiveness theories, a person is responsible only for actions issuing from attitudes or processes that are reasons-responsive. People with Scrupulosity are motivated by their anxiety in a way that keeps them from being adequately responsive to reasons, at least in some cases. They might sometimes not be able to recognize reasons against their anxieties that they should recognize as reasons, e.g., leading a person with Scrupulosity to continue to worry that he violated a religious fast by swallowing his own saliva, even after multiple reassurances by his rabbi (Abramowitz, 2002). As long as their anxiety persists, they are motivated to act on that anxiety. Our initial conclusion, then, is that, to the extent that people with Scrupulosity respond to reasons based on their own anxiety but not to genuine reasons, or to the extent that they respond to reasons only to the degree that those reasons reflect their own anxieties and not the weightiness of the reasons, they are not really responsive to some reasons. That explains why they are less than fully responsible.

Second, to the extent that people with Scrupulosity do react to reasons, they often over-react. Compare people with a phobia about flying in airplanes. There is a possibility one's airplane will crash when one flies. However, the danger is slight and is less than the danger of driving much shorter distances in a car. Thus, people who drive a long distance instead of flying simply because they are phobic about flying are over-reacting to the danger of flying and under-reacting to the danger of driving. They do react to reasons but not proportionately or appropriately.

Similarly, there is a slight but real chance that the store made a mistake in Adam's favor. Even if he checked his receipts before, there is still a very slight chance that he missed a mistake in his favor. And if the store did make a mistake in his favor then he has some reason to try to correct that mistake. The problem is not that he has no reason at all but instead that he over-reacts to a very small reason to recheck his receipts. In cases of Scrupulosity like these, then, agents appear to react to reasons, but they do not react appropriately.

Notice that the issue here is reactivity rather than receptivity. People with Scrupulosity do not usually have higher degrees of belief or of confidence. Indeed, they often have chronic doubts about their beliefs. Instead of over-believing, they over-react. Still, this lack of appropriate reactivity is enough to undermine reasons-responsiveness and responsibility, according to most reasons-responsiveness theories of responsibility.

People with Scrupulosity can respond to reasons inappropriately in many other ways as well. They often continue to take something to be a sufficient reason even when it no longer is. Or they take it to be a sufficient reason even when it is outweighed or overridden by more important reasons. Or they take it to be a reason for a large action (e.g., repeating each line of the prayer multiple times to get it right) when it is in fact only a reason for some much smaller action (e.g., pausing to collect one's thoughts before starting or before saying the most important line of the prayer). Each of these is an example of responding to reasons, but not responding appropriately: overreacting, perseverating, exaggerating the weight of the reason, or exaggerating the response needed.

What best explains these inappropriate responses by people with Scrupulosity is the way in which their underlying anxiety shapes their thoughts and actions. This separates cases of Scrupulosity from the cases in which, say, a person reacts inappropriately to reasons and yet his responsibility remains intact. The bank robber Willie Sutton is reported to have said that he robbed banks "because that's where the money is."[34] Sutton

---

[34] For what it's worth, Sutton denied having said this. In fact, he said: "Why did I rob banks? Because I enjoyed it. I loved it. I was more alive when I was inside a bank, robbing it, than at any other time in my life. I enjoyed everything about it so much that one or two weeks later I'd be out looking for the next job. But to me the money was the chips, that's all" (Sutton, 1976).

responded inappropriately to the fact that there is money in a bank that can be removed for one's own needs, and he was responsible.

In contrast, the *capacity* to respond appropriately to reasons is required for responsibility.[35] To see why, recall the airplane phobic. Most people would not hold an airplane phobic entirely responsible for not flying to a family reunion, for example, because the airplane phobic is not capable of responding to reasons appropriately. The same grounds would justify denying or reducing responsibility in cases of Scrupulosity when agents are equally incapable of responding to reasons appropriately.

The third way in which people with Scrupulosity fail to respond to reasons involves fixation on a few reasons to the exclusion of others. This is because the underlying anxiety of Scrupulosity leads its sufferers to soothe their anxiety, which prompts them to fixate on those reasons that seem most relevant to their anxiety, to the exclusion of other reasons that can be more important, which they should notice and respond to. For example, Peter responds to his concerns about pregnancy and parenthood but ignores the overwhelming reasons to give his ex-girlfriend her privacy. He is not failing to respond to the reasons that he *does* notice; he is failing to notice and respond to those other reasons.

Even if people with Scrupulosity do recognize reasons not to act as they do, they can find it excruciatingly difficult to pay sufficient attention to those other reasons because their anxiety makes them fixate on the reasons that they believe are directly related to their anxiety. Indeed, on Neil Levy's account of OCD more generally, it is a related inability to keep their attention focused correctly that is the defining feature of those with OCD (Levy, 2018). Imagine, by illustration, learning that your feelings of pain do not reliably correspond at all to harmful features of the world, that you feel pain during events that are perfectly fine, so, to function well, you should therefore ignore your pain when acting. This is unrealistic for almost any of us, at least for any sustained length of time. Pain serves as such a strong motivator and indicator of problems that it would be an unreasonable burden to expect people indefinitely to ignore their pain. If they could stop the pain, even if the only way they had to stop it was itself to act unreasonably, we would understand that.

---

[35] This lack of capacity might seem to supply not only an excuse but an exemption, comparable to the exemption from responsibility accorded to young children because of their incapacities. However, as mentioned above, the incapacities of people with Scrupulosity are not as pervasive as those of young children. The incapacities that come with Scrupulosity affect only some actions on some occasions. That is why we see them as excuses rather than exemptions.

Similarly, although people with Scrupulosity might in theory be able to ignore their anxiety and respond to reasons, it is unrealistic and unreasonable to expect them both to be aware of the problem and to ignore the anxiety they feel (cf. Levy, 2011; Yaffe, 2011). Anxiety, like pain, is a strong motivator and directs attention, even when one realizes that it is misguided.

This fixation on some reasons to the exclusion of others results in a lack of reasons-receptivity rather than reactivity. If people with Scrupulosity fail to notice or to pay attention to reasons not to act as they do, then they are not able to recognize or to be receptive to those reasons, even if they would be able to react to those reasons if they ever did notice them.

The problem of fixation thus differs from the problem of over-reaction in at least two ways. First, fixation leads to lack of receptivity rather than reactivity, whereas over-reaction is a problem of reactivity rather than receptivity. Second, the problem with fixation is about failure to recognize reasons *against* actions, whereas over-reaction is over-reaction to reasons *for* actions. Despite these differences, however, both fixation and over-reaction result from anxiety and undermine reasons-responsiveness and, hence, responsibility.

Those with Scrupulosity thus lack reasons-responsiveness in at least three ways. Sometimes persons with Scrupulosity respond to their anxieties instead of real reasons for or against their actions and beliefs. Sometimes they respond to reasons but not appropriately. And sometimes they respond to only a small subset of the relevant reasons. The point is not just that they do not respond to reasons in these ways, but that they *cannot* respond to reasons because of their anxiety. These inabilities show why agents with Scrupulosity are not fully responsible for actions that result from their mental illness, according to the theory that responsibility requires reasons-responsiveness. We suspect that this conclusion seems more plausible to most people than the view that those with Scrupulosity are entirely responsible for their actions and for harms that they cause. To the extent that this conclusion is correct, it also speaks in favor of reasons-responsiveness as an account of responsibility.

Degrees of Responsibility

As we said at the start of this chapter, Scrupulosity—like many other conditions—seems to reduce but not completely remove responsibility.

People with Scrupulosity have some kinds of responsibility but not others, and the motivational role of anxiety would explain—at least on a reasons-responsive account of responsibility—why those with Scrupulosity have an intermediate degree of accountability in particular.

The reasons-responsiveness account can explain degrees of responsibility because responsiveness to reasons comes in degrees. Some people are responsive (receptive and reactive) to more kinds of reasons than other people are. They might, for example, not respond to financial incentives but still respond to emotional harm to their families. Some people need to exert more effort and find it more difficult and costly to respond to reasons than other people do. People with Scrupulosity pay a high price in anxiety for avoiding their compulsive behaviors, and they need to exert constant effort in order to recognize and react to reasons when their thoughts become obsessive and pervade their lives. Thus, people with Scrupulosity might retain some ability to respond to reason, but the difficulty and costs of exerting that ability still show that their control, ability, and capacity are at a lower level than for those people without such a mental illness.

Circumstances also matter. When discussing treatment in the next chapter, we will see that Scrupulosity patients in treatment are sometimes able to do acts that they see as immoral. Their therapists ask them to do such acts during therapy sessions, and the patients often comply. Nonetheless, this ability to do an act in a therapist's office does not show that they have the ability to act that way consistently in everyday life. Just as an alcoholic might be able to stay sober when at an Alcoholics Anonymous meeting but not in a bar, so those with Scrupulosity might be able to refrain from compulsive behaviors in some circumstances (the therapist's office) but not in others (the workplace). The range of circumstances in which they have the ability to respond to reasons then indicates another dimension along which responsiveness to reasons varies by degree.

Degrees of responsiveness to reasons lead to degrees of responsibility because the more responsive to reasons a person is regarding an act, the more responsible that person is for that act. That is how responsiveness to reasons explains responsibility.

Because responsibility and responsiveness to reasons come in degrees, it is usually a mistake to ask simply *whether* an agent is responsible or not. Instead, we should ask *how* responsible that person is for that act. Agents could be responsible in some ways and not others, but they can also be responsible to different degrees even within a single kind of responsibility, such as accountability.

Insofar as we allow degrees of responsibility, our view differs from dichotomous reasons-responsiveness theorists, including Fischer and Ravizza (1998), who claim that agents are either fully responsible or not at all responsible. To maintain this dichotomy, Fischer and Ravizza specify a threshold of moderate reasons-responsiveness and claim that moderately reasons-responsive agents are responsible, whereas weakly reasons-responsive agents are not responsible. In reply, critics have presented cases where agents who are only weakly reasons-responsive seem responsible (McKenna, 2012). Our hope is to avoid this whole debate by saying that people who are weakly but not moderately responsive to reasons are weakly but not moderately responsible. By allowing degrees of responsibility, we avoid the need for any arbitrary threshold.

Now apply this point to Scrupulosity. Are Ezekiel, Bridget, and others with Scrupulosity responsible or not? Neither answer seems accurate, even restricting our attention to accountability. They seem only partly responsible, but why? What explains their position on the continuum from complete responsibility to complete lack of responsibility? One suggestion is that their reduction in responsiveness to reasons explains why they are not fully responsible for the acts that result from their Scrupulosity. They are still partly responsible to the degree that they are responsive to reasons, but the difficulties and costs that they face when they try to nullify their obsessions and avoid their compulsive acts explain why they are less responsive, and thus why their responsibility is reduced.

It also explains why we have mixed feelings about Ezekiel, and so does Ezekiel's wife. Ezekiel did hurt his wife, but we doubt that she would judge him (or be justified in judging him) to be as responsible as he would have been if he had neglected her out of a lack of concern for her that was not motivated by pathological anxiety. She would not be justified in feeling as much indignation as she would feel if he neglected her because he preferred to play video games. On the other hand, she might well have felt some indignation in the real case, more than she would have felt if he had hurt her as the result of some seizure or tumor. In the real case, she probably did and should have held him responsible to some intermediate degree (between video games and seizure). Her feelings and our feelings would be mixed, and her ambivalence seems justified and right.

But where exactly between the extremes does Ezekiel lie? We lack detail about the case, and Ezekiel's responsiveness probably varies from one time to another, so it would be hard to say much more than this about any particular case—or more about responsibility in Scrupulosity in general. Some people with Scrupulosity have much greater foresight and insight and are a lot more reasons-responsive and responsible than others. Despite these complications, a reasons-responsive account of responsibility can still explain why people with Scrupulosity in general have *some* responsibility but are less than fully responsible for the acts that reflect their mental illness.

Of course, people can change. Although these people are less than fully responsible now, Scrupulosity (like other forms of OCD) does respond to treatments, both medication and therapy. These treatments might make them more responsible in the future than they are at present. That depends on how well treatments work. The following chapter will address that topic.

Tracing Responsibility

Before turning to treatment, we need to respond to one potential complication with everything that we have said about responsibility. So far, our discussion has been ahistorical. We have focused only on the agent at the time of the act rather than on all that went before. The question of responsibility (especially accountability) becomes more complex when we look at how the agent got into the condition that currently seems to reduce responsibility.

Compare alcoholism. Even if we assume that alcoholics are unable to respond to reasons against drinking, we may still hold them responsible because they are responsible for creating their own inability to respond to those reasons. Imagine that an alcoholic father misses his child's concert because he passes out drunk at home. Our complex reaction involves some pity in addition to some indignation and resentment, but probably more pity and less indignation and resentment than in a non-addictive case of parental neglect. The alcoholic father does not seem as responsible as a negligent father who simply ignores the concert because he does not care about his child. Nevertheless, the alcoholic father still seems more responsible than a kidnapped father who is physically restrained from going to his child's concert. The degree of responsibility of the alcoholic father thus falls somewhere between the negligent father and the kidnapped father. Our mixed reactions probably reflect our understanding that the alcoholic's condition is brought about largely through his own past misbehavior. Whatever genetic or other propensities the alcoholic had, he could have avoided alcoholism by never having a drink—or, if that seems overly strict, at least by never drinking very much or not regularly drinking to intoxication.

Contrast those with OCD. We generally do not hold people with OCD responsible for their compulsive actions. When a mother misses her child's performance because she had to check the door lock hundreds of times before being able to leave home, we usually think that she deserves pity and not indignation or resentment (or at least not as much resentment as the negligent father or the alcoholic father), because we think that the OCD mother is not responsible (or at least less responsible than the negligent father or the alcoholic father) for missing the concert. There is no ambivalence analogous to that in our assessment of the alcoholic, because the person with OCD did not bring about her present condition—or, at least, that is the common assumption.

That assumption, however, is sometimes false. The actions of those with OCD, including Scrupulosity, often play some role in sustaining and even increasing the anxiety at the root of the disorder. Remember how OCD develops in those disposed to develop such anxiety. Long before people develop OCD, when they first feel anxiety about a door that they just locked, their anxiety is not as strong, and they may even have insight into its irrationality. At that early point, it is much easier for them to refuse to act to soothe their anxiety than it will be later. Resistance at the earlier time is uncomfortable but clearly possible, just as it's uncomfortable but possible for most people not to go back to check the stove when they know it's off but can't shake the feeling that it's still on. If they make the choice not to check the lock, then their anxiety is much less likely to begin developing into the compulsive actions characteristic of full-blown OCD (Abramowitz, 2002).

In contrast, if people succumb to their anxiety and check the lock anyway, then they reassure themselves. But the reassurance is only temporary. Ironically, they also reinforce their anxiety by reinforcing their belief that the anxiety was legitimate, one that they should not ignore, which makes it more likely to arise again and makes it easier for them to justify checking when it rearises. By checking the lock to quell their anxiety, they start a vicious cycle. The more they check the lock to reassure themselves and ease their anxiety, the more they reinforce their anxiety about the lock. Worse, the more they check, the more routine each checking becomes, so any distinctive feeling that would have signaled that the checking was successful becomes more elusive to achieve (van den Hout & Kindt, 2004). Therefore, the compulsive checking serves to ease anxiety in the short term, but, in the long term, it reinforces and increases the obsession and, thus, the compulsive action.[36]

If compulsive rituals temporarily diminish anxiety while also serving to sustain and even increase the anxiety over time, then OCD resembles alcoholism more than most people assume. The alcoholic is currently unresponsive to reasons as a result of past actions, such as regular, heavy drinking. Those past actions that created the later problem might themselves have been responsive to reasons, including reasons both for and against drinking so much. The way in which alcoholics responded to those reasons in the past is a large part of what makes them now substantially unresponsive to reasons in the way they are. If they had instead dealt with their past problems by talking to a therapist, or by eating junk food and watching television, then they would not now be alcoholic. Thus, for the alcoholic as well as the person with OCD or Scrupulosity, their own past actions are part of what made them presently less responsive to reasons.

If these cases are similar in these respects, then why should we distinguish the responsibility of the alcoholic from that of the person with OCD or Scrupulosity? A Tracing (or Transfer) principle holds that a person is responsible for later behavior that the person is not able to control if the act or inability results from earlier actions that the individual could have controlled and was responsible for (cf. Fischer & Ravizza, 1998). This principle implies that, because both the alcoholic and the person with Scrupulosity are responsible for creating conditions that led to their present disabilities and behaviors, they are both responsible via the Tracing principle for their current behaviors, despite their current disabilities.

One response is that those with OCD did not realize and saw no reason to expect or foresee that checking the lock would increase their lock-checking anxiety. Similarly, people with Scrupulosity do not realize that repeating a prayer to get the wording or intention right would increase anxiety and

---

[36] A similar story could be told about some phobias. Fear of flying sometimes seems to result from (or at least get magnified by) an individual's repeated refusal to get on a plane. If the phobic was able to get on the plane early on but became less willing to do so as the fear increased, then the current inability can be due in part to the person's own previous choices and actions.

doubt to irrational levels. When Ezekiel found himself doubting that he said a particular prayer with the correct wording or intention, he had no reason to foresee a future in which his many hours of prayer lead his wife to threaten to leave him. Hence, although his past actions did create present conditions in which his responsiveness to reasons is diminished, he did not and could not reasonably be expected to foresee these results of his past actions, so he is not responsible for his present actions.

It is true that the relevant results of past actions are never entirely foreseeable. This is partly because not all people are predisposed to such disorders (to addictions, to OCD, or to Scrupulosity), and, given a widespread understanding of addiction and lack of understanding of anxiety disorders, this unforeseeability might hold more often for anxiety disorders than for addictions. Someone will not likely foresee that easing anxieties by checking locks or repeating prayers could actually increase anxiety.

But we should be careful here. Many people do not foresee that drinking regularly will make them alcoholics. After all, most people who drink regularly do not become alcoholics. Even if addiction is a slim possibility, drinking is not an obviously worse way of dealing with stress and disappointment than some commonly used alternatives, such as eating junk food and watching television, even if there is some risk of addiction. Moreover, if our assessments of people's responsibility depend on what they foresaw, then do we need to know how much they actually foresaw? Or how much they *should* have foreseen? *Could* have foreseen? How much a "reasonable person" in that situation could have foreseen? These questions might all affect our assessments of a person's responsibility.

What we want to emphasize here is primarily that alcoholics and people with OCD and Scrupulosity are similar in that foreseeability appears to affect their responsibility. That means either that both of them are generally responsible because of the foreseeability of their condition, or that neither of them is generally responsible because their condition was not foreseeable (or not foreseeable in the right way), or that there is something about the foreseeability of their conditions that distinguishes them. It seems harsh and insensitive to hold that those with OCD and Scrupulosity are responsible because their later conditions were foreseeable: they inspire pity as much as resentment, indignation, moral anger, or blame, so they do not meet the conditions in the above definition of accountability. But if OCD and Scrupulosity sufferers are not fully responsible, and alcoholism is similarly foreseeable, then alcoholics also cannot be held fully responsible, merely on the grounds that they created their present condition. At least one of those positions—holding OCD sufferers responsible or not holding alcoholics responsible—is likely to strike most people as counterintuitive.

A better reply to this conundrum might be to deny the Tracing principle. Past responsibility for making oneself presently unresponsive to reasons does not in itself make one presently responsible. Indeed, there is independent reason to doubt the Tracing principle. Imagine someone who takes a drug just for pleasure knowing that it has a small chance of making her blind. She does go blind as a result, and later a child crawls into a swimming pool right in front of her. She cannot rescue the child that she cannot see, and her blindness is traceable to her own actions and their potentially foreseeable consequences. Thus, according to the Tracing principle, she is responsible for letting the child drown. Does she seem accountable for letting the child drown? If she seems accountable in this case, imagine that she took the drug initially not for pleasure but in order to treat a painful but not fatal condition, one that she could have lived with. Now is she responsible for the child's drowning? It's still a result of her own choices that she's blind. Our intuitions here might, of course, be due to our feeling sorry for her, but then we need to ask why we do not also feel sorry for the alcoholic whose condition also results from past negligence, who began drinking either for pleasure or for self-medication. For these reasons, we doubt the Tracing principle as a general principle of responsibility.

This lesson applies to Scrupulosity. Consider Ezekiel long before he developed Scrupulosity. When he first repeated a prayer because he doubted that he had said it perfectly, his repetition contributed to his Scrupulosity much later in his life (cf. Bonchek & Greenberg, 2009). Suppose he knew of the small risk of his developing this rare disorder, perhaps because he had heard of others who were overly concerned about religious ritual. (It's not unheard of in conservative religious communities.) That is not enough to show that he is now responsible for regularly abandoning his wife for his lengthy prayers. The Tracing principle suggests otherwise. So much the worse for the Tracing principle.

Of course, defenders of the Tracing principle can respond, perhaps by restricting or qualifying their Tracing principle or redefining foreseeability in some way, but it is not clear whether the needed qualifications will make the revised principle inapplicable to alcoholism. In any case, such qualifications will reveal, as we hope also to have shown, that the original, unqualified principle was indefensible. For these reasons, then, people with

Scrupulosity are not responsible as a result of their foreseeing in the past that their choices created a risk that they could someday develop Scrupulosity.

We could also consider a different kind of past action. Those with Scrupulosity who did not seek treatment that would have helped to reduce the severity of their Scrupulosity now have an increased risk of harming others. The same point applies to OCD or alcoholism. But Scrupulosity makes a person often unable to see the need for treatment, especially in ego-syntonic cases. If such individuals were not able to see any adequate reason to seek treatment, then it seems unfair to hold them accountable for failing to seek treatment, or for the later actions that they would not have done if they had sought treatment. We could also consider analogues of the blindness counterexample from before. Imagine that the person who is blind and unable to save the child is blind not from drug use but from untreated glaucoma. Does the past failure to seek treatment make her presently responsible for her inability to save the child? We think not.

Of course, any discussion about the responsibility that comes from a failure to seek treatment assumes that treatment is itself justified. And that depends on the probability that the treatment will succeed, on the personal costs of seeking treatment, and on when and how psychiatrists are justified in treating such conditions. These difficult issues are addressed in the next chapter, so the discussion there will shed further light backward on the responsibility of persons with Scrupulosity.

8

Treatment

João gave almost all of his income to strangers who were worse off, putting himself below the poverty line and passing up most of the goods and opportunities that his peers took for granted. Zell Kravinsky similarly gave away most of his fortune and a kidney. Devout Jains sweep the sidewalk as they walk to make sure they don't accidentally step on an insect. Aaron Pitkin (profiled in MacFarquhar, 2015) dedicated his life—sacrificing his money, health, and at least one serious relationship—to improving the conditions of chickens raised for food. It's doubtful that all of these people have Scrupulosity. Should we try to talk any of them into caring less or giving less to the needy? Few of us give this much, but is there a problem with them or with us? It seems backward to advise them to become more like us. If anything, they should advise us to be *more* generous.

What if someone who is equally generous has Scrupulosity, though? Should we advise those who are extraordinarily generous and who also have Scrupulosity to become more like us? Should we encourage them to lower their standards? Should we try to make them care less about morality? If psychiatric treatment could accomplish these goals, but they do not want to become more like us (because they view that result as making them less moral), then should we put pressure on them to accede to treatment anyway? What kind of pressure is warranted? When, if ever, do people need psychiatric treatment for being too concerned with morality or for having moral standards that are too high?

The answers might seem simple because, in addition to the anxiety, there are clear drawbacks to being moral in an immoral world. If you are in a competitive situation where others lie and break their promises, your moral qualms about doing the same can keep you from succeeding. Psychiatric treatment could relieve these costs.

But is relieving those costs enough to justify treatment? If Scrupulous people honestly believe that they are morally required to act as they do, isn't it intrusive, presumptuous, and moralistic of us to impose our own lax standards on them and try to change their moral beliefs into ours?

Does this set a dangerous precedent for indoctrinating those who have moral standards that we disagree with? And what exactly would it be to "cure" them?

Our focus throughout this book has been on people with Scrupulosity, contrasting them with people who are morally virtuous, have non-pathological scrupulous traits, make ordinary moral judgments, have ordinary moral motives, and are responsible for their actions. We will continue that focus, but here we will ask what we should do about their differences. We are now concerned in particular with what we are allowed to do to change persons with Scrupulosity. Just because the Scrupulous are not moral saints doesn't mean that we are allowed to rebuild them in our image or that they can't make moral objections to our attempts to change them. If they do raise moral objections to treatment, then how should we respond? Should we respect their objections to treatment or is it permissible for us to insist on treating them regardless of what they want?

The Scrupulosity patients discussed so far have all been in treatment already. Some of them sought treatment on their own, and others were pressured into treatment by friends and family. Still, even while treatment is ongoing, and even after consent was given, that psychiatric treatment still might not be justified if there is no adequate reason to continue it. It might be just as inappropriate and moralistic to keep trying to change them as it was to start trying to change them in the first place, especially if they continue to see themselves as more moral than we are.

These problems raise two main questions: Is any treatment justified? Even if we can justify some treatment, which kinds of treatment are justified? This chapter will address both of these questions in turn.

Specifying the Issue

These problems are easier in some cases. Suppose that a woman with Scrupulosity decides on her own (with no pressure from anyone else) to try to reduce her anxiety and chronic doubt. She asks a psychiatrist for help, the psychiatrist explains what he can do to treat her, and she freely consents. He offers treatment, but he does not pressure her or even tell her that she needs or ought to get treatment. In this case (which does happen sometimes), there are no special problems. There is nothing wrong with a psychiatrist offering to treat anyone who freely seeks help, perhaps even someone without any mental illness. There might be questions about whether the insurance company should be required to pay for the treatment if the patient is not mentally ill, but psychiatrists can and perhaps should help when they are able. Scrupulosity is no exception. We assume that no particular issues arise from a psychiatrist or therapist simply offering to treat someone with Scrupulosity (Pickard, 2016). We also assume that there is nothing objectionable about a person seeking or accepting treatment for Scrupulosity—no more than accepting treatment for any other condition, or even "treatment" to become a better person.

The opposite extreme is another easy case. Imagine that siblings of a man with Scrupulosity tell a psychiatrist that their brother needs help for Scrupulosity. Their brother refuses to consent to treatment, because he thinks his siblings are morally lax and are only annoyed by his reminding them of what they really are morally required to do, which is to give up their loose and luxurious lives. (Imagine Little John as an adult.) Nonetheless, the psychiatrist sides with the siblings against the brother, restrains the brother physically in a straightjacket, and transports him involuntarily into a mental facility that he cannot escape until he is "cured." Unless there is a lot more to the story, this coercion is clearly wrong.

Physical force is not the only bad way to force someone into treatment. Except perhaps in very rare cases, it would also be wrong for the psychiatrist to declare the brother mentally incompetent in order to block his access to his own money until he agrees to treatment. And (again except perhaps in very rare cases) it would be wrong for the psychiatrist to threaten to deny the brother custody of his children or visits with them until he accepts treatment.

The extreme cases are easy on both sides. Offering therapy is almost never problematic, and forcing therapy almost always is. The rare cases where legal measures (denying competence or custody) might be justified have already been discussed extensively elsewhere with respect to when other mental illnesses justify various liberty deprivations. Hence, we will not say any more about these extreme cases.

Between these extremes, though, lie many more moderate forms of manipulation and pressure. Our topic is whether these moderate measures are justified. Are therapists, friends, and family members, for example, entitled to pressure people with Scrupulosity to get them into treatment? Would it be legitimate to hassle them by arguing, pleading, cajoling, insinuating, making ourselves a nuisance, not letting the issue drop, and enlisting others to do all of these same things? For example, would it be legitimate for Bob's wife to demand that he go into treatment, because she is sick and tired of changing all of their daughter's diapers? What if she threatened to divorce him or to complain publicly to all their friends?

We usually shouldn't apply such pressure to people who are entitled to make their own decisions, even if we disagree with their positions. Part of what it means to respect people's autonomy is that you don't continue to try to get them to change their position after they've made it clear that they have no intention of revising it, unless circumstances change. Philosophers may forget this sometimes in our professional fervor, but annoying other people with arguments about what they should do has a moral cost that we must justify, even if our intentions are entirely pure.

Sometimes we can carry this burden—we can give adequate reasons to pressure people into treatment. Still, these cases are quite complex. The first complication is that psychiatric treatment is often much less efficacious when the patient objects, so we need to determine the treatment's likelihood of success with a recalcitrant patient. If treatment won't help, then it would be self-defeating to pressure the person into treatment. We will assume, therefore, that treatment of Scrupulosity has some chance of success for whatever person we're considering.

Another complication is that we need to determine how to get a person to submit to treatment over objection. Sometimes repeated attempts at persuasion and pressure are needed, but how many times and how forcefully should we apply pressure?

A third complication arises because the person might object to treatment by certain people. Paranoid individuals might have special objections to being treated by the therapist who is best able to help, if they believe that this particular psychiatrist is part of a conspiracy against them. Similarly, a person with Scrupulosity might want treatment only if it is sanctioned or administered by a certain religious leader or in accordance or with a certain religious view (Huppert & Siev, 2010; Huppert, Siev, & Kushner, 2007).

We will ignore many of these complications and ask the general questions of whether, when, and why some kind of psychiatric treatment for Scrupulosity is justified, on the assumption that it is likely to have some positive effects. We will also assume in each case either that the patient is in therapy already or that nothing more than an initial interview has taken place. Thus, we are asking whether the therapist is justified in beginning or continuing treatment of this particular condition.

Finally, we will focus on only one special ground for opposition to psychiatric treatment, namely, *moral* objection. There are many reasons that people could cite against treatment: they think the money would be better spent elsewhere, or they are lost causes already, or they don't like psychiatrists. What interests us is that people with Scrupulosity might object to psychiatric treatment for specifically moral reasons. People might think, for example, that psychiatric treatment will make them morally worse, even if it succeeds in making them less distressed. They see the moral benefits of their condition as worth the personal costs. Our question is whether some treatment can be justified if persons object for such moral reasons.

Compare a loved one who eats way too much unhealthy food. We may tell him that we think he has a problem, ask him why he eats so much, and even suggest that he talk to a professional psychiatrist (or nutritionist or physical trainer). If he is a child, then we might be permitted to put more pressure on him, withdrawing privileges if he does not eat properly; but if he is an adult, then we are not entitled to exert as much, if any, pressure on him—depending on our relationship with him and how old and knowledgeable he is. The danger in our exerting unjustified pressure here is that we treat him paternalistically, making a decision that we believe is in his own interest regardless of what he thinks.

The situation with Scrupulosity is somewhat different. The unhealthful eater objects that those who pressure him think that they know what is good for him better than he does. He objects that others are interfering with his autonomy. But he does not object that they are trying to make him morally worse. In contrast, the person with Scrupulosity knows that his behaviors are costly to himself, but he still thinks that they are morally required. Those with Scrupulosity could object that people who pressure them into treatment are trying to make them less moral.

Because this particular objection is peculiar to Scrupulosity, we will focus on it. Therefore, our question is when, if ever, other people (including psychiatrists, friends, and family) are justified in pressuring (with repeated arguing, cajoling, pleading, and mild threats) a person with Scrupulosity (not just scrupulous traits) to enter or continue treatment (by a psychiatrist or therapist) over moral objections (especially the objection that treatment will make the person less moral, in the view of the person with Scrupulosity). The question is more general, as people can make moral objections to treatments for other conditions, but our focus is only on Scrupulosity.

Justifications for Treatment

If Scrupulosity is a form of OCD, and if psychiatrists are justified in treating OCD, then aren't they also justified in treating Scrupulosity for the very same reasons? There are two major problems with this simple deduction. First, the features of OCD that justify treating other forms of OCD might not be present in Scrupulosity. Second, the methods of treating Scrupulosity might have costs that do not arise when treating other forms of OCD. We'll consider these two problems in order.

Mental Illness

The first argument for treating Scrupulosity therapeutically is simply that Scrupulosity, like other forms of OCD, is a mental illness or disorder. We argued for this premise in Chapter 3. The question here is whether this premise provides enough support for the conclusion that Scrupulosity should be treated.

This argument is too simple. For one thing, just as with physical illnesses, some mental illnesses lead to only minor problems that, if they take any significant effort to treat, are not worth the effort to treat. For example, a claustrophobic man who lives on an open farm far from civilization might be happy and only rarely feel anxiety from his mental illness, so treating him might not be worth the effort of his traveling regularly to see a therapist. Similarly, some people with OCD might be able to control their anxiety at little cost, for example, by checking their locks or washing their hands more than necessary but not enough to cause significant distress. Again, some people with Scrupulosity might be able to control their anxiety simply by looking at the frames instead of the pictures inside the frames (as Jennifer did), by checking receipts at night (as Adam did), or by greeting co-workers (as Big John did).

Furthermore, whether a condition is labeled a mental illness can depend on one's social environment. It has not been very long since homosexuality was classified as a mental illness by the *DSM*, and some scholars have argued that schizophrenia is culturally valued in some circumstances (Krippner, 2002). These examples are complicated and debatable, of course, but they remind us to be cautious in assuming that our existing categories of mental illness alone are enough to show that a condition should be treated. Even if mental illness usually should be treated, we need to ask what it is about each mental disorder that warrants treatment.

Harm to Self or Others

Treatment is sometimes warranted in the case of mental illness because a mentally ill person is a threat to herself or to others. What constitutes "harm" is difficult to define. There are clear cases—cutting or self-mutilation, depression with suicidal ideation, severe anorexia, and delusions that one can fly create serious risks of harm that treatment can prevent. Other cases are less clear, like self-sabotage of one's goals, destroying friendships, and depriving oneself of fulfilling life experiences. All of these losses would justify treating a person with a mental illness if that person seeks or at least does not object to treatment, but the justification becomes less clear when potential patients object to treatment.

People with Scrupulosity almost never pose a significant risk of death or permanent physical harm to themselves. Bridget might lose her job, Bob's home life might deteriorate, and Mary's health might worsen from her sleep deprivation, but they are not likely to die or seriously injure themselves from Scrupulosity. The risks that they pose to themselves are more often of less serious harms, like losing access to goods that others enjoy, disadvantaging themselves in competitions, or sabotaging their life goals. While those harms make their lives worse, they are present in many people without mental illnesses, too. Thus, if these kinds of harms to self are enough to justify treatment of people with Scrupulosity over their objections, then they must also justify treating many people without Scrupulosity or any other mental illness who cause themselves similar harms but object to treatment. That would justify pressure for treatment way too broadly.

The same problem applies to harm to others as a justification for treatment. Ezekiel did drive his wife to contemplate divorce, so he caused her harm. This harm might have extended to their children, if they had any. And some parents with Scrupulosity might be inattentive or neglectful— think of chronically sleep-deprived Mary and her three children. However, many spouses act in ways that lead to divorce and parents disadvantage their children, but this alone is not enough to justify psychiatric treatment over objection in those cases, so it also cannot be enough to justify treatment of people with Scrupulosity despite their moral objections.

Distress

A more specific harm that would justify treatment for most mental illnesses, including OCD, is distress. Addicts suffer the distress that comes from increasing drug use and dependence. Paranoid schizophrenics suffer the distress of imagining that their world conspires against them. Likewise, OCD creates the distress of easily triggered, stubbornly maintained, or regularly and deeply felt anxiety. When mental illness leads to so much distress, this second argument asserts, treatment is justified at least in part as a way to alleviate that distress. We should consider the probability of the treatment succeeding, the benefits of successful treatment, and the costs of treatment (successful or unsuccessful). Nonetheless, allowing for such cost-benefit calculations, this second argument for treatment is relatively straightforward.

Alleviating distress won't always justify treatment. Even when benefits otherwise outweigh costs, we need to consider the potential patient's autonomy. Typically, a distressed person wants to alleviate that distress by changing something about herself, such as her addiction, her schizophrenia, or her anxiety disorder. Some patients with Scrupulosity share this desire for relief, and the justification for their treatment is then that they are in distress, they request treatment, and treatment will probably bring more benefits than costs. It is easy to justify treatment in those cases. However, this justification is inadequate for those in distress who do not initiate treatment or who even refuse it. Their recalcitrance forces the therapist (as well as caregivers, loved ones, and others) to balance a desire to alleviate the patient's distress with respect for the patient's (perhaps limited) autonomy. The patient might not recognize her own distress, might prefer the distress to the costs of treatment, or might even prefer her current condition to the condition that therapy aims to bring about. The patient's distress alone is not enough to justify treatment over objection in those cases. These difficult cases are the ones that interest us here.

It is hard to see how treatment in such cases could be justified merely by the distress and anxiety felt by people with Scrupulosity. Morality and religion often require personal sacrifice and make people anxious about living up to moral and religious standards. It is distressing for honest people to keep a promise that they wish they could break, or even to see someone else break a promise. It is difficult for a caring person to be polite or helpful to a jerk. Good people also can feel some anxiety about whether they are doing the right thing. These bad feelings don't show that such people need therapy, but only that they are willing to endure some personal cost in order to adhere to their moral norms. Likewise, persons with Scrupulosity might be distressed about many aspects of their lives—that they are sinners, have harmed someone inadvertently, or have had wrongful thoughts—but that distress by itself is not enough to justify therapy over objection, especially when they see these personal costs as morally required.

Of course, people with Scrupulosity might feel greater distress and anxiety than most others. Even this greater degree of distress, however, would not be a general justification for their treatment. It is always problematic to make an assessment that a person is in enough distress to justify treatment over objection (Wakefield, 1992). If a woman with Scrupulosity thinks that her distress is warranted by her own moral standards, then it is particularly problematic to claim that she is wrong (either because her standards are wrong or because she interprets them wrongly). The job of psychiatrists and clinical psychologists is, on the common view, not to make moral evaluations of their patients, their views, or their judgments (cf. Pearce & Pickard, 2009; Pickard, 2011, 2016). Likewise, her professional capacity doesn't extend to changing people's views to those that she believes are more moral, except when she has some other justification for that change. Yet the evaluation that a person is in distress over her moral views is not enough to justify the therapist's trying to change those views if the patient morally objects. So, the justification of distress is problematic at best. If the therapist is to respect the moral beliefs that the patient cites in objecting to her treatment—even when the therapist disagrees with them—then we need a different justification.

Future Gratitude

Another possible justification for treatment over moral objection is a prediction of future gratitude. Although people with Scrupulosity are distressed by the slightest possibility of sin, this distress and assessment of sin are due to their mental illness. After successful treatment, they would have less anxiety, distress, and chronic doubt; and they would see their former anxiety levels as unjustified because they would then have less stringent moral standards. After a treatment works, they understand why treatment was in their best interests, and they would be at least understanding, perhaps even grateful, that they had received the treatment despite their earlier objections.

This justification is problematic for people with Scrupulosity. It assumes that patients are better off after successful therapy because they are no longer as distressed by what was previously distressing. But what *should* a person find distressing? Before treatment, people with Scrupulosity might recognize that they will be happier after treatment, but they might see this happiness as the result of lower moral standards, and they might be willing to sacrifice their happiness for the sake of moral goodness. Of course, a therapist might be able to convince them that their moral standards are incorrect or even that some other moral standards are correct, in which case the patients could be talked out of their objection. But, while they continue to object, it remains hard to see how the therapist could justify treatment over moral objection. Such treatment seems too close to indoc-trination into a lax moral culture or to an imposition of the therapist's own moral standards. Even if the patient could be convinced of the therapist's standards, the therapist ventures onto shaky ground when she must rely so explicitly on her own assessment of how moral a person should be.

Community Standards

Yet another justification, which avoids this problem, cites the moral standards of a relevant community. A therapist who applies the standards of the patient's own moral or religious community need not rely on the therapist's own standards, since the therapist need not be a member of that community or endorse its standards. Still, how and how well this jus-tification works depends on the relation between the community's moral standards and the patient's own moral standards.

Consider first a patient, like Jacob, who is trying to meet the standards of his community.[37] He sees his own standards—those he would argue for and defend—as morally or religiously ordinary standards. For example, Jacob insists on being physically clean and in an environment that is also free from any trace of feces before praying. If Jacob believes that this is what his community requires, and he is wrong about what his community requires,

---

[37] The desire to meet community standards is suggested when patients seek reassurance from a community leader, such as in the example cited above of a patient who repeatedly sought his rabbi's reassurance that he had not sinned by swallowing his saliva on a day of fasting (Abramowitz et al., 2002).

then the therapist (perhaps with help from community leaders) can point out this error in Jacob's interpretation of his community's standards without endorsing those community standards and, hence, without imposing the therapist's own standards.

In contrast, there is no justification for treatment over moral objection for persons who are trying to exceed their community's standards or to endorse and meet a higher standard. Imagine Jacob knows that his community requires only that one make reasonable efforts to be clean, but he personally sees that standard as too lax. He thinks that his community should endorse a more stringent requirement closer to his own. He believes that he and other members of his community are really required to meet this more stringent standard. In this situation, the therapist cannot simply appeal to the community standard, because Jacob knows and rejects that standard. The therapist could not justify treatment over objection without assuming that the community is right and Jacob is wrong about the proper standards. Treatment then again seems too close to indoctrination, regardless of whether Jacob feels distress.

Jacob's mistake is about religious community standards, but what if the person is wrong instead about what morality requires? Does that error justify therapy? Not if the person is trying to exceed the community's standards, for the same reasons as with Jacob. Admittedly, moral errors can be very dangerous. It may be grounds for enforced psychiatric treatment or even preventive detention (perhaps in prison) if someone is wrong about moral issues in ways that endanger others, e.g., someone who believes that killing is morally good—at least if there is enough danger that the person will act on that belief. And someone's being radically wrong about obvious moral issues suggests some underlying psychological problem. It's hard to imagine someone who endorses murdering innocents but has no underlying psychopathology. However, we will focus primarily on religious examples, since those standards are often easier to identify, and being or failing to be religious is not itself indicative of psychopathology.

Internal Coherence

How, then, could a therapist who respects autonomy justify treatment over objection for persons whose actions reflect abnormally stringent moral or religious standards? We'll suggest three justifications, each of which cites an internal incoherence in the patient's beliefs or standards. Because the incoherence is internal to the patient's own views, the therapist's own standards are not imposed on the patient. In each case, that incoherence is best explained as the patient's attempt to soothe her own anxiety. As a result, the therapist can justify treatment by citing the patient's own moral or religious standards: the ones that the patient would hold if anxiety and doubt had not distorted the standards so as to make them incoherent. This justification therefore appeals to internal coherence of the patient's standards instead of the therapist's own moral or religious standards.

Our three justifications do assume that incoherence is worse than coherence. It might seem that one could object on behalf of someone with Scrupulosity, or on behalf of others with mental illnesses, that coherence is just one value among many others, perhaps overridden by moral requirements. Whether one could *argue* that incoherence is no worse than coherence is doubtful, given that coherence is a criterion of any good argument; but, for similar reasons, one may also have difficulty arguing *against* that view (though see Davidson, 2004; Fogelin, 2002). This difficulty suggests why we are safe in assuming that incoherence should be minimized when possible: coherence is fundamental to our having any values at all and to interacting with others. If I claim to value honesty while also claiming to value dishonesty, and I can't tell a story to make the two coherent (in different situations?), then you and I both don't know what I really value. We couldn't conclude that I simply value both honesty and dishonesty, because that would be unintelligible, so it's not clear that we could conclude anything about what I value.

In any event, even if coherence were simply one value among many, it is a value that those with Scrupulosity show themselves to endorse already, and it is one that is quite fundamental to them as well as to us. Minimizing incoherence at least does not impose an arbitrary or idiosyncratic value.

The first justification of this new kind appeals to internal incoherence that arises from the patient's inability to coherently defend her actions or her standards. Imagine that Mary is asked to defend her praying 18 times after each meal. She might cite a standard that she knows is abnormal. But then how could she defend her abnormal standard? Is there some biblical or rabbinic source for saying 18 prayers? Is it required for everyone? Does someone sin by praying only once for each meal? Is everyone else, including her friends and family as well as religious exemplars and leaders in her community, a sinner many times over? Questions like these will often reveal that Mary's own views are incoherent because they are arbitrary.

Arbitrariness reveals incoherence because coherence is more than mere logical consistency (Sinnott-Armstrong, 2006, Chapter 10). A belief that there are six planets around every star, because six is a perfect number, is logically consistent. It is not coherent, though, with any evidence or theory that a person could accept without radically revising ordinary beliefs about the cosmos. Those kinds of connections to evidence and to laws governing related phenomena are required for coherence. That is why arbitrary views like Mary's are incoherent.

How did Mary end up with such arbitrary and incoherent standards? The answer seems to be that she chose standards that would soothe her anxiety rather than choosing standards she could best justify. The description of her case is not detailed enough to know for sure, but here's a suggestion of how Mary arrived at her rituals as a response to her anxiety. Mary had "persistent doubts" that led her to engage in prayers "repeatedly until satisfied that they had been performed correctly" (Abramowitz, 2008). She had doubts about whether she had said a prayer adequately (cf. Bonchek & Greenberg, 2009). She repeated parts of it to reassure herself; then, she repeated all of it. As repeating the entire prayer started to feel ordinary, she felt a need to repeat the entire prayer again. Finally, she decided to try 18 repetitions, since 18 is a number important in her religion, and 18 repetitions did soothe her anxieties. In this story, Mary *feels compelled* to exceed her standards (which require only one prayer said adequately) only because she *doubts* that she has fulfilled that standard, and she feels *anxious* if she does not repeat her prayers.

Notice that this doubt might not only make her exceed her own standards; it might even make her adopt the higher standards and even believe they are required. If she comes to think that she is in fact required to pray 18 times without any error after each meal, those higher standards are part of her understanding as to why she feels so much anxiety and doubt after saying the prayer only once. This rationalization can explain and thus make her anxiety and doubt easier to deal with. However, she settles on these higher standards only in order to explain or cope with her anxiety, not because she has engaged in a theological investigation. In general, then, Mary's abnormal standards and the actions that reflect those standards end up being incoherent because they are motivated primarily by her need to relieve her doubts and anxieties.

This first form of incoherence—when one acts on or endorses standards without justification[38] but only from the motivation to soothe one's anxieties—is a justification for treatment over moral objection because the patient cannot coherently defend her own standards, and the underlying explanation for this incoherence is something amenable to psychiatric treatment. To justify treatment in such cases, the therapist does not need to rely on the therapist's own standards but can instead cite the patient's own desire for coherence plus the source of that incoherence in the desire to avoid anxiety as justification for changing the patient's views so as to become more coherent. What get treated are not the patient's moral views or standards themselves but instead the anxiety that is the source of those standards. Of course, treatment will not be justified unless the patient suffers significant distress, but the point here is that therapists can justify relieving that distress over moral objections when those objections are arbitrary and motivated to soothe anxiety.

A second type of incoherence arises from a conflation of ideals with requirements. Again, consider Jacob, who agrees with his community that one should not begin prayer when very dirty, when one smells of feces, or when one has not showered in a long time. That is a minimal requirement, a standard below which it is not permissible to pray.[39] In contrast, the ideal level of cleanliness is to be free from every speck of dirt and feces (and bacteria? and dead skin cells?). This ideal is practically unobtainable—and probably hazardous to try to obtain—though one can approach it to varying degrees. It might be better to come closer to the ideal and not settle for the bare minimum. However, if one thinks that the ideal is not only better but *required*, then one will never feel permitted to pray, because that ideal standard cannot be met. Even if it could be met, one could never know whether one has met it on a particular occasion. Jacob, for example, could never be sure that he is entirely clean, so he cannot begin praying until he

[38] To be clear, Mary probably could give *some* justification as to why she should pray 18 times after a meal, but that justification is best explained as a rationalization of the desire to alleviate anxiety, i.e., if the person weren't trying to alleviate anxiety, she would likely not even herself find her justification persuasive. Certainly, those in her community will find it to be a weak and narrowly focused justification. As a short-hand, then, we will say that there is no justification, but that should be understood as meaning that the justification is weak and primarily a rationalization of an underlying desire.

[39] Interestingly, what we now take to be a minimal standard of cleanliness probably exceeds what would have counted as thoroughly clean even a couple of centuries ago. One standard of cleanliness articulated in the 1500-year-old Talmud, a work that observant Jews like Jacob take very seriously, is that, after defecation, one could clean oneself with three small, smooth stones (tractate Shabbat). Jacob would exceed this ancient standard with even the most minimal of modern hygienic practices.

is no longer anxious or doubtful about whether he has reached an ideal that he treats as required—and similarly for many others with Scrupulosity who treat ideals as required.

If patients' extreme behaviors or standards result from a failure to distinguish ideals from requirements, and if that failure is again the result of an underlying desire to soothe their anxiety, and if this condition causes great enough distress, then treatment can be justified without imposing the therapist's own standards. The therapist relies on the patients' standards and helps the individuals to see that they have confused their own ideals with requirements. The therapist relies only on a conceptual distinction, so the therapist's own standards are unimportant in resolving this confusion. This justification does not question the patients' views about what is morally or religiously ideal. It simply reminds them that what is ideal need not be required. Hence, treatment over moral objection may be justified in many such cases without presumptuously imposing outside standards.

A third kind of internal incoherence results from perseveration or fixation. People with OCD, including those with Scrupulosity, often focus exclusively on a small number of (often unimportant) issues at the expense of many other (more important) issues. Those with Scrupulosity focus primarily on the features that relieve their anxiety in the short term, not on features that further their professed goal to be more moral or religious. As a result, people with Scrupulosity are more moral or religious in select areas, but their actions are morally or religiously distorted, in ways we showed in previous chapters. Like Ezekiel and Mary, they might be far more observant about making sure no word of a prayer is said incorrectly, but that extra time can lead to problems in other areas, for example, in devoting enough time to one's family. Or consider again Bridget, who fixated on the solvents that were almost impossible to get into the customers' meals, instead of her job of getting their meals out to them. In cases like this, a therapist can justify treatment by appealing to standards that the patient herself endorses but which she has forgotten because she is so fixated on only one part of her overall view.

How to Justify Treatment Over Moral Objection

These three types of incoherence—arbitrariness, conflation, and fixation—are important in establishing that the therapist is not imposing the therapist's own goals or standards. But a justification for treatment over moral objection also requires that the patient suffers significant distress and that the underlying explanation of the patient's incoherence is that she is trying to reduce her own anxiety. The extra conditions regarding distress and anxiety are needed to explain why our argument would not justify treating people without Scrupulosity who still display extreme religious devotion (Taylor, 2002). As described in Chapter 5, a devout Catholic might regularly pray the rosary to imitate favorite saints or to carry out the penance prescribed by a priest during confession. In contrast, a Catholic with Scrupulosity might pray the rosary as a way of preventing bad thoughts or events that would increase anxiety.

Altogether, then, we have argued that treatment of Scrupulosity over moral objection can be justified in various cases by citing incoherence, a source in anxiety, and significant distress. Different justifications might apply in different cases of Scrupulosity, and separate justifications might need to work together. When a person has an abnormally high moral standard, that by itself is not enough to justify treatment over moral objection. In contrast, when that higher standard is both incoherent and also an attempt to soothe anxiety, and this leads to distress for the person, then there is a justification for treatment over moral objection.

What if only one of these conditions is met? Someone with incoherent moral or religious standards but whose standards are not motivated by a desire to relieve anxiety seems to need education rather than psychiatric treatment. Similarly, someone whose moral or religious standards are motivated by a desire to relieve anxiety may benefit from psychiatric treatment, but such treatment cannot be compelled if those standards are not incoherent or otherwise defective, or if they lead to no distress, even if they are abnormally stringent. Thus, three conditions—incoherence, the motivation to relieve anxiety, and significant distress—are all necessary in order to justify treatment over moral objection. The separately necessary conditions are sufficient only jointly.

This triple requirement responds, then, to the puzzle at the outset: Why should we treat those with high moral standards? Shouldn't we instead praise them? Our answer is that we _do_ and _should_ praise them in some cases: when their high standards are coherent and they are motivated by recognizably moral motives instead of just the need to soothe their own anxiety, then we should not treat them (unless they want treatment). Zell Kravinsky, who gives away much of what he has, including a kidney, to help the needy makes the case for why his actions are morally good, maybe even why they are morally required. Most of us will not act as he does, so his actions are statistically abnormal. Perhaps there is even something defective about his actions. He may, for instance, focus too much on material donations to charity over other moral requirements. Or, his gifts might cause problems for his family and friends. Nevertheless, his actions are aimed at helping others and not just at soothing his own anxiety, so he is not blinded by his anxiety to other areas that he should and does also care about. If his standards are wrong, then we should address this with reasoned debate and discussion, pointing out competing moral requirements or unanticipated consequences of his actions. If he were offered therapy that he refused for moral reasons, then there is no justification in trying to pressure him into treatment over his moral objections.

Thus, we are not justified in treating people *just because* they have higher moral standards. But we can still be justified in treating some people who have extremely high moral standards when these standards are incoherent, when the underlying motivation—to soothe anxiety—is what explains those standards, and when the people suffer significant distress. That justification will apply to many, though not all, cases of Scrupulosity.

Types of Treatment

This justification for treatment in general still leaves open the question of which specific kinds of treatment are justifiable. As with treatments for physical illnesses, some forms of treatment might raise special problems, even if they are effective. We will consider some of those here.

Treatments Without Distinctive Ethical Issues

There are many possible treatments, most of which don't raise any distinctive ethical issues. Consider first the treatments that engage with the content of Scrupulosity. What it means to engage with the content of Scrupulosity is that the treatment engages with the Scrupulous thoughts in a way that takes them seriously as beliefs, not as rationalizations or underlying anxiety or mental illness. For example, if Mary tells her rabbi that she must pray 18 times after eating, her rabbi might engage with her by talking about why she thinks the prayer is required 18 times, what other extreme religious beliefs she holds, and whether there is some underlying misunderstanding that would explain all of these. He might help Mary see how her position differs from what is required, how it is inconsistent with her other positions, or morally relevant problems that she is causing by her actions.

This approach might not seem like a form of treatment, and it certainly doesn't have to be. Mary's rabbi, for example, might think that Mary has nothing more seriously wrong with her than a misunderstanding about what she needs to do, which he can correct. But the rabbi might instead understand very well that Mary has a deeper problem. He might have talked to Mary about many such issues and know that Mary's praying forms part of a pattern of Scrupulous action. Nevertheless, he might determine that the best way to help Mary is to take each of her thoughts seriously, engage with it as if it is a genuine belief reached on the basis of evidence, and try to use evidence to show how it is mistaken. Because Scrupulosity is a disorder brought about and sustained by underlying anxiety, not just a set of mistaken beliefs, we suspect this treatment isn't going to be successful very often. It does nothing to address the underlying anxiety itself. But our goal here is not to consider the efficacy of treatments but only the ethical issues they raise. This form of treatment raises no particular ethical issues.

One could also engage with the content of Scrupulosity without engaging with the content of each of the Scrupulous beliefs. For example, Mary's rabbi might instead point out to her that her actions, regardless of their justification (or lack of justification) are in fact detracting from her religious obligations in general, since she is passing up other obligations by staying up late repeating prayers. This takes Mary seriously as someone who is fundamentally motivated by her desire to do what is religiously or morally best overall, and it highlights the costs of her actions, rather than asking whether her beliefs are correct. Again, the rabbi might or might not believe that Mary has an underlying mental illness, but this treatment engages with Mary as if her fundamental motivation is to do what's right.

These treatments raise no distinctive moral problems because they engage with the person in the terms that the person would use and endorse. "Treatment" in this sense more closely resembles an ordinary discussion about what one ought to do. As with any discussion of what a person ought to do, there are plenty of relevant ethical concerns to be aware of: coercion, manipulation, deception, and so on. But these ethical concerns aren't peculiar to Scrupulosity.

A second family of therapeutic strategies addresses the Scrupulous person's anxiety more directly, either invoking religious or moral terms as part of the therapy or considering Scrupulosity solely as an anxiety disorder. Some of these strategies raise no special moral issues, e.g., helping the person to "reconsolidate" anxious memories so they no longer prompt anxiety (Lane, et al., 2015). But others of these therapies do in fact raise special moral issues.

One therapeutic strategy to address the disorder in terms that the Scrupulosity patient will understand also directly targets the underlying anxiety disorder by using both religious or moral terms. One example is a treatment strategy used by Father Thomas M. Santa, a Roman Catholic priest with decades of work treating Scrupulosity. One common problem for people with Scrupulosity within the Catholic tradition is that, because of their Scrupulosity, they believe that they are constantly in a state of sin, and, as a result, are unable to take communion. Ordinarily, Catholics who believe they are in a state of sin would go to confession and perform acts of penance, if required, and would then be free to take communion. Those with Scrupulosity, however, are not relieved of this feeling that they are sinful even after confession and penance—perhaps also believing that they failed to confess everything or confess properly, or perhaps worried that they committed subsequent sins, like having blasphemous thoughts, that again rendered them unfit to take communion. Father Santa's approach is to explain that they have a mental illness, and, as such, they are eligible to have their sins forgiven in the same way as others who are sick, viz., by Anointing of the Sick (or "Unction"). This Catholic sacrament can be used to bring these individuals back into a good relationship with the Church, enabling them to take communion and not believe that they are excluded from religious and spiritual life.

We omit some details of Father Santa's approach, and it is beyond our expertise to assess its religious merit. What is notable for our purposes is how this technique uses religious concepts like sin and forgiveness as well as an understanding of Scrupulosity as a mental illness. If people believe themselves to be genuinely sinful instead of having a mental illness, then they will be unwilling to ask for Anointing of the Sick: they don't think they're sick! But if they believe themselves to be only mentally ill but not sinful, then they would feel no need to ask for forgiveness. This therapeutic strategy therefore trades on the individuals' understanding their disorder as both religiously relevant and also a mental illness.

Similarly, a therapist, whether religious or not, might make a religious case to patients that their actions lack religious merit if they are motivated by Scrupulosity or anxiety. Of course, this therapy, like the last, requires that patients have insight into their own condition, at least enough to know that their motivation is something other than a religious motivation and that it could be different. This again uses their religious or moral interests as well as their understanding of their underlying motivation to encourage change. If patients want to do what is morally right, but can be made to see that their underlying motivation actually detracts from their doing what is morally right, then they might be convinced to do something about their underlying motivation. This technique, too, relies on patients' understanding of their Scrupulosity as a mental illness, and their wanting to be morally or religiously better.

These therapies also don't raise distinctive ethical questions. They help patients understand the religious or moral implications of their underlying disorder, and we might disagree about what the implications of Scrupulosity in fact are, but that's not a problem peculiar to therapy. Even if the therapist (or religious practitioner who employs these forms of therapy) doesn't entirely believe what she tells the patient when using these techniques, that's again not an ethical problem distinctive of these techniques. There is a larger conversation to be had about the role of honesty and manipulation in therapy in general, but that discussion is not about treatment of Scrupulosity in particular.

Treatments with Distinctive Ethical Issues

The therapeutic techniques that do raise distinctive ethical issues are those in which the therapist asks patients to do something that they (and maybe also the therapist) judge immoral or potentially immoral, and asks them not to do anything to make up for the things that they believe they have done wrong. That raises one ethical worry that is distinctive of treatment for Scrupulosity. A second worry is that, in the long term, successful therapy might make a patient less sensitive to morality in general. Such costs could be significant, so it is worth looking at these therapeutic techniques more closely.

One of the most effective means of treating various forms of OCD, often in combination with medication, is Exposure and Response Prevention. This therapy requires exposing OCD patients to something that, given their OCD, will provoke their anxiety, then having them follow instructions not to perform compulsive actions that they would ordinarily perform in order to soothe their anxiety. For a lock-checking form of OCD, the therapist might instruct the patient to leave the door unlocked for a while, and not to perform any rituals, including mental rituals, that would soothe anxiety about the unchecked lock. By experiencing and noticing that this action brings about anxiety but then not doing anything to ease that anxiety, the patient avoids reinforcing the anxiety with compulsions and may come to recognize that the anxiety will diminish naturally over time (Abramowitz, Deacon, & Whiteside, 2012; Abramowitz, 1996).

For patients with Scrupulosity, the exposure is to an action or omission that they see as at least potentially immoral. For example, Adam's psychiatrist might ask him to throw away his receipts without checking whether he was undercharged. Mary's therapist might ask her to say a ritual blessing only once, without repeating any prayers at night. Other therapists might ask their patients to blaspheme or to touch something they find ritually unclean. In some cases, the action seems immoral even to most other people, including the therapist. One patient was anxious about inadvertently blurting out racist slurs in public, so the therapist advised this patient to utter racist slurs out loud during therapy sessions—and not apologize. This kind of exposure and response prevention sounds problematic. Should a therapist instruct a patient to do something that the patient (and others, including even the therapist) judges to be potentially immoral, particularly given the additional instruction not to do anything to compensate for the supposed moral transgression?

The short-term costs seem less problematic if we remember the justification for treatment, which is first explained to patients before they begin this form of treatment. Their extreme view of moral or religious obligations reflects their attempts to soothe their own anxiety. Their compulsive behaviors also aim at reducing anxiety. Thus, if they do what seems immoral without performing those compulsive behaviors, then they will learn that the anxiety will subside even without the compulsive acts. In addition, their moral view is incoherent in ways discussed above (arbitrary, conflated, fixated). Unless the therapist is also a religious authority, the therapist and the patient might need to consult a relevant religious authority to testify to this incoherence in particular cases.[40] Given this justification for treatment, the therapist does have some flexibility to ask the patient to act in a way that the patient prefers not to act for moral or religious reasons, but which is not immoral overall by the standards of the patient or of the patient's community. If the patient remains concerned about the immorality of the action that the therapist requests, then the therapist can remind the patient of the larger goals and techniques of this form of therapy, which are important to make clear to the patient. This reminder should not itself be a form of reassurance, but the patient should be made to understand that the goal of treatment is not to make the patient act immorally. The short-term costs of such treatment then seem minimal in light of the justifications for treatment.

Similar points could be made for another form of treatment, often called "radical acceptance" or "Dialectical Behavior Therapy" (DBT).[41] In this form of treatment, patients aren't asked to do something they think is wrong, but they are asked not to do anything to make up for doing something they think is wrong when it does happen. So, for example, patients might not be instructed to blaspheme, but they agree with the therapist not to do anything the next time a blasphemous thought springs to mind. As with Exposure and Response Prevention, patients stop themselves from responding to what they think they have done wrong, and instead accept the feeling of anxiety and discomfort of having done something wrong. Because they don't do anything to nullify the perceived wrongdoing, like praying or performing a ritual, they might believe that they remain deliberately sinful. This raises the same ethical problems that we just discussed, though they are here less acute since the patient didn't do anything deliberately sinful during therapy to provoke the feeling, and the therapist did not encourage the patient to do such an action. The short-term costs here are therefore even more justifiable than the similar costs in Exposure and Response Prevention.

---

[40] Consulting respected authorities is a common part of treatment for Scrupulosity (Huppert & Siev, 2010). However, a therapist must be careful not to let the consultations with a religious authority serve as reassurance to the patient. That would defeat the response-prevention aspect of the treatment. The therapist should also be aware that asking the patient to replace the prayer repetitions with more religiously acceptable activities would similarly risk turning those replacements into their own anxiolytic compulsions.

[41] Thanks to Laura Crosskey for discussing this and the previous form of therapy, and to Liz Sinnott-Armstrong for discussion on this form of therapy, as well as discussing treatment for those with Scrupulosity more generally.

Potential long-term risks are another matter. Treatment—exposure therapy, radical acceptance, or any other form of treatment for Scrupulosity—might potentially make a person less sensitive to real moral or religious obligations. Even if the patient's moral views are abnormal, there might be no way to target only those disproportionate moral positions. If Bridget comes to be less anxious about harming others, this will keep her from checking unnecessarily for poisons, but she might also become less attentive to harms that a moral exemplar would continue to worry about. If Adam becomes less sensitive to mistakes in his favor, then he might also become less sensitive to actively lying or cheating in his favor. If Big John becomes less inclined to greet co-workers, he might become less sensitive to insulting them. These dangers arise because such patients' moral and religious practices are motivated (at least in part) to soothe some underlying anxiety. If therapy is successful in reducing that anxiety, then their motivation to be moral or religious in other ways might also decrease, and perhaps not just in the misguided or disproportionate cases. In becoming less sensitive to their extreme moral standards, they might become immoral by ordinary moral standards.

Luckily, most people are likely not moral or religious primarily as a way of soothing anxiety. Philosophers and psychologists debate what exactly motivates people to be moral, but there is good reason to think that anxiety is not the only or the primary motivation for most people. Similarly, there are motivations other than the desire to soothe anxiety (such as concern for others and love of God) that lead people to be religious. Most people are capable of being moral and religious regardless of their anxiety. This suggests that successful therapy need not eliminate an adequate motivation to be moral and religious.

Nevertheless, for some patients who are motivated largely by their anxiety, there is theoretically some threat that the long-term effects of reducing anxiety might be to reduce their moral or religious motivation more broadly. With less motivation to be moral, they might start to act immorally more often at least in certain circumstances, such as when they are tempted by self-interest. We are unaware of any research showing this to be a real danger, so we suggest it only as a theoretical possibility. It is nevertheless instructive to consider how to address even this theoretical danger.

One way to diminish this theoretical danger is to supplement therapy with steps to help patients calibrate their moral responses to the moral and religious responses that they or those in their community consider normal and justified. (Remember that those with Scrupulosity exceed even their own moral standards in many cases.) In the case of morality, their regular interactions with ordinary people over time could calibrate their moral responses, and they can learn over time how to discuss what is morally required without doing so simply to reassure their own anxiety. For example, if Big John becomes too insensitive to others, then it might help him if he talks with other employees about what makes for a friendly coworker.

If the therapist can continue discussions of how best to negotiate morally fraught situations without thereby simply reassuring the patient, then this role might be appropriate for the therapist. It would require the therapist to take substantive moral stands, and the therapist should exercise caution in doing so. In the religious case, a religious authority or community could serve a similar role. Indeed, there are sometimes even support groups for people with Scrupulosity within religious communities, such as the Roman Catholic Scrupulous Anonymous (Ciarrocchi, 1995). These groups provide discussions with people who understand what it is like to hold extreme moral standards and to feel chronic doubt and anxiety, but whose moral standards are fixated in different areas, so they might benefit by noticing how different people are sensitive to violations in different areas. Discussions with other people who understand and broadly endorse the same religious and moral standards can thereby reduce the theoretical dangers of treating Scrupulosity.

Conclusion

Initial appearances might incline some to think of people with Scrupulosity as exceedingly moral or religious. In contrast, we have argued that Scrupulosity is, instead, a form of mental illness, specifically a kind of OCD. Even so, there remains a question of whether this particular form of OCD warrants therapeutic treatment. We argued that such therapy cannot be justified simply by pointing out that Scrupulosity is a mental illness, that it causes harm or distress, that the patients will be grateful after therapy, or that persons with Scrupulosity go beyond what their communities require. Nonetheless, therapy for Scrupulosity can be justified, sometimes even over moral objection. Therapists need not invoke their own moral or religious judgments or claim that Scrupulosity patients are too moral or religious. The reason is that, as a result of the underlying anxiety that they try to soothe, persons with Scrupulosity are disproportionately and inflexibly concerned with certain areas of morality and religion at the expense of others that they themselves often recognize as important, so their views become internally incoherent. Thus, their treatment can be justified on the basis of the significant discrepancy between the moral or religious standards to which they themselves are ostensibly committed and their behavior manifesting their obsessions and compulsions, due to that underlying anxiety. Finally, we considered a potential short-term cost of exposure therapy, that the individuals are asked to do something that they see as immoral, as well as one possible long-term cost of any form of treatment, that they may in fact become less moral. We argued that neither potential cost is terribly concerning.

We conclude that, contrary to initial appearances, treatment of persons with Scrupulosity even over their moral objections is morally justified in many cases. Of course, this does not mean that everyone with scrupulous traits should be pressured into psychiatric treatment, nor that every type of pressure is warranted. However, when people suffer anxiety and distress as a result of the mental illness of Scrupulosity, then psychiatrists, friends, and family members are often justified in pressuring them to get psychiatric help, and psychiatrists are justified in providing that help in the form of treatment.

Epilogue

Rationality

Our philosophical reflections on Scrupulosity have revealed several important complexities. In particular, they have shown how mental illness is much more complicated than just the absence of rationality. People with Scrupulosity sometimes hurt themselves and their loved ones, apparently for no adequate reason. However, they are trying to relieve their anxiety, so their actions might be instrumentally rational, at least from a certain point of view, and given the alternatives open to them (Sinnott-Armstrong, 1987).

What about their moral judgments? People with Scrupulosity adopt positions about moral obligations that might—taken case by case—be reasonable and defensible. What is wrong with their moral judgments isn't that they can't think about moral or religious issues: they are often quite knowledgeable and reflective about the issues that most concern them and us. The distortions that anxiety causes in those judgments might not be detectable until we step back a little and see how their judgments fit their entire situation.

These complexities arise because moral actions, character traits, and judgments cannot be evaluated in isolation. When I decide whether to return something that I inadvertently took from you, we might agree that returning it is the moral thing to do. However, genuine moral decisions aren't considered so narrowly. If what I took is only a replaceable ballpoint pen, and returning it to you requires me to abandon my family for a week to fly across the country, then I cannot decide to return the pen or judge that I am morally required to return it unless I focus on just that one moral issue to the exclusion of all of the more relevant and obvious moral considerations. I am thinking about moral issues in making my decision, but I am not thinking rationally. This failure to view moral considerations in context is part of what goes wrong in Scrupulosity.

It is also what gets treated in therapy. Therapists who work with those with Scrupulosity help them understand that, while they genuinely aspire to be better and often more religious persons, this goal is in fact undermined by the way they approach their moral or religious life. It's not just that they don't get any joy from doing the right thing—perhaps a moral life will always be somewhat anxious. The problem is that they are so focused on themselves and on managing their own anxiety that they don't look at the world around them to see what a genuinely moral life requires. They might know how to make themselves more confident that their prayer of thanks for some food was said correctly, but they haven't been able to think enough about the food or how lucky they are to have it to become genuinely thankful.

The various aspects of Scrupulosity that we have surveyed thus raise complex issues about morality, religion, sainthood, character, mental illness, responsibility, rationality, and so on. Our goal in reflecting on Scrupulosity was not, however, to resolve these complexities or to demonstrate any single, grand conclusion about them. Our goal was instead to illustrate various ways that our thinking about these issues is complicated and illuminated by reflecting about this real psychiatric case. Such cases and reflections are instructive about how hard and sometimes subtle it is to draw a clear line between this disorder—and perhaps many other disorders—and ordinary, rational moral life.

References

Abramowitz, J. S. (1996). Variants of exposure and response prevention in the treatment of obsessive-compulsive disorder: A meta-analysis. *Behavior Therapy*, *27*(4), 583–600.

Abramowitz, J. S. (2002). Treatment of scrupulous obsessions and compulsions using exposure and response prevention: A case report. *Cognitive and Behavioral Practice*, *8*(1), 79–85.

Abramowitz, J. S. (2008). Scrupulosity. In *Clinical handbook of obsessive compulsive disorder and related conditions* (pp. 156–172). Baltimore, MD: Johns Hopkins University Press.

Abramowitz, J. S., Deacon, B. J., & Whiteside, S. P. H. (2012). *Exposure therapy for anxiety: Principles and practice*. New York: Guilford Press.

Abramowitz, J. S., Huppert, J. D., Cohen, A. B., Tolin, D. F., & Cahill, S. P. (2002). Religious obsessions and compulsions in a non-clinical sample: The Penn Inventory of Scrupulosity (PIOS). *Behaviour Research and Therapy*, *40*(7), 825–838.

Abramowitz, J. S., Taylor, S., & McKay, D. (2009). Obsessive-compulsive disorder. *The Lancet*, *374*(9688), 491–499.

Abramowitz, J. S., & Jacoby, R. (2014). Obsessive-Compulsive Disorder in the *DSM-5*. *Clinical Psychology: Science and Practice*, *21*(3), 221–235.

American Psychiatric Association & American Psychiatric Association Task Force on DSM-IV. (2000). *Diagnostic and statistical manual of mental disorders: DSM-IV-TR* (4th ed.). Washington, DC: American Psychiatric Association.

American Psychiatric Association. (2013). *Diagnostic and statistical manual of mental disorders: DSM-5*. Washington, DC: American Psychiatric Association.

Amir, N., Freshman, M., Ramsey, B., Neary, E., & Brigidi, B. (2001). Thought-action fusion in individuals with OCD symptoms. *Behaviour Research and Therapy*, *39*(7), 765–776.

Arpaly, N. (2003). *Unprincipled virtue: An inquiry into moral agency*. Oxford: Oxford University Press.

Baron, M. (2002). Character, immorality, and punishment. In W. Sinnott-Armstrong & R. Audi (Eds.), *Rationality, rules, and ideals; Critical essays on Bernard Gert's moral theory with reply* (pp. 243–258). Lanham, MD: Rowman & Littlefield.

Berkson, J. (1946). Limitations of the application of fourfold table analysis to hospital data. *Biometrics Bulletin*, *2*(3), 47–53.

Berle, D., & Starcevic, V. (2005). Thought-action fusion: Review of the literature and future directions. *Clinical Psychology Review*, *25*(3), 263–284.

Berman, N. C., Abramowitz, J. S., Pardue, C. M., & Wheaton, M. G. (2010). The relationship between religion and thought–action fusion: Use of an in vivo paradigm. *Behaviour Research and Therapy*, *48*(7), 670–674.

Berman, N. C., Wheaton, M. G., & Abramowitz, J. S. (2013). Rigid rules of conduct and duty: Prediction of thought action fusion. *Journal of Cognitive Psychotherapy*, *27*(2), 83–95.

Bommarito, N. (2018). *Inner virtue.* Oxford: Oxford University Press.

Bonchek, A., & Greenberg, D. (2009). Compulsive prayer and its management. *Journal of Clinical Psychology, 65*(4), 396–405.

Boorse, C. (1975). On the distinction between disease and illness. *Philosophy and Public Affairs, 5*(1), 49–68.

Cefalu, P. (2010). The doubting disease: Religious scrupulosity and obsessive-compulsive disorder in historical context. *Journal of Medical Humanities, 31*(2), 111–125.

Ciarrocchi, J. W. (1995). *The doubting disease: Help for scrupulosity and religious compulsions.* Mahwah, NJ: Paulist Press.

Clucas, J. G. (1988). *Mother Teresa.* New York: Chelsea House.

Cohen, A. B., & Rozin, P. (2001). Religion and the morality of mentality. *Journal of Personality and Social Psychology, 81*(4), 697–710.

Coles, M. E., Pinto, A., Mancebo, M. C., Rasmussen, S. A., & Eisen, J. L. (2008). OCD with comorbid OCPD: A subtype of OCD. *Journal of Psychiatric Research, 42*(4), 289–296.

Doris, J. (2015). *Talking to ourselves: Reflection, ignorance, and agency.* New York: Oxford University Press.

D'Cruz, J. (2015a). Rationalization as performative pretense. *Philosophical Psychology, 28*(7), 980–1000.

D'Cruz, J. (2015b). Rationalization, evidence, and pretense. *Ratio, 28*(3), 318–331.

Davidson, D. (2004). Incoherence and irrationality. In *Problems of rationality* (pp. 189–198). Oxford: Oxford University Press.

Egan, S. J., Wade, T. D., & Shafran, R. (2011). Perfectionism as a transdiagnostic process: A clinical review. *Clinical Psychology Review, 31*(2), 203–212.

Eisen, J. L., Sibrava, N. J., Boisseau, C. L., Mancebo, M. C., Stout, R. L., Pinto, A. et al. (2013). Five-year course of obsessive-compulsive disorder: Predictors of remission and relapse. *Journal of Clinical Psychiatry, 74*(3), 233–239.

Erikson, E. (1958). *Young man Luther: A study in psychoanalysis and history.* New York: W. W. Norton.

Fergus, T. A. (2014). Mental contamination and scrupulosity: Evidence of unique associations among Catholics and Protestants. *Journal of Obsessive-Compulsive and Related Disorders, 3*(3), 236–242.

Fischer, J. M., & Ravizza, M. (1998). *Responsibility and control: A theory of moral responsibility.* Cambridge: Cambridge University Press.

Flanagan, O. J. (1993). *Varieties of moral personality: Ethics and psychological realism.* Cambridge, MA: Harvard University Press.

Fogelin, R. J. (2002). Why obey the laws of logic? *Philosophic Exchange, 32*(1), article 3.

Frankfurt, H. (1988). Freedom of the will and the concept of a person. In *The importance of what we care about* (pp. 11–25). Cambridge: Cambridge University Press.

Freud, S. (1973). Obsessive actions and religious practices. In *Collected works, standard edition (1907)* (Vol. 9, pp. 115–128). London: Hogarth Press.

Friedman, R. A. (2012). Grief, depression, and the DSM-5. *New England Journal of Medicine, 366*(20), 1855–1857.

Frost, R. O., & Steketee, G. (2002). *Cognitive approaches to obsessions and compulsions: Theory, assessment, and treatment.* Oxford: Pergamon Press.

Fulford, K. W. M., Davies, M., Gipps, R., Graham, G., Sadler, J., Stanghellini, G., & Thornton, T. (Eds.). (2015). *The Oxford handbook of philosophy and psychiatry.* New York: Oxford University Press.

Ganss, G. E. (Ed.). (1991). *Ignatius of Loyola: The spiritual exercises and selected works*. New York: Paulist Press.

Garcia, H. A. (2008). Targeting Catholic rituals as symptoms of obsessive compulsive disorder: A cognitive-behavioral and psychodynamic, assimilative integrationist approach. *Pragmatic Case Studies in Psychotherapy*, 4(2), 63–74.

Gert, B., & Culver, C. M. (2004). Defining mental disorder. In J. Raden (Ed.), *The philosophy of psychiatry: A companion* (pp. 415–425). Oxford: Oxford University Press.

Gert, B., & Duggan, T. J. (1979). Free will as the ability to will. *Noûs*, 13(2), 197–217.

Graham, G. (2010). *The disordered mind: An introduction to philosophy of mind and mental illness*. New York: Routledge.

Graham, G. (2015). Words, worlds, and addictions. *Philosophy, Psychiatry, & Psychology*, 22(1), 45–47.

Graham, J., Haidt, J., Koleva, S., Motyl, M., Iyer, R., Wojcik, S. P. et al. (2013). Moral foundations theory: The pragmatic validity of moral pluralism. *Advances in Experimental Social Psychology*, 47, 55–130.

Grayson, J. (2014). *Freedom from obsessive compulsive disorder* (updated edition). New York: Penguin.

Greenberg, D. (1984). Are religious compulsions religious or compulsive: A phenomenological study. *American Journal of Psychotherapy*, 38(4), 524.

Greenberg, D., & Huppert, J. (2010). Scrupulosity: A unique subtype of obsessive-compulsive disorder. *Current Psychiatry Reports*, 12(4), 282–289.

Greenberg, D., Witztum, E., & Pisante, J. (1987). Scrupulosity: Religious attitudes and clinical presentations. *British Journal of Medical Psychology*, 60(1), 29–37.

Hacking, I. (1996). The looping effects of human kinds. In D. Sperber, D. Premack, & A. J. Premack (Eds.), *Causal cognition: A multidisciplinary debate* (pp. 351–394). New York: Oxford University Press.

Haidt, J. (2012). *The righteous mind: Why good people are divided by politics and religion*. New York: Pantheon Books.

Hare, R. M. (1952). *The language of morals*. Oxford: Oxford University Press.

Hart, H. L. A. (1968). *Punishment and responsibility*. Oxford: Clarendon.

Henderson, A. J. Z., Landolt, M. A., McDonald, M. F., Barrable, W. M., Soos, J. G., Gourlay, W. et al. (2003). The living anonymous kidney donor: Lunatic or saint. *American Journal of Transplantation*, 3(2), 203–213.

Hobbes, T. (1651). *Leviathan*.

Huppert, J. D., & Siev, J. (2010). Treating scrupulosity in religious individuals using cognitive-behavioral therapy. *Cognitive and Behavioral Practice*, 17(4), 382–392.

Huppert, J. D., Siev, J., & Kushner, E. S. (2007). When religion and obsessive–compulsive disorder collide: Treating scrupulosity in ultra-orthodox Jews. *Journal of Clinical Psychology*, 63(10), 925–941.

Hurka, T. (1993). *Perfectionism*. Oxford: Oxford University Press.

Inozu, M., Clark, D. A., & Karanci, A. N. (2012). Scrupulosity in Islam: A comparison of highly religious Turkish and Canadian samples. *Behavior Therapy*, 43(1), 190–202.

Jone, H., & Adelman, U. (1959). *Moral theology*. Westminster, MD: Newman Press.

Kane, Robert. (2011). *The Oxford handbook of free will* (2nd ed.). New York: Oxford University Press.

Kant, I. (1997). *Groundwork of the metaphysics of morals* (M. Gregor, Trans.). Cambridge: Cambridge University Press.

Kean, S. (2015, May). The man who couldn't stop giving. *Atlantic Monthly*.

Kennett, J. (2014). Just say no? Addiction and the elements of self-control. In N. Levy (Ed.), *Addiction and self-control* (pp. 144–164). Oxford: Oxford University Press.

Kiehl, K., & Sinnott-Armstrong, W. (Eds.). (2013). *Handbook on psychopathy and law.* New York: Oxford University Press.

Kincaid, H., & Sullivan, J. A. (Eds.). (2014). *Classifying psychopathology: Mental kinds and natural kinds.* Cambridge, MA: MIT Press.

Kohlberg, L. (1973). The claim to moral adequacy of a highest stage of moral judgment. *Journal of Philosophy, 70*(18), 630–646.

Korsgaard, C. (2009). *Self-constitution: Agency, identity, and integrity.* New York: Oxford University Press.

Kozuch, B., & McKenna, M. (2016). Free will, moral responsibility, and mental illness. In D. Moseley & G. Gala (Eds.), *Philosophy and psychiatry: Problems, intersections and new perspectives* (pp. 89–113). Milton Park, Abingdon-on-Thames, UK: Taylor and Francis.

Krippner, S. C. (2002). Conflicting perspectives on shamans and shamanism: Points and counterpoints. *American Psychologist, 57*(11), 962–978.

Kurth, C. (2015). Moral anxiety and moral agency. In *Oxford studies in normative ethics* (Vol. 5). Oxford: Oxford University Press.

Kurth, C. (2018). *The anxious mind.* Cambridge, MA: MIT Press.

Lane, R. D., Ryan, L., Nadel, L., & Greenberg, L. (2015). Memory reconsolidation, emotional arousal, and the process of change in psychotherapy: New insights from brain science. *Behavioral and Brain Sciences, 38*, 1–80.

Levy, N. (2011). Resisting 'Weakness of the Will'. *Philosophy and Phenomenological Research, 82*(1), 134–155.

Levy, N. (2016). Have I turned the stove off? Explaining everyday anxiety. *Philosophers' Imprint, 16*(2), 1–10.

Levy, N. (2018). Obsessive-compulsive disorder as a disorder of attention. *Mind & Language, 33*(1), 3–16.

MacFarquhar, L. (2015). *Strangers drowning: Grappling with impossible idealism, drastic choices, and the overpowering urge to help.* London: Penguin.

Manne, K. (2017). *Down girl: The logic of misogyny.* New York: Oxford University Press.

McKenna, Michael. (2012). *Conversation and responsibility.* New York: Oxford University Press.

Marsh, A. A., Stoycos, S. A., Brethel-Haurwitz, K. M., Robinson, P., VanMeter, J. W., & Cardinale, E. M. (2014). Neural and cognitive characteristics of extraordinary altruists. *Proceedings of the National Academy of Sciences, 111*(42), 15036–15041.

Mele, A. R. (2000). *Self-deception unmasked.* Princeton, NJ: Princeton University Press.

Melli, G., Chiorri, C., Carraresi, C., Stopani, E., & Bulli, F. (2015, April). The role of disgust propensity and trait guilt in OCD symptoms: A multiple regression model in a clinical sample. *Journal of Obsessive-Compulsive and Related Disorders, 5*, 43–48.

Miller, C. H., & Hedges, D. W. (2008). Scrupulosity disorder: An overview and introductory analysis. *Journal of Anxiety Disorders, 22*(6), 1042–1058.

Molden, D. C., & Higgins, E. T. (2005). Motivated thinking. In K. J. Holyoak & R. G. Morrison (Eds.), *The Oxford handbook of thinking and reasoning* (pp. 390–411). Oxford: Oxford University Press.

Moore, J. (1963). Of religious melancholy: A sermon preach'd before the Queen at White-Hall, March the 6th, 1692. In R. Hunter & I. Macalpine (Eds.), *Three hundred years of psychiatry, 1535–1860* (pp. 252–253). London: Oxford University Press.

Moore, E. L., & Abramowitz, J. S. (2007). The cognitive mediation of thought-control strategies. *Behaviour Research and Therapy, 45*(8), 1949–1955.

Mora, G. (1969). The scrupulosity syndrome. *International Psychiatry Clinics, 5*(4), 163.

Nadelhoffer, T., & Sinnott-Armstrong, W. (2013). Is psychopathy a mental disease? In N. Vincent (Ed.), *Legal responsibility and neuroscience* (pp. 227–253). Oxford: Oxford University Press.

Nagel, T. (1970). *The possibility of altruism.* Princeton, NJ: Princeton University Press.

Nelson, E. A., Abramowitz, J. S., Whiteside, S. P., & Deacon, B. J. (2006). Scrupulosity in patients with obsessive-compulsive disorder: Relationship to clinical and cognitive phenomena. *Journal of Anxiety Disorders, 20*(8), 1071–1086.

Nietzsche, F. (1966). *On the genealogy of morals* (W. Kaufman, Trans.), *Basic writings of Nietzsche.* New York: Modern Library.

Noggle, R. (2016). Belief, quasi-belief, and obsessive-compulsive disorder. *Philosophical Psychology, 29*(5), 654–668.

O'Connor, K., & Robillard, S. (1995). Inference processes in obsessive-compulsive disorder: Some clinical observations. *Behaviour Research and Therapy, 33*(8), 887–896.

Olatunji, B. O., Abramowitz, J. S., Williams, N. L., Connolly, K. M., & Lohr, J. M. (2007). Scrupulosity and obsessive-compulsive symptoms: Confirmatory factor analysis and validity of the Penn Inventory of Scrupulosity. *Journal of Anxiety Disorders, 21*(6), 771–787.

Olatunji, B. O., Sawchuk, C. N., Lohr, J. M., & de Jong, P. J. (2004). Disgust domains in the prediction of contamination fear. *Behaviour Research and Therapy, 42*(1), 93–104.

Olatunji, B. O., Tolin, D. F., Huppert, J. D., & Lohr, J. M. (2005). The relation between fearfulness, disgust sensitivity and religious obsessions in a non-clinical sample. *Personality and Individual Differences, 38*(4), 891–902.

Olbert, C. M., Gala, G. J., & Tupler, L. A. (2014). Quantifying heterogeneity attributable to polythetic diagnostic criteria: Theoretical framework and empirical application. *Journal of Abnormal Psychology, 123*(2), 452–462.

Parker, I. (2004). The gift. *The New Yorker, 80*(21), 54–63.

Pearce, S., & Pickard, H. (2009). The moral content of psychiatric treatment. *British Journal of Psychiatry, 195*(4), 281–282.

Pereboom, Derk. (2001). *Living without free will.* Cambridge: Cambridge University Press.

Pickard, H. (2009). Mental illness is indeed a myth. In M. Broome & L. Bortolotti (Eds.), *Psychiatry as cognitive neuroscience: Philosophical perspectives* (pp. 83–101). New York: Oxford University Press.

Pickard, H. (2011). Responsibility without blame: Empathy and the effective treatment of personality disorder. *Philosophy, Psychiatry, & Psychology, 18*(3), 209–223.

Pickard, H. (2016). Scrupulosity and the shady morality of psychiatry. In D. Moseley & G. Gala (Eds.), *Philosophy and Psychiatry: Problems, Intersections, and New Perspectives* (pp. 180–188). New York: Routledge.

Pinto, A., Eisen, J. L., Mancebo, M. C., & Rasmussen, S. A. (2007). Obsessive-Compulsive Personality Disorder. In J. Abramowitz, D. McKay, & S. Taylor (Eds.), *Obsessive-Compulsive Disorder: Subtypes and Spectrum Conditions* (pp. 246–270). Oxford: Elsevier Science Ltd.

Pinto, A., Steinglass, J. E., Greene, A. L., Weber, E. U., & Simpson, H. B. (2014). Capacity to delay reward differentiates obsessive-compulsive disorder and obsessive-compulsive personality disorder. *Biological Psychiatry, 75*(8), 653–659.

Plutarch. (1951). *Plutarch: Selected lives and essays* (L. R. Loomis, Trans.). Roslyn, NY: Walter J. Black.

Rachman, S., & de Silva, P. (1978). Abnormal and normal obsessions. *Behaviour Research and Therapy, 16*(4), 233–248.

Rassin, E., & Koster, E. (2003). The correlation between thought-action fusion and religiosity in a normal sample. *Behaviour Research and Therapy, 41*(3), 361–368.

Rassin, E., & Muris, P. (2007). Abnormal and normal obsessions: A reconsideration. *Behaviour Research and Therapy, 45*(5), 1065–1070.

Rosen, Gideon. (2004). Skepticism about moral responsibility. *Philosophical Perspectives, 18* (Ethics), 295–313.

Sachs-Ericsson, N., & Blazer, D. G. (2015). The new DSM-5 diagnosis of mild neurocognitive disorder and its relation to research in mild cognitive impairment. *Aging & Mental Health, 19*(1), 2–12.

Salkovskis, P. M. (1999). Understanding and treating obsessive-compulsive disorder. *Behavior Research and Therapy, 37*(supplement), s29–s52.

Salkovskis, P. M., & Harrison, J. (1984). Abnormal and normal obsessions—a replication. *Behaviour Research and Therapy, 22*(5), 549–552.

Salwen, K., & Salwen, H. (2010). *The power of half: One family's decision to stop taking and start giving back.* Boston: Houghton Mifflin Harcourt.

Santa, T. M. (2007). *Understanding scrupulosity: Questions, helps, and encouragement.* Liguori, MO: Liguori/Triumph Publishers.

Scadding, J. G. (1990). The semantic problems of psychiatry. *Psychological Medicine, 20*(2), 243–248.

Scanlon, T. M. (2008). *Moral dimensions: Permissibility, meaning, blame.* Cambridge, MA: Belknap Press.

Scheffler, Samuel. (1993). *Human morality.* New York: Oxford University Press.

Schroeder, T. (2015). Obsessive-compulsive disorder and moral agency. In D. Shoemaker (Ed.), *Oxford studies in agency and responsibility* (Vol. 3, 85–103). New York: Oxford University Press.

Schwitzgebel, E. (2010). Acting contrary to our professed beliefs or the gulf between occurrent judgment and dispositional belief. *Pacific Philosophical Quarterly, 91*(4), 531–553.

Schwitzgebel, E., & Ellis, J. (2017). Rationalization in moral and philosophical thought. In J.-F. Bonnefon & B. Trémolière (Eds.), *Moral inferences* (170–190). New York: Routledge.

Sedgwick, P. (1973). Illness: Mental and otherwise. *Hastings Center Studies, 1*(3), 19–40.

Shafran, R., & Mansell, W. (2001). Perfectionism and psychopathology: A review of research and treatment. *Clinical Psychology Review, 21*(6), 879–906.

Shafran, R., Thordarson, D. S., & Rachman, S. (1996). Thought-action fusion in obsessive compulsive disorder. *Journal of Anxiety Disorders, 10*(5), 379–391.

Shoemaker, D. (2011). Attributability, answerability, and accountability: Toward a wider theory of moral responsibility. *Ethics, 121*(3), 602–632.

Shoemaker, D. (2015). *Responsibility from the margins.* Oxford: Oxford University Press.

Sidgwick, H. (1981). *The methods of ethics* (7th ed.). Indianapolis: Hackett.

Sinnott-Armstrong, W. (1987). Insanity and irrationality. *Public Affairs Quarterly, 1*(3), 1–21.

Sinnott-Armstrong, W. (2005). You ought to be ashamed of yourself (when you violate an imperfect moral obligation). *Philosophical Issues, 15, Normativity*, 193–208.

Sinnott-Armstrong, W. (2006). *Moral Skepticisms*. New York: Oxford University Press.

Sinnott-Armstrong, W. (Ed.). (2008). *Moral psychology*, Vols. 1–3. Cambridge: MIT Press. (Vol. 4, 2014; Vol. 5, 2017).

Sinnott-Armstrong, W. (2016). The disunity of morality. In S. Matthew Liao (Ed.), *Moral brains: The neuroscience of morality* (pp. 331–354). New York: Oxford University Press.

Sinnott-Armstrong, W., & Summers, J. S. (2018). Defining addiction: A pragmatic perspective. In H. Pickard & S. Ahmed (Eds.), *The Routledge handbook of philosophy and science of addiction* (123–131). New York: Routledge.

Sinnott-Armstrong, W., & Summers, J. S. (2019). Are mental illnesses biopsychosocial? In W. Davies, J. Savulescu, & R. Roache (Eds.), *Psychiatry reborn: Biopsychosocial psychiatry in modern medicine*. New York: Oxford University Press.

Smith, A. M. (2015). Responsibility as answerability. *Inquiry*, 58(2): 99–126.

Sripada, C. (2010). The deep self model and asymmetries in folk judgments about intentional action. *Philosophical Studies*, 151(2), 159–176.

Sripada, Chandra. (2016). Self-expression: A deep self theory of moral responsibility. *Philosophical Studies*, 173(5),1203–1232.

Strohminger, N., Knobe, J., & Newman, G. (2017). The true self: A psychological concept distinct from the self. *Perspectives on Psychological Science*, 12(4), 551–560.

Summers, J. S. (2017). *Post hoc ergo propter hoc*: Some benefits of rationalization. *Philosophical Explorations*, 21(sup.1), 21–36.

Summers, J. S., & Sinnott-Armstrong, W. (2014). Scrupulous agents. *Philosophical Psychology*, 28(7), 947–966.

Summers, J. S., & Sinnott-Armstrong, W. (2015). Scrupulous judgments. In M. Timmons (Ed.), *Oxford studies in normative ethics* (129–150). Oxford: Oxford University Press.

Summers, J. S., & Sinnott-Armstrong, W. (2017). Scrupulous characters and mental illness. In I. Fileva (Ed.), *Questions of character* (pp. 283–296). Oxford: Oxford University Press.

Sutton, W., & Linn, E. (1976). *Where the money was*. New York: Ballantine Books.

Szasz, T. S. (1961). The myth of mental illness. *American Psychologist*, 15, 113–118.

Szasz, T. S. (1999). Is mental illness a disease? *The Freeman*, 49, 38–39.

Taylor, C. Z. (2002). Religious addiction: Obsession with spirituality. *Pastoral Psychology*, 50(4), 291–315.

Taylor, S. E., & Brown, J. D. (1988). Illusion and well-being: A social psychological perspective on mental health. *Psychological Bulletin*, 103(2), 193.

Taylor, S. E., & Brown, J. D. (1994). Positive illusions and well-being revisited: Separating fact from fiction. *Psychological Bulletin*, 116(1), 21–27.

Tek, C., & Ulug, B. (2001). Religiosity and religious obsessions in obsessive-compulsive disorder. *Psychiatry Research*, 104(2), 99–108.

Tolin, D. F., Abramowitz, J. S., Kozak, M. J., & Foa, E. B. (2001). Fixity of belief, perceptual aberration, and magical ideation in obsessive-compulsive disorder. *Journal of Anxiety Disorders*, 15(6), 501–510.

Traig, J. (2004). *Devil in the details: Scenes from an obsessive girlhood*. New York: Little, Brown.

Tsang, J.-A. (2002). Moral rationalization and the integration of situational factors and psychological processes in immoral behavior. *Review of General Psychology*, 6(1), 25–50.

van den Hout, M., & Kindt, M. (2004). Obsessive-compulsive disorder and the paradoxical effects of perseverative behaviour on experienced uncertainty. *Journal of Behavior Therapy and Experimental Psychiatry*, 35(2), 165–181.

Wakefield, J. C. (1992). Disorder as harmful dysfunction: A conceptual critique of DSM-IIIR's definition of mental disorder. *Psychological Review*, 99(2), 232–247.

Watson, G. (1975). Free agency. *Journal of Philosophy*, 72(8), 205–220.

Wells, A., & Davies, M. I. (1994). The Thought Control Questionnaire: A measure of individual differences in the control of unwanted thoughts. *Behaviour Research and Therapy*, 32(8), 871–878.

Wolf, S. (1982). Moral saints. *Journal of Philosophy*, 79(8), 419–439.

Wolf, S. (2003). Sanity and the metaphysics of responsibility. In G. Watson (Ed.), *Free will* (2nd ed., pp. 372–387). Oxford: Oxford University Press.

Yaffe, G. (2011). Lowering the bar for addicts. In *Addiction and responsibility* (pp. 113–138). Cambridge, MA: MIT Press.

Yorulmaz, O., Gençöz, T., & Woody, S. (2009). OCD cognitions and symptoms in different religious contexts. *Journal of Anxiety Disorders*, 23(3), 401–406.

Zimmerman, A. (2007). The nature of belief. *Journal of Consciousness Studies*, 14(11), 61–82.

Index